D0604494

The Cooking of the British Isles

LIFE WORLD LIBRARY
LIFE NATURE LIBRARY
TIME READING PROGRAM
THE LIFE HISTORY OF THE UNITED STATES
LIFE SCIENCE LIBRARY
GREAT AGES OF MAN
TIME-LIFE LIBRARY OF ART
TIME-LIFE LIBRARY OF AMERICA
FOODS OF THE WORLD
THIS FABULOUS CENTURY
LIFE LIBRARY OF PHOTOGRAPHY

Foods of the World

The Cooking of the British Isles

by

Adrian Bailey

and the Editors of

TIME-LIFE BOOKS

photographed by Anthony Blake

TIME-LIFE BOOKS, NEW YORK

THE AUTHOR: Adrian Bailey *(near left)* has spent most of his life in London, but acquired his extensive knowledge of British gastronomy while touring the United Kingdom as a member of a Royal Air Force publicity unit after World War II. He has been at various times a road-construction laborer, television scriptwriter, photographer's assistant and free-lance artist and writer. His interest in food began when, as a teen-ager, he invaded the kitchens of hotels owned by his father to cook his own experimental dishes. He has contributed articles on cooking and other subjects to many leading British publications, notably *Queen* magazine. Mr. Bailey drew the marginal illustrations scattered through the book.

THE PHOTOGRAPHER: Anthony Blake *(far left)*, also a Londoner, spent five years as an R.A.F. photographer. Today one of Britain's most distinguished food photographers, he spent a year traveling in the country and later worked in the *Foods of the World* kitchens in New York taking the pictures for this book.

THE CONSULTING EDITOR: Michael Field, one of America's leading culinary experts, supervised the testing, adapting and writing of recipes for this book. He conducts a cooking school and writes on food for several leading magazines. His books include *Michael Field's Cooking School, Michael Field's Culinary Classics and Improvisations* and *All Manner of Food.*

THE CONSULTANT: José (pronounced Josie) Wilson began learning about British cooking as she learned her ABCs in her native Cumberland village. After working for women's magazines in London, she came to the United States and in 1953 joined *House & Garden*. She edited *House & Garden's New Cook Book* (1967).

THE COVER: Britain's deservedly long-reigning favorite, a rib roast of beef cooked with potatoes, and served with the classic accompaniments of Yorkshire pudding and horseradish sauce, is displayed against the coat of arms of the British Crown. For the recipes for roast, pudding and sauce see the Recipe Index.

TIME-LIFE BOOKS

EDITOR: Jerry Korn
Executive Editor: A. B. C. Whipple
Planning: Oliver E. Allen
Text Director: Martin Mann
Art Director: Sheldon Cotler
Chief of Research: Beatrice T. Dobie
Picture Editor: Robert G. Mason
Assistant Text Directors: Ogden Tanner, Diana Hirsh
Assistant Art Director: Arnold C. Holeywell
Assistant Chief of Research: Martha T. Goolrick
Assistant Picture Editor: Melvin L. Scott

PUBLISHER: Joan D. Manley
General Manager: John D. McSweeney
Business Manager: John Steven Maxwell
Sales Director: Carl G. Jaeger
Promotion Director: Beatrice K. Tolleris
Public Relations Director: Nicholas Benton

FOODS OF THE WORLD
SERIES EDITOR: Richard L. Williams
EDITORIAL STAFF FOR THE COOKING OF THE BRITISH ISLES:
Associate Editor: Jay Brennan
Picture Editor: Donald Hinkle
Designer: Albert Sherman
Assistant to Designer: Elise Hilpert
Staff Writers: Geraldine Schremp, Ethel Strainchamps
Chief Researcher: Helen Fennell
Researchers: Sarah B. Brash, Sondra Albert, Malabar Brodeur, Marjorie Chester, Susan Grafman, Julia Johnson, Don Nelson
Art Assistant: Gloria duBouchet
Test Kitchen Chef: John W. Clancy
Test Kitchen Staff: Fifi Bergman, Sally Darr, Leola Spencer

EDITORIAL PRODUCTION
Production Editor: Douglas B. Graham
Quality Director: Robert L. Young
Assistant: James J. Cox
Copy Staff: Rosalind Stubenberg, Eleanore W. Karsten, Florence Keith
Picture Department: Dolores A. Littles, Joan Lynch

Published simultaneously in Canada.
Library of Congress catalogue card number 69-19833.

The text for this book was written by Adrian Bailey, the recipe instructions by Michael Field, the picture essays and appendix material by members of the staff. Valuable assistance was provided by the following individuals and departments of Time Inc.: Editorial Production, Robert W. Boyd Jr., Margaret T. Fischer; Editorial Reference, Peter Draz; Picture Collection, Doris O'Neil; Photographic Laboratory, George Karas; TIME-LIFE News Service, Murray J. Gart; Correspondent Margot Hapgood (London).

Contents

The Recipe Booklet that accompanies this volume has been designed for use in the kitchen. It contains all of the 86 recipes at the ends of the chapters plus 24 more. It also has a wipe-clean cover and a spiral binding so that it can either stand up or lie flat when open.

A Warming Cuisine Rooted in Rural Simplicity

British cooking is not noted for saucing and subtleties. It depends on the excellence of the raw materials, the rhythm of the seasonal crops and a simple style of preparation that permits the flavors of the food to come through. Fish from the rivers, lakes and coastal waters is one of our great prides. Never more than a few hours from the net to the fishmonger's slab and the housewife's pot, it remains always fresh enough to retain its true taste—the main reason we cook it so plainly. To sully a Dover sole, a matchless fish, with a rich sauce would be a negation of nature's intent.

The indigenous and characteristic aspects of British cooking that have earned it a culinary niche in the world's cuisines date back centuries. As great meat eaters, we perfected the art of roasting. We have evolved splendid specialties: steamed puddings and raised pies; potted, jellied and pickled meats and fish; and an enormous range of breads and cakes.

Because of the rural, regional nature of our islands and their close-knit peoples our food is intrinsically what it always has been—home-grown, home-reared, homemade. Unlike the French, we have no *grande cuisine* or custom of elegant, highly contrived restaurant eating. There was nothing about our eating patterns to occasion it: almost everyone, from king to commoner, ate the same foods, however fancied-up or plain. The kitchens of the royal courts and great country houses merely drew on a wider variety of foodstuffs in greater quantities. A wealthy imperial nation and a world-wide trader since the 16th Century, England could afford to import the best the world had to offer, from tea, coffee and rice to exotic spices and fruits, and all these found their way into home cooking.

British food is uncomplicated, reassuring to the palate, a repository of familiar, cherished flavors. There are no gastronomic flourishes to upset the delicate balance of digestion. In essence it is nostalgic and evocative, intertwined with memories, heightened by time, of snowy Dickensian Christmases when the goose sputtered in the oven, the pudding simmered on the stove, and trays of mince pies cooled tantalizingly in the pantry. It is substantial food, designed to stoke the inner fires in a country that, though never arctically cold, is frequently raw and bone chilling and has yet to embrace wholeheartedly the delights of central heating. Armored with a good breakfast of sausage, bacon, grilled tomato and fried egg washed down with cups of strong, sweet, milky tea, anyone can start the day with a flush of warmth and well-being. And at the end of a cold, gray winter afternoon there is the promise of tea with scones and jam, and crumpets oozing butter. For British food is, above all, comforting food, the kind you turn to when you are tired, cold, hungry, miserable or sick. Not for nothing has it been affectionately dubbed "nursery food," and the names of certain dishes have a schoolboy ring about them—toad-in-the-hole, bubble and squeak, spotted dog.

I was lucky enough to grow up in the British countryside in the county of Cumberland in the days when almost everything could be bought from the local farms, market, garden and butcher, and to have a mother who was a fine North Country cook with the lightest of hands for pastry and cakes. We bought practically nothing at the confectioners', except perhaps a few "fancy" cakes for Saturday tea. Friday was baking day and I would ensconce myself in the kitchen to watch the bread and teacakes being set to rise, hungrily sniffing the smell of gingerbread baking in the oven.

In the summer, when we had desserts and pies made from the garden fruits, I was sent to the neighboring farm to buy cream to pour over them, so thick and yellow that I was warned not to swing the can on the way home or it would turn to butter. It was at the farm, in those days before World War II, that we also bought eggs and chickens, milk, and freshly churned butter that was shaped into one-pound bricks and stamped with the image of a friendly cow. The color and taste of the butter changed with the seasons—in winter it was pale, almost white, with the faintest of flavors. In summer, when the cows were turned out to pasture in meadows carpeted with buttercups, it became yellow and rich as a golden sovereign. The war killed that particular piece of tradition in Cumberland. Milk and eggs were sent to a central marketing board and the farmers found that it was easier to hand over their produce than to sell it themselves.

Now in Cumberland the butter is packaged, the eggs are stamped, the milk bottled and the chickens frozen. A generation is growing up that has never tasted the glories of British country food, although it is still possible to find it if you take a little time and trouble.

There is a tendency, understandable enough, to favor foreign dishes over the native product. The young people are cooking *risotto* and *boeuf à la mode* and, although they may still make potted shrimp or steak-and-kidney pie, there are few who will bake bread or mix a Christmas pudding when it can be bought just down the road. It is, one has to admit, the way of the world. Yet a tradition of food is a seemingly sturdy but actually vulnerable thing that must be nurtured to survive. Let tastes change and customs shrivel, and in no time at all a good part of a centuries-old tradition will have disappeared, never to return. That is why I was delighted to be asked to serve as consultant for this book in the FOODS OF THE WORLD series. Here was a chance to record and, hopefully, to perpetuate a type of cooking that is strongly interwoven with the British heritage, countryside and character, lovingly and lucidly described in Adrian Bailey's text. The recipes in this book were chosen to illustrate the full range of British cooking, eliminating only those that could not, in all honesty, be duplicated, or that required foodstuffs such as fresh herring that are difficult to obtain here. With few exceptions, British recipes are easy to reproduce in the United States. You can make potted shrimp with the tiny West Coast variety or, in a pinch, use the Icelandic canned ones, and there is no reason to salt your own beef for boiled beef and carrots when corned brisket gives the same result.

It is therefore with a great deal of pride that I invite you into the world of British cooking. *José Wilson, foods editor and consultant*

I

The Great Creations of Country Cooks

In a tiny, quarry-tiled kitchen in northern Wales, Mrs. Jones (in northern Wales everyone is either Jones or Evans) watches her husband eat the following: a plate of freshly boiled ham with *tatws slaw* (mashed potatoes with buttermilk), three tomatoes, some buttermilk cakes called *crempog,* a few slices of *bara brith,* a bread filled with currants, fresh from the oven and thickly spread with good Welsh butter, and a piece of spongecake, all washed down by gallons of scalding tea.

"Flippin' 'eck," exclaims Mrs. Jones crossly, her voice rising in a querulous cadence. "You surely haven't finished that already?" Mr. Jones looks at her from under black, bushy eyebrows. "Bloomin' wimmin," he thinks, "always going on." What he says aloud is, "That was lovely, Gwinny. I'll be late, Gwinny," and dashes off to the workingmen's club where, for the rest of the evening, he will argue vociferously (in Welsh) about politics and the new reservoir that the Liverpool Council is building in a distant valley.

And Mrs. Jones, clearing away the dishes, smiles to herself. Although her husband has given no outward sign of pleasure or satisfaction (in Britain, few people ever do) save the dutiful, "That was lovely," she knows that her cooking rarely fails to please. Were Mr. Jones deprived of her baking for more than one week he would become morose and irritable. There is probably little difference between her *bara brith* and that of Mrs. Evans, wife of Evans the Electric, who repairs their radio, but to Mr. Jones it is unique, although he would never say so, "not in a million years, boy!"

Mrs. Jones's cooking—very individual, entirely simple, marked by its regional accent and ancestral heritage—is British food at its best. The creativity

When summer is a-coming in, the gardens of England burgeon with seasonal delights. Among these delights are strawberries just off the vine, served with rich cream and a freshener of champagne, like these displayed on the grounds of Petersham House, a Georgian architectural masterpiece in Surrey.

of country cooks like Mrs. Jones, working in their own kitchens, has given the dishes of the British Isles the originality and rich flavor that belie the occasional carpings from foreign visitors who have not really experienced British cooking. For it is primarily in the home that the breadth of British cuisine can be appreciated. A dinner, perhaps, of a thick juicy slice of rare roast beef and Yorkshire pudding, followed by the delicate gooseberry dessert called fool. Or a tea. Only the British make tea a meal, with minuscule shrimp tasting of sea spray, jam-filled tarts and, of course, tea itself—strong, rich, scalding hot. Even a plain lunch of sharp Cheddar cheese with freshly baked bread and a pint of bitter braces a man for the day's work remaining.

If you could tour homes throughout the British Isles, you would be served many meals like that. Often you would be introduced to a dish you had never met before, a regional specialty, for Britain is a land of immense variety on a small scale, and country cooks, of course, always deal with the ingredients closest to hand. Most of the dishes served you would be hearty; it must be remembered that Britain was once wholly an agricultural land. The great majority of the people were country folk—farmers and laborers. They were hardy and always hungry, and appetites, stimulated by long hours of work, were enormous. Their filling dishes, evolved from the intermingling of Celtic, Germanic and Norman cultures, survived to become the foundation of British cooking, a solid cuisine tempered with lively trifles and sweets.

A land of immense variety on a small scale, I have written. A county that rides a chain of hills lies next to one of extraordinary flatness. The weather (Britain has no climate, only weather) changes by the minute, and by the mile. There are rural areas that have altered little since the 18th Century; a villager from five miles away is a foreigner, even though the villagers play cricket against one another and drink in the pubs together. There are larger divisions as well. Ireland is an island on its own. Scotland and Wales are set off from England by customs as well as geography. From the Midlands through the North Country and into Scotland runs the spine of England, the heaving Pennine Chain that divides the open fields of the northeast from those of the northwest. Beyond the plains just south and north of the Pennines the land again becomes mountainous, often harsh yet always beautiful, a landscape matched by the trenchant, no-nonsense character of its native Celtic people in Wales, Cornwall and Scotland.

The poet A. E. Housman once described summertime in the county of Shropshire in the west: "Here of a Sunday morning/My love and I would lie,/And see the coloured counties,/And hear the larks so high/About us in the sky." The "coloured counties" of this area are variegated hues of green and gold; fields and meadows are precisely bisected by hedgerows or neat stone walls. The clouds cast shadows that travel swiftly over the ground. The larks trill, rising and falling, over the waving acres of wheat, oats and barley. East Anglia, the rump of England, and once an area of reed-choked fens, is as flat as a board. Below London the southeast, on the other hand, with its gently undulating landscape, has long been rich farmland. Indeed, the county of Kent is often referred to as the garden of England.

It is in this fertile corner of the southeast that the seed of England's cooking was first sown. Here the Germanic invaders who came from Northern Europe in the Fifth Century eventually settled and began to farm the Weald of Kent and the broad back of the Sussex Downs. They found a land of thick forests profuse in wildlife, rich in oak, beech, alder and elm, sharp-leaved holly and barbed hawthorn, and slowly they made it into a garden.

To these Angles, Saxons and Jutes, who were followed by Danes, the land was similar in many ways to their own country. Those who went to East Anglia in summer recognized the deep, booming call of the bittern, a bird that nested in the reedbeds of the Norfolk fens, where the wind sighed like a ghost through the rushes, and the brilliant yellow swallowtail butterflies hovered and danced. The black-and-white wading birds called avocets were the same as those back home, delicately picking their way across the salt marshes, probing their upturned bills into the mud.

The men made homesteads in their own fashion, houses that looked like upturned boats. They ventured into the surrounding woods to find deer and wild boar, partridge, hare and rabbit, and in the streams and rivers, fish. The land yielded wild strawberries and blackberries; sour crab apples and small, hard pears; cobnuts and fungi.

Despite such abundance, life was hard. Though rich and fertile the soil needed taming, and the tools and methods of these warrior-farmers were primitive. Their pigs were long-nosed and skinny, their cattle and sheep stunted and long-haired. Summers were warm, but winters were damp and very cold. The people prepared, as best they could, against the capricious humor of the island weather—against the mists that clung to the low ground, against the thin, sharp wind that penetrated the coarsely stitched gaps in their clothing, and blew through the open windows and doors of their houses.

The wind followed the contours of the downs. It swept through Ashdown Forest and lifted the dried leaves in a spiral, scattering them over the fields. It blew across Hampshire and over Salisbury Plain, flattening the wild oat grass around prehistoric Stonehenge and on to the West Country and Cornwall, where the dark-browed Celts crouched. When the wind's cold cry warned of winter's coming, most of the livestock were killed for food, for they could not be supported through the dark season. Then, too, the women went out to gather herbs, wild fruits and nuts, and began to store the stock of barley, wheat and oats.

Yet life was certainly not entirely barren, gastronomically speaking. These Anglo-Saxons had brought from their Continental homelands the arts of brewing and baking and the techniques for making butter and cheese. They made ale from their barley, and milked their ewes and cattle to make cheese. They cultivated cider-apple trees and kept bees for honey. From the washings of the honeycombs the Saxons made the sweet, fermented, herb-flavored mead, drink of the gods of Valhalla. Did those Saxon cooks actually enjoy cooking, I wonder, or was it just part of the daily routine—rearing children, repairing their houses and clothes, collecting food, grinding grain and churning the milk to make butter? Did it give them pleasure to work the coarse bran flour to a dough with water and cook it on flat stones before the fire—as prehistoric tribes had done, even before Stonehenge was erected? While ale worked in the jar, and butter came in the churn, did they pause to think of new ways with the wild fruits, the herbs and the meats? Certainly the Saxons enjoyed eating, and the size of some of their banquets perhaps indicates that they enjoyed preparing the food, too.

One basic ingredient in their feasts was game. With short bows they shot the wild deer and the boar and hung the carcasses in the trees, away from the wolves. Throughout the green seasons of the year, when food was in plentiful supply, the iron pot and the roasting spit were in constant use. Over the fire of wood and furze the whole carcass of a boar would slowly revolve, the boar's tough skin crackling and singeing, while the fat and juices dripped, spluttering, into the red embers. With iron knives the men carved hunks of herb-flavored meat from the ribs of the pig. The meat was good, the skin crisp; it burned the fingers and the mouth, but tasted delicious.

The Saxons needed no excuse for a feast. They ate as often as they could, and drank mighty drafts of foaming mead and ale. Over the carcass of the boar they passed around horn drinking tumblers that had pointed bases and so could not be put down until the last drop was drained. This was story time, and from such feasts our English literature was born. While the flames of the fire cast dancing shadows on the walls, men would repeat the old tale of Beowulf and his fight with the monster Grendel, who lived with his mother at the bottom of the lake. Those who sat and listened on the outer circle of the fire cast glances over their shoulders, toward the open door and the forest where the wolves moved in packs, and where the sudden shriek of the owl could set the heart pounding.

The men slept (some uneasily) on the rushes that were strewed across the floor. In the morning they breakfasted upon ale, cold pork and coarse, dark bread. This was the food that was destined to break British fasts for the next thousand years—a tradition rooted, like many traditions, in economy and expediency. Meat, bread, cheese and ale were all available and nourishing; it was only natural that they became staples. I think it more than likely that out of similar expediency the Saxons invented haggis, now a Scottish specialty but known in Ireland and in England long before it reached the Highlands. To the Saxon, livestock was his most precious commodity. When he killed a sheep, he used its skin for clothing and ate the rest. The offal would be boiled, chopped up and perhaps mixed with a handful of oats or barley and some dried herbs. Having noticed that the resilience of the sheep's stomach resisted all attempts at boiling, what was more natural than to stuff the stomach with the meat-and-cereal mixture, and set it to boil in the pot? The haggis

Islands Full of Delectable Names

From the hindle wakes of Lancashire to the fat rascals of Yorkshire, either of which might be found today on a North of England tea table, dozens of the regional foods of Britain bear names so ancient that their origins have become confused or have long been forgotten. However, the recipes—and the taste—for the foods have been handed down intact from generation to generation, in some cases evidently since prehistoric times. A few of the foods on this culinary map have gained national popularity; many more, including some of the most delectable ones, are still little known outside the places whose names they bear.

Cheese
ORKNEY
CAITHNESS
SUTHERLAND
HEBRIDES ISLANDS
ROSS AND CROMARTY
Colcannon
NAIRN
MORAY
BANFF
Fried Kippers
Baked Haddock
Loch Ness
Malt Whisky
ABERDEEN
Aberdeen Sausage
Parkin
INVERNESS
KINCARDINE
ATLANTIC OCEAN
Scones
ANGUS
NORTH SEA
PERTH
Dundee Orange Marmalade
ARGYLL
Petticoat Tails
FIFE
Loch Lomond
KINROSS
CLACKMANNAN
STIRLING
Haggis
EAST LOTHIAN
DUMBARTON
WEST LOTHIAN
Edinburgh Black Bun
Glasgow Tripe
MIDLOTHIAN
BERWICK
RENFREW
LANARK
PEEBLES
BUTE
Dunlop Cheese
SELKIRK
ROXBURGH
Bannock
AYR
Granny Loaf
DUMFRIES
NORTHUMBERLAND
KIRKCUDBRIGHT
Singing Hinny
DONEGAL
LONDONDERRY
ANTRIM
Potato Cakes
WIGTOWN
CUMBERLAND
DURHAM
TYRONE
Loch Neagh
Belfast Ham
Cumberland Sauce
WESTMORLAND
Fat Rascals
DOWN
FERMANAGH
ARMAGH
Haggis
Grasmere Gingerbread
Wensleydale Cheese
Ripon Spice Bread and Wilfra Tarts
SLIGO
MONAGHAN
ISLE OF MAN
Dumb Cake
Lancashire Cheese
YORK
York Hams
LEITRIM
CAVAN
MAYO
ROSCOMMON
LOUTH
Fig Pie
Parkin
Yorkshire Pudding
Hindle Wakes
Gingerbread
IRISH SEA
LONGFORD
MEATH
Stout
DUBLIN
Wet Nelly
LANCASHIRE
Soused Mackerel
GALWAY
WEST MEATH
Bolton Hot Pot
Liverpool Lobscouse
Eccles Cakes
Prawns
Brandy Snaps
Colcannon
OFFALY
KILDARE
Dublin Coddle
ANGLESEY
CHESHIRE
DERBY
FLINT
NOTTINGHAM
LAOIGHIS
CAERNARVON
DENBIGH
Cheshire Cheese
LINCOLN
CLARE
WICKLOW
Pancakes
Bakewell Tarts
MERIONETH
STAFFORD
NORFOLK
CARLOW
Bara Brith
Stilton Cheese
Melton Mowbray Pork Pie
TIPPERARY
LEICESTER
RUTLAND
LIMERICK
KILKENNY
SHROPSHIRE
Cheese
Dumplings
WEXFORD
MONTGOMERY
Coventry Godcakes
HUNTINGTON
Irish Soda Bread
Simnel Cake
NORTHAMPTON
KERRY
WORCESTER
SUFFOLK
RADNOR
WARWICK
CAMBRIDGE
CARDIGAN
Pax Cakes
Whigs
Harvest Cakes
WATERFORD
HEREFORD
Banbury Cakes
CORK
BEDFORD
Boiled Lobster
Cider
BRECKNOCK
PEMBROKE
BUCKINGHAM
CARMARTHEN
Bara Ceirch
GLOUCESTER
OXFORD
ESSEX
Cork Drisheen Sausages
HERTFORD
Irish Whiskey
Mustard Sauce
Sausage
GLAMORGAN
MONMOUTH
Cheese
MIDDLESEX
Boiled Beef and Carro
Caerphilly Cheese
Bacon
London Jellied Eels
Sally Lunn Cakes and Bath Buns
BERKSHIRE
WILTSHIRE
Richmond
Flead Cakes
Cheddar Cheese
Devizes Pie
Maids of Honour
KENT
Huffkins
ENGLAND
SURREY
Lardy Cakes
Fruit Tarts
SOMERSET
HAMPSHIRE
Cider
Cider
SUSSEX
DORSET
Steak-and-Kidney Pudding
WALES
Cornish Pasties
DEVON
Blue-Veined Cheese
Cheese
ISLE OF WIGHT
Doughnuts
Saffron Cake
Cream
SCOTLAND
CORNWALL
Grilled Mackerel
ENGLISH CHANNEL
Stargazey Pie
NORTHERN IRELAND
SCILLY ISLANDS
FRANCE
EIRE
0
100 Miles
CHANNEL ISLANDS
Simnel Biscuits
Jersey Bean Jar

is, after all, merely a form of sausage and would keep for some days.

Taking the haggis a stage further, these same cooks may have invented the famous English meat pudding. Flour, mixed with shredded suet from the sheep, and made into a stiff dough with water, led to the Sussex and Kentish suet pudding, and the Norfolk dumpling. Meat or fish was encased in this suet crust, wrapped in a cloth, and boiled. The pudding gave nourishment and protection against the weather; it was hot and filling.

Such expediency also created other typically English things: those envelopes of pastry containing a mixture of meat and potatoes (at one time meat and cereal) called Cornish pasties. Because the meat and vegetables are contained in an edible case, a whole meal can readily be carried to work.

By the 11th Century the Anglo-Saxons had established the basis of a national cuisine—solid, yeomanlike fare: meat, bread, cheese, puddings and pies designed to sustain a man and keep him warm inside and out. Most of them were unaware that another influence was about to have its effect, and not only on their cooking. In 1066 William the Conqueror, or William the

Guarded by a mounted shepherd on one side and a large sheep dog on the other, a flock of young lambs grazes on a rugged hillside in Wales. Spring lambs from this mountain grassland in the Brecon Beacons are the finest in the British Isles.

Bastard as he was sometimes called (although never in his presence), landed at Pevensey Bay in Sussex at the head of an army of Norman barons and knights and French mercenaries. For five years he terrorized the South and North of England as he conquered the land.

The mercenaries left little to remember them by, save fire and sword. But the Norman barons and knights, with their educated speech and curious table manners, revolutionized the Saxon way of life forever, especially in the kitchen. The Norman cooks were inventive and good, preparing such delicacies as tripe and onions, and dishes made with wonderful pastry. Their bread was much better than that of the Saxons, especially that known as *guastel.* Their meat was served in slices on "trenchers"—platters of metal or wood or slices of coarse bread. The word derives from *tranchouoir,* Old French for "to cut, or slice." After the Norman trencherman had eaten his fill of meat, the soaked slices of bread were given to the poor. The Normans actually had salt and even pepper on their tables, whispered the Saxon slaves! They flavored their dishes, not only with herbs, but with strange-tasting spices that the Saxons later came to know as ginger, cloves, nutmeg and cinnamon. These Normans puzzled the Saxon servants by their insistence on having food in separate, well defined courses. There were, however, compensations. Out in the scullery the servants could clean the cream bowls with their fingers, and quarrel over the scraps of pancakes, and cherries cooked in batter. In Kent they still make a cherry batter pudding, strewed with sugar, not unlike the *clafoutis* made in many French provinces.

Under the influence of the Normans the simple cooking of England was embellished with glamor, although what was glamorous to them would not be glamorous to you and me. Perhaps few of us would enjoy one of the favorites of the year 1430—a pie with pastry containing three or four egg yolks, colored by saffron and covered with bone marrow, ginger, raisins and sugar. But pies became standardized fare, filled with all manner of things such as chopped chicken and pork, flavored with cloves, mace and sugar. And there were simple dishes like "petticoat tails"—a flat ring of Scottish shortbread, divided into wedges the shape, some maintain, of the pattern for a 16th Century petticoat. It has been suggested that the name petticoat tails comes from *petit guastel* (pronounced *petty-goh-tel),* perhaps a combination of the Norman word for a fine wheat bread and the French word *petit,* or small. But nobody really knows.

It is impossible today to trace the origins of all of our dishes, although all arise out of the past, and out of specific regions of the nation. Some of them, like steak-and-kidney pudding, Yorkshire pudding and Lancashire hot pot, have strayed beyond the borders of their respective counties of origin and have become national. But most remain regional, even parochial. Scouse, for example, a word related to "Scouser," a nickname often bestowed on those who admit to coming from Liverpool, is a kind of thin, poverty-stricken stew, said to have been introduced into that city by the Irish. Scouse has never, as far as I know, penetrated very far beyond the Liverpool suburb of Knotty Ash, and neither has "wet Nelly," a Liverpudlian pudding of pastry and cake scraps soaked in syrup.

Across the sea in Ireland you will find that, in all probability, Paddy O'Connor eats a lot of fish and potatoes, partly because he is a Roman Catholic, and partly because a lot of fish and potatoes are produced in Ireland. Both Ireland and Wales are inclined to cling to the past and its strictly local recipes far more than other areas of the British Isles. In Kerry, the magic county, the country lanes in the early morning are full of flat-topped carts, each supporting a huge milk churn, pulled by aged horses. In the case of Ireland, this positive refusal to step out of the early 19th into the 20th Century is backed by the undoubtedly accurate belief that many people, tourists in particular, prefer it that way. It is in the interest of Ireland to preserve that romantic image, nursed by millions of expatriate Irish men and women all over the world, of a green checkerboard land covered with whitewashed cottages. In such a cottage Mother Machree stoops to lift a loaf of soda bread—a crisp loaf baked, by tradition, over a peat fire—and says, "Cup o' tea—or a glass of stout?"

The romantic image is perfectly accurate, of course. I used to visit an old couple in their cottage by the side of a hill in County Kerry. The surrounding countryside had a fierce beauty that took your breath away,

An Irish farm wife and her son dig a few potatoes for supper from their family patch in County Galway. Ever since potatoes were first brought to Ireland from the New World in the 17th Century, they have been a mainstay of the Irish diet.

especially during one of the coastal storms that swept across the Bay of Kenmare, when the landscape changed color from a soft green to a dense blue. The mountains, whose flanks were of peat, collected the water and turned it brown—the color of Irish whiskey. It ran in torrents past the cottage and down the hill. The old woman seemed always to be baking soda bread on the peat fire. Her husband, a lieutenant in the Sinn Fein during "the troubles" of 1914-1921, when the Irish fought so hard to win their independence from England, was forever drinking tea or stuffing his pipe with the black, treacly "Mick McQuaid" shag. I believe that they lived on tea, stout, soda bread, potatoes and an occasional fish from the sea. This diet was supplemented, now and then, with a dish of eggs, bacon and fried liver. Meat as a rule was scarce and expensive. Their cottage had no electricity, no gas. They never read a paper or a book and neither did they have a radio, but they did own a donkey and a small boat. They kept a few hens, a cow and a pig, and their cottage was by the sea, where the wild fuchsia grew, and it was in Ireland, so what more did they want?

Continued on page 20

Caithness Cheese

On the bank of a Lowland loch rests a rich sampling of Scottish specialties *(details overleaf)*.

The Anglo-Saxon and Norman invaders and their descendants established only nominal rule over the Irish, and the other Celtic inhabitants of the Isles—Scots, Welsh and Cornish—were never really subdued either, but merely segregated as they were pushed back into the mountains. The Celts adopted but few of the English dishes, preferring to create their own. The evening meal known as high tea, for example, is a monument of Scottish invention. Its leading feature is a pile of hot scones, crisp and brown on the outside and soft and white when you split them open. Scones are made of flour leavened with baking powder and are eaten spread with butter. Tea bread, speckled with currants, stands on the table next to a pile of wedge-shaped shortbread. There are kipper toasts—smoked haddock with a poached egg sitting on the fish's golden flanks. There are potted herring, Dundee cake black with fruit, raspberry jam and oatcakes.

Cornish food is another example of Celtic rural fare that has remained stubbornly and proudly independent. Only a little more than a century ago the Cornish language, a Celtic dialect, was a familiar tongue west of the Tamar River. Cornwall is in the West Country, down in the bottom left-hand corner of England. It is the foot of England that sticks out into the warm Cornish sea, warm because the Gulf Stream brushes past, and spring comes early, softening the harsh wind-blown landscape with flowers. Gorse blooms in January, and the woods near St. Ives are full of blue hydrangeas.

Cornwall is a land of smugglers, pirates and pixies, of magpies, magic and mines. All around the town of Truro the crumbling ruins of the old tin mines dot the tumbled land. In some pubs there are collection boxes for people who have strayed off the road and injured themselves by falling down disused mine shafts. To those of us who live in other parts of England, Cornwall is famous for two things: Cornish cream, thick and yellow like butter and very rich, and the Cornish pasty.

The pasties, pronounced "pah-stees," are pastry cases with a number of different fillings, most commonly meat. They originated, it is said, as a tin miner's portable lunch: a small envelope of pastry, pointed at both ends and designed to be carried in the pocket. Everyone eats them—for lunch, for tea, for supper. There's an old Cornish saying that goes, "The Devil is afraid to come into Cornwall, for fear of being baked in a pasty."

Cornwall is the place for mackerel, but the fish shops are also full of other local seafood such as ling, hake, turbot, gurnard, herring, lobster, scallops and prawns. There are several fish pies, especially the stargazey pie, made with pilchards. There are pigeon pie and conger-eel pie and lots of different cakes: Cornish heavy cakes, fairings, saffron cake, even a pie cake. Some dishes have strange names: figgy obbin, grovey cake, meaty fuggan, currany obbin, Gerty Grey, shenagrum, and likky pie. But the pasty reigns supreme. An old Cornish woman showed me how to make a pasty, and then told me that I would never succeed because "only a true Cornish woman can make a proper pasty."

The more rural and independent the area, the more such recipes survive, not only because of the stubborn inflexibility of the people, but because the food exactly suits the demands of the open-air life and the tastes it inspires.

Yet those British tastes that were so firmly established over a thousand years ago by the invasion of different cultures are once again being changed,

The Scottish specialties pictured by Loch Chon on the two preceding pages are *(proceeding clockwise in the outer circle from bottom left):* brown-and-white rolls; Dundee cake; black bun, which is like a rich fruitcake except that it is wrapped in dough; fruit bread; soda scones, to be eaten hot; drop scones, which are similar to pancakes; whole-meal bread and (on the same plate) oatcakes and the large, round breakfast rolls known as baps; honey and unsalted butter; the large cookies made of oatmeal and syrup known as parkin; and the dish known as haggis, a stuffed sheep's stomach. In the center are *(from left):* a package of Highland hard-curd cheese; shortbreads resting on the mold in which they were cooked; a scoop of oatmeal; and herring fillets in oatmeal.

The cliff-hung Cornish coast provides an appropriate setting for one of Cornwall's other delights: Cornish pasties, turnovers made of pastry with a meat-and-vegetable filling. Beef, potatoes, turnips and onions are among the ingredients frequently used in the pasties.

by a subtler yet no less persuasive invasion: canned and frozen food, packaged meat, mass-produced poultry and factory-made bread. Since we are no longer an agricultural country (only one worker in 60 now tills the land), our urban environment has radically altered our tastes.

You will not, for instance, find many Kentish bakers who still bake Kentish huffkins. Neither will you find many people in London who can cook for you a clipping-time pudding, enjoyed by the sheepshearers of Cumberland, and I know only one man who will prepare a Jersey bean jar, and regularly sends back home to the Channel Isles for a fresh supply of beans to cook this dish.

Most of the recipes in this book are survivors from the past. They deserve to survive, and their continued happy use in many homes in Britain is a tribute to the English housewife,that archetype of English cooks, with her rosy cheeks, her floral-print apron, her plump arms covered with white flour, and at her disposal the finest fruits, vegetables and meats of the land.

The British picnic, a venerable institution whose main course may be something as simple as cold pork pie, reaches its apex of elegance in the annual outing at the Glyndebourne Opera Festival in Sussex. Here, in formal attire, opera lovers repair between acts to the grounds of the Glyndebourne estate, where the festival takes place, for refreshments they may have brought with them or have ordered from a caterer. This group, with a green salad and a bowl of peaches at hand, is enjoying wine before beginning the main course of huge, meaty, cold Cornish lobster *(left)*. They have also brought along assorted pâtés, Melba toast, mayonnaise, strawberry cake and, in the wicker basket, bread and additional wine.

II

Breakfasts to Rouse Sluggards from Sleep

Hot off the stove, a traditional British breakfast sizzles in an up-to-date skillet. Two kinds of bacon accompany the eggs (and in practice would be cooked before the eggs). The British call the bacon at the upper left and bottom "streaky" and refer to the wider, leaner slices as "middle-back." The bread is fried last and at high heat so it will absorb less fat.

Slices of bacon sizzle on the stove, cooking in their own snow-white fat that turns first transparent, then brown and crisp. Warm plates are stacked above the stove to receive the rashers as they are lifted sputtering from the pan. A delicious and compelling breakfast aroma fills the house and drags the sluggard from sleep into wakeful, eager anticipation; bacon is an everyday luxury of which we never tire.

The frying pan must be allowed to cool a little before the eggs are added, for if the pan is too hot the egg white will scorch and become tough. Crack! and the egg is emptied from its shell into the pan. While it gently fries we must baste it with the fat in the pan, covering the egg with a residue of minute scraps of burned bacon, turning the surface speckled and opaque.

Now for the fried bread, the essential accompaniment to this classic dish. Sometimes we garnish our bacon and eggs with fried mushrooms or with grilled tomatoes, but almost always we add a slice or two of fried bread. Raise the heat beneath the pan, for the fat must be really hot so as to quickly seal the surface of the bread, which otherwise will soak up all the fat, a circumstance most surely to be avoided.

Plunge the slice into the hot fat, and quickly bring it to a rich, warm brown on both sides. Place the egg on top, and surround with the bacon. Now to the table, and eat!

The salty, smoky flavor of the bacon contrasts perfectly with the bland, smooth egg and the crisp, crunchy bread.

Hot toast follows, accompanied by bittersweet marmalade, its irregular chunks of orange peel held in suspension by a thick, golden jelly with a citric, caramel perfume. Tea has long been the companion beverage to such a breakfast and remains so today.

If the bacon and eggs had been preceded by either oatmeal porridge or a breakfast cereal like cornflakes, we would have a typical British breakfast of the 20th Century. Variations on this original theme might include fish, such as haddock or those split and smoked herrings called kippers. Some of us demand fruit juice with our breakfasts. Others request stewed prunes, or a half grapefruit in whose center the British hotel chef invariably plunges a sticky, meretricious *glacé* cherry.

Abroad, the British breakfast has gained a formidable reputation. The French consider it perfectly barbaric, a meal to be approached with caution, for how can we start the day with fish and that strange gray glue called porridge? The fact is that the English breakfast is the result of a long process of evolution, of the slow amalgamation of foods from places other than England. For those who can afford the leisure in this hurried age to indulge in it, it is the finest meal of the day. As Somerset Maugham once observed, the best way to eat well in England is to take breakfast three times a day.

The "English" breakfast owes much in particular to the Scots. They eat even more substantial breakfasts than do the English, the Welsh or the Irish. They consume quantities of porridge and a considerable amount of bread (in the form of a soft breakfast roll called a bap) and drink prodigious quantities of tea on winter mornings (sometimes laced with whisky). Oatmeal porridge is a Celtic invention, and the Scottish influence on our breakfasts is evident every time we eat a kipper or reach for the marmalade.

Aberdeen was the birthplace of a breakfast sausage (and also of my grandfather), while Dundee is the home of marmalade *(Recipe Index)*, without which no breakfast is complete. Orange marmalade, according to legend, was introduced into Scotland in the 16th Century by the French cook of Mary, Queen of Scots. It is more likely that orange marmalade was invented at a considerably later date; a British cookbook published in 1669 contains several recipes for marmalades, but none made from oranges. Most were made from quinces. (In Europe the name given to the quince was *marmelo*, a Portuguese word from which the confection marmalade took its name.) Orange marmalade was first produced commercially in the 1790s by the firm of Keiller of Dundee. It became a well-loved preserve, and still is. It is, of course, not the only marmalade favored in Scotland; the Scots even produce a whisky-flavored marmalade.

If our breakfasts today seem substantial, they were even more so in the past. A few years ago I read of a general in the British Army who, on one of his infrequent visits to London, made an early-morning appearance at his club, and demanded breakfast.

"Will you start with porridge, sir?" the waiter asked. "Or would you prefer cornflakes?"

"Cornflakes?" roared the General. "Cornflakes be damned! Bring me a plate of cold, underdone roast beef and a tankard of ale!"

This request from another age would be considered highly eccentric nowadays in most British homes. Attempts to revive the classic breakfast would today surely fail, because our eating habits have changed—not once but several times. For centuries, however, the British breakfast remained unchanged, as stable as the cycle of the seasons. In the Middle Ages, the very wealthy, who actually slept in nightshirts between sheets, got out of bed when it suited them. They breakfasted on good bread, boiled beef and mutton, cheese, salt herring and ale or wine. But it should be borne in mind that any history of British eating habits must be divided by the rule for the rich and the rule for the poor. So rigid were the social and economic patterns of life that it is impossible to generalize about the eating habits of the entire nation.

The poor rose with the first light of dawn, getting up from the straw upon which they had been sleeping (fully dressed), and snatched whatever kind of food they could get. Bread, certainly. If they were lucky, a piece of salt pork or bacon, fish on Fridays, and a mug of ale. This meat-and-ale diet persisted for more than 500 years.

Even toward the end of the 18th Century, breakfast remained an essentially masculine meal. For one thing, it was usual among the gentry and the middle class for husband and wife to breakfast separately. When the ladies at the manor house chatted over their morning meal—chocolate and cakes—the time was 10 o'clock and the squire had already taken an earlier breakfast of cold meat, pies and ale or claret.

Down in the village the farmers and plowmen were up before the squire, consuming their spartan meal of bread, cheese and ale. Parson Woodforde, an East Anglian Anglican who carefully recorded the details of 18th Century country life, was among those who fared rather better. He noted that his breakfast of October 7, 1794, included: "Chocolate, green & brown Tea, hot Rolls, dried Toast, Bread & Butter, Honey, Tongue and ham grated very small."

A quarter of a century later, breakfasts were becoming even more formidable. In his *Sketch Book* of 1820, the American author Washington Irving wrote: "Our breakfast consisted of what the Squire denominated true old English fare. He indulged in some bitter lamentations over modern breakfasts of tea and toast which he censured as among the causes of modern effeminacy and weak nerves, and the decline of the old English heartiness, and though he admitted them to his table to suit the palates of his guests, yet there was a brave display of cold meats, wine, and ale on the sideboard."

The forebodings of Irving's friend were unwarranted, for many people continued to breakfast heartily. From those chatty tea-chocolate-and-cakes ladies' breakfasts of the late 18th Century, society developed the important, time-consuming, highly conversational family meal that was to remain popular right through Victorian times and the Edwardian era that ended with the onslaught of World War I. The diplomat and author Harold Nicolson remembered the Sunday breakfasts of Edwardian society as very substantial and social affairs: "On a table to the right between the windows were grouped Hams, Tongues, Galantines, Cold Grouse, ditto Pheasant, ditto Partridge, ditto Ptarmigan. No Edwardian meal was complete without Ptarmigan. Hot or Cold. Just Ptarmigan. . . . Edwardian breakfasts were in no sense a hurried proceeding. The porridge was disposed of negligently, people walking about and watching the rain descend upon the Italian garden. Then would come whiting [one variety of codfish], and omelette and devilled kidneys and little fishy messes in shells. And then tongue and ham and a slice of Ptarmigan. And then scones and honey and marmalade. And then a little melon,

Continued on page 30

Solid Start for a Day: Kedgeree, Kippers, Kidneys

On leisurely weekends in some of the stately homes of England, breakfasts reminiscent of Victorian times and appetites still take the chill off British mornings. The heart of such a breakfast remains eggs with bacon or ham, but these are preceded by a fruit-and-cereal course and then a fish course. For those who still feel a few lingering pangs of hunger before facing the rest of a stately-home day, the hostess might offer still another course to be eaten cold, such as tomatoes and ham. The fare arranged on the antique sideboard above includes coffee, tea and cream (on the silver tray) and from left, top row: rolls; a platter of bacon, sausage and mushrooms; boiled eggs; cold ham and tomatoes; toast; kedgeree (flaked, smoked fish with rice) and butter curls. On the bottom row, from left, are stewed prunes, kidneys, broiled kippers, fried eggs and scrambled eggs.

and a nectarine or two, and just one or two of those delicious raspberries."

Nicolson's remembered morning banquet was the culmination of customs begun in the previous century. It was the Victorians' tendency toward family solidarity and early breakfasting that had influenced the quality, quantity and content of their meals. They were the empire builders. One cannot build an empire by lying slug-abed and breakfasting late on coffee and rolls. In the households that maintained servants, the members of the family helped themselves to food that had been cooked and set to keep warm in covered chafing dishes on the sideboard, because the servants took their breakfast in the kitchen at the same time as the family.

Some chafing dishes would contain bacon, all crisp and brown and curly, and delicious, freshly gathered field mushrooms. A ceramic dish, often in the shape of a fat hen, would contain a clutch of soft-boiled eggs. Silver salvers might reveal, when their gleaming, polished covers were lifted, a selection of fish, such as smoked haddock seethed in milk, or fine Scottish kippers.

There would be deviled kidneys *(Recipe Index)*, a variety of breakfast sausages, potted meat, fresh fruit, honey and Dundee marmalade. And then there was kedgeree. The English brought the recipe back from India, and adapted it to their own taste. In India kedgeree was made of rice, lentils, onions, eggs and spices. The English added smoked fish, usually haddock, and kedgeree became a breakfast dish *(Recipe Index)*.

Pots of tea, black coffee, milk and cream stood by. Assorted hot rolls and breads were to be had, and from the past came the legacy of meat cutlets in a sharp sauce, game pies, cold ham and ale.

This was the "new breakfast," still a meal enjoyed by a privileged minority. At the beginning of Victoria's reign perhaps as much as a third of the population had suffered from malnutrition and deficiency diseases. The workhouse pauper would breakfast on thin porridge and stale bread; as elsewhere, the diets of the rich and the poor were still sharply divided, most noticeably in the big industrial towns.

Some agricultural workers were more fortunate, being to a certain extent self-supporting. They slaughtered their own pigs and cured their own bacon. The pig was an essential member of every country family. The 20th Century chronicler Flora Thompson described how a family ensured its future supply of bacon, feeding the pig on a mixture of boiled potatoes and barley meal: "The family pig was everybody's pride and everybody's business. Mother spent hours boiling up the 'little taturs' to mash and mix with the pot liquor, in which food had been cooked, to feed to the pig for its evening meal and help out the expensive barley meal. The children, on their way home from school, would fill their arms with sow thistle, dandelion and choice long grass, or roam along the hedgerows on wet evenings collecting snails in a pail for the pig's supper."

Bacon is, by origin, entirely English. Ham, which also often figures on the breakfast table, is the pig's cured hind leg, while bacon comes from the cured carcass. Only the English cured the carcass of the pig, usually by salting, while the rest of Europe ate the carcass fresh. Centuries ago, the word bacon was applied to all pork, both the fresh and the cured. One had either "bacon" or "salt bacon." The distinction between the meanings of the words bacon and pork did not occur until much later.

Before the curing of ham and bacon became a centralized industry, each farm had its own curing techniques. The simplest method of curing hams was to rub them in quantities of dry salt and cover them with the salt for two or three days. Some farmers then immersed them in a pickling solution that contained a variety of preservative ingredients and flavorings, the mixture varying according to the district. Usually the pickle consisted of common salt, saltpeter, coarse brown sugar, black treacle, stout and vinegar. Some people added juniper berries, apple pulp left over from cider making, herbs and spices. The hams lay in the brew for several weeks, and then were hung to dry, after which they might be smoked, often in the chimney, and left to mature in the cellars, or under the high roofs of the barns, where cool air circulated. On some farms, particularly along the coast, hams and bacon were smoked over seaweed fires.

Bacon and hams were made in many areas of the country, those from York destined to become the most famous. The old York hams, cured by smoking, were reputed to have obtained their flavor from the smoke of the burning sawdust of the oak timbers cut for the construction of York Minster. The story may indeed be true; the church took 250 years to build, long enough for a custom to have become established, and what else was to be done with all that sawdust?

Wiltshire, on the plains of southwest England, acquired its fame as a producer of hams not only from the local pigs, the fat, Wessex saddlebacks, but also from pigs from abroad. Before the construction of the Great Western Railway, which connected the port of Bristol to London, huge herds of pigs imported from Ireland were driven up the main highway that ran eastward across the Wiltshire Downs past Stone-Age Stonehenge. One of the resting places for the drovers was the town of Calne, where the inhabitants were driven mad by the nocturnal squeals of a thousand Irish porkers. Some of these pigs were acquired by the local curing industry, and Wiltshire ham and bacon became world-renowned.

Most of our English hams are mild and delicately flavored. From Chippenham, another Wiltshire town, comes a tasty example, the black-skinned Bradenham. This ham is dry-salt-cured, after which it is subjected to a costly process of curing and maturing with special applications of molasses and spices. The recipe, which originated in 1781, has been handed down from generation to generation, and is known, it is said, to only two people in the Wiltshire Bacon Company. Another local specialty is the Seager ham from Suffolk. Treated by immersion in brine and syrup, the ham is matured for several weeks, smoked, and then hung for about three months to allow the meat to develop its characteristic sheen.

When the time came for the ham to be cooked, ingredients similar to those that were used in the pickle were added to bring out the full flavor. Here, for instance, is an ancient and well-loved recipe still frequently used in the county of Westmorland: "Line a large pan with sweet hay, and put in one of every kind of root vegetable, such as celery, carrots, onions, etc., the greater variety the better. Put in the ham and cover with cold water, adding two bottles beer. Add a large tablespoonful of syrup. Allow 20 minutes for each 1 lb. weight of the ham and simmer very gently. Cover with fresh water (cold) letting it boil fast. When cooked let the ham remain standing in the liquor . . . for at least 12 hours. This allows it to retain the full flavour."

When Britain was a wholly agricultural nation and the clean country air encouraged mighty appetites, ham and bacon were essential breakfast dishes, having the value of being easily digested foods full of calories that are quickly assimilated. Oatmeal, too, has these advantages—hence the popularity of porridge and other cereals. In Scotland, porridge is traditionally eaten without sweetening; each spoonful is dipped into a bowl or cup of cold milk. Most English people today eat their porridge with sugar or golden syrup. The milk, either hot or cold, is poured over the porridge in the dish, a custom that the Scots regard with utter contempt. Porridge has sustained the Irish, the Welsh and the Scots for centuries. The Scottish troops that fought for Charles I in the 17th Century Civil War were able to march great distances over rough country and go into battle nourished mainly on a handful of oatmeal a day, which they carried with them and made into porridge.

The Welsh, on the other hand, obtained their early-morning energy by consuming quantities of siot, an oatcake soaked in buttermilk, and brewis, an oatmeal broth. In England the place of porridge was long taken by a concoction called frumenty, which some claim to be among the oldest-known dishes in England, along with beans and bacon.

Frumenty was made by soaking whole-wheat or barley grains in a bowl of water that was kept in a warm oven for three days. The grains, absorbing the water, swelled and burst, a process known as creeing (from the French

Irish soda bread, traditionally baked over an open peat fire and served hot or cold with sweet butter and perhaps jam or jelly, is a biscuitlike loaf featured on Ireland's breakfast and tea tables. Mrs. John T. Clarke of County Mayo starts her soda bread an hour before teatime. As her peat fire glows, she mixes the ingredients: flour, salt, soda and buttermilk. Then she puts the dough into a heavy iron pot suspended over the fire *(center)*, covers the pot, and finally lifts the lid to find the bread steaming and brown.

crever, to burst). The starch thus released turned the whole mass into a thick jelly in which the grains were suspended. Creed wheat, as frumenty is also known, was eaten with honey, or sugar and hot milk, for a fortifying wintertime breakfast.

In remote and rural areas of England the tradition of making frumenty still continues. In the north, spices are added; in the south and west dried fruit and eggs are often mixed with the creed wheat, which is served as a pudding. It is a wonder to me that frumenty, which takes time to prepare, has survived the breakfast invasion of prepackaged cereals. Regional tastes, however, die hard. Potato cakes, made of yesterday's cold boiled potatoes mixed with flour, butter and milk, and fried in bacon fat, are still eaten regularly in the West Country. Slices of blood sausage, which is known as black pudding, fried with bacon, and sometimes served with fried apple rings, are a favorite throughout Lancashire.

The last stronghold of the British breakfast will be in the country, probably the rural corners of the north and west. Our urban complexes continue to expand in ever-widening circles, as they do elsewhere in the world. In the cities we hurry more than ever before, and, of course, there are considerably fewer of us who now do heavy work in the open air. That is one of the reasons that we have evolved from meat and beer, through eggs and bacon, and are moving toward tea and toast. The next stage must surely be the continental breakfast of coffee and rolls. Hardly worth getting up for. . . .

CHAPTER II RECIPES

How to Prepare and Seal Canning Jars

To ensure consistent results in home canning, use standard canning jars or jelly glasses with matching lids. An airtight seal is imperative. Examine each one carefully and discard those with covers that do not fit securely or those with edges that have cracks or chips.

Wash the jars, glasses, lids and rings in hot, soapy water and rinse them with scalding water. Place them in a large, deep pot and pour in sufficient hot water to submerge them completely. Bring to a boil over high heat. Then turn off the heat and let the pan stand while you finish cooking the food that you plan to can. The jars or glasses must be hot when the food is placed in them.

To be ready to seal the glasses, grate a 4-ounce bar of paraffin into the top of a double boiler (preferably one with a pouring spout), and melt it over hot water. Do not let the paraffin get so hot that it begins to smoke; it will catch fire easily.

When the food is ready for canning, remove the jars or glasses from the pot with tongs and stand them upright on a level surface. Leave the lids and rings in the pot until you are ready to use them. Fill and seal the jars one at a time, filling each jar to within 1/8 inch of the top and each glass to within 1/2 inch of the top. Each jar should be sealed quickly and tightly with its ring and lid.

The jelly glasses should also be sealed at once. Pour a single thin layer of hot paraffin over the surface of jelly, making sure it covers the jelly completely and touches all sides of the glass. If air bubbles appear on the paraffin prick them immediately with a fork or the tip of a knife. Let the glasses rest until the paraffin cools and hardens; then cover them with metal lids.

NOTE: If there is not enough food to fill the last jar or glass completely, do not attempt to seal it. Refrigerate and use it as soon as possible.

Deviled Kidneys

To serve 4

8 whole lamb kidneys, peeled and trimmed of fat
2 teaspoons bottled mango chutney, finely chopped
1 tablespoon prepared mustard
1 1/2 teaspoons dry English mustard
2 teaspoons fresh lemon juice
1/2 teaspoon salt
Pinch of cayenne pepper
1 tablespoon butter, softened
4 slices hot buttered toast

With a large, sharp knife, split the kidneys in half lengthwise without cutting all the way through. For the marinade, combine the chutney, prepared mustard, dry mustard, lemon juice, salt and cayenne pepper in a large mixing bowl, and stir until thoroughly mixed.

Add the kidneys and turn them about with a spoon to coat them evenly on all sides. Set the kidneys aside at room temperature to marinate for 1 hour, stirring them from time to time.

Remove the broiler pan from the oven and, using a pastry brush, coat it with softened butter. Setting the pan aside, preheat the broiler to its highest point. Then remove the kidneys from the marinade and spread them out flat on the pan, cut side up. Broil the kidneys 3 inches from the heat for 3 minutes. Turn them over with tongs and broil them 3 minutes more. Spread about 1/2 teaspoon of the marinade on each slice of toast, arrange the kidneys in pairs on the toast, and serve at once.

Finnan Haddie

To serve 4

1 small onion, cut into 1/8-inch slices and separated into rings
1 teaspoon whole black peppercorns
2 pounds smoked haddock, cut into 4 pieces
3 cups milk
Mustard sauce *(page 126)*

Strew the onion rings and peppercorns over the bottom of a heavy 10-inch skillet, and arrange the pieces of smoked haddock on top. Pour in the milk. The milk should just cover the fish; add more if necessary. Bring to a boil over high heat, then reduce the heat to low. Cover and simmer undisturbed for about 10 minutes, or until the fish flakes easily when prodded with a fork. Do not overcook.

With a slotted spatula, transfer the fish to a heated serving platter and discard the milk, onions and peppercorns. Serve the Finnan haddie at once, accompanied by a bowl of mustard sauce.

Kedgeree

CURRIED FINNAN HADDIE (FINDON HADDOCK) WITH RICE

To serve 2

3 tablespoons salt
1 cup long-grain rice
1 pound smoked haddock
4 tablespoons butter
1 tablespoon curry powder, preferably imported Madras curry powder
1/4 teaspoon cayenne pepper
4 hard-cooked eggs, rubbed through a sieve
2 tablespoons finely chopped parsley

Bring 6 quarts of water to a boil in a large heavy pot, add the salt, then pour in the rice in a thin, slow stream so that the water never stops boiling. Reduce the heat to moderate, and boil the rice uncovered for 15 minutes, or until the grains are tender but still slightly firm to the bite. Taste periodically to make certain.

Meanwhile, in a heavy 8- to 10-inch skillet, cover the haddock completely with cold water. Bring to a boil over high heat, reduce the heat to low and simmer uncovered for 10 minutes. With a slotted spatula transfer the fish to a plate and break it up into large flakes with a fork, discarding any bones you find. Cover and set aside.

In a heavy 3- to 4-quart saucepan, melt the butter over moderate heat. When the foam has almost subsided, sprinkle in the curry and cayenne pepper. Lower the heat and cook, stirring constantly, for about a minute. Then drain the rice in a colander and stir it into the butter with a fork. Add the flaked fish and return the saucepan to low heat.

Tossing the rice and fish together gently but thoroughly, cook for a minute or two, until the fish is heated through. Stir in half of the sieved eggs, and taste for seasoning. Transfer the kedgeree to a deep heated platter or a serving bowl, sprinkle with the remaining sieved eggs and the parsley, and serve at once.

Irish Soda Bread

To make one 8-inch round loaf

1 tablespoon butter, softened
4 cups all-purpose flour
1 teaspoon baking soda
1 teaspoon salt
1 to 1 1/2 cups buttermilk

Preheat the oven to 425°. With a pastry brush coat a baking sheet evenly with the tablespoon of softened butter.

Sift the flour, soda and salt together into a deep mixing bowl. Gradually add 1 cup of the buttermilk, beating constantly with a large spoon until the dough is firm enough to be gathered into a ball. If the dough crumbles, beat up to 1/2 cup more buttermilk into it by the tablespoon until the particles adhere.

Place the dough on a lightly floured board, and pat and shape it into a flat circular loaf about 8 inches in diameter and 1 1/2 inches thick. Set the loaf on the baking sheet. Then with the tip of a small knife, cut a 1/2-inch-deep X into the dough, dividing the top of the loaf into quarters.

Bake the bread in the middle of the oven for about 45 minutes, or until the top is golden brown. Serve at once.

The bittersweet of a perfect grapefruit marmalade is the reward of care in marrying the flavors of rind and juice with sugar. Even the first step in making the marmalade, peeling the fruit *(top, left)*, is critical. Using a sharp knife, remove only the thin yellow outer coat, taking as little as possible of the underlying bitter white membrane. Then slice the peel into match-size strips *(top, center)*, and set them aside. Now cut away the white membrane *(top, right)*, and slice the fruit in half. Wrap each half separately in cheesecloth and wring out the juice *(above)*. When the peel, squeezed fruit, and juice are recombined with sugar, cooked to the jellying stage, and ladled into a jar *(right)*, they make the golden marmalade *(opposite)* that will brighten breakfast in the months to come.

Grapefruit Marmalade

To make about 4 pints

3 large, ripe grapefruit
2½ to 3 quarts cold water
8 to 10 cups sugar, preferably superfine

Wash the grapefruit and pat dry with paper towels. With a knife or rotary peeler remove the skins without cutting into the bitter white pith. Cut the peel into strips about 1 inch long and ⅛ inch wide. Cut away and discard the white outer pith. Slice the fruit in half crosswise, wrap the halves one at a time in a double thickness of damp cheesecloth, and twist the cloth to squeeze the juice into a bowl. Wrap the squeezed pulp in the cheesecloth and tie securely. Add enough cold water to the bowl to make 3½ quarts of liquid. Drop in the bag of pulp and strips of peel. Let the mixture stand at room temperature for at least 12 hours.

Pour the entire contents of the bowl into an 8- to 10-quart stainless-steel or enameled pot, and bring to a boil over high heat. Reduce the heat to low and, stirring occasionally, simmer uncovered for 2 hours. Discard the bag of pulp and measure the mixture. Add 1 cup of sugar for each cup of mixture, stir thoroughly, and bring to a boil over moderate heat. When the sugar has dissolved, increase the heat to high and, stirring occasionally, boil briskly for about 30 minutes, until the marmalade reaches a temperature of 220° (or 8° above the boiling point of water in your locality) on a jelly, candy or deep-frying thermometer. Remove from the heat. With a large spoon, skim off the surface foam. Ladle the marmalade into hot sterilized jars or jelly glasses *(directions, page 34)*. To prevent the peel from floating to the top, gently shake the jars occasionally as they cool.

To serve 4

- 1¾ cups regular oatmeal
- ¼ teaspoon baking powder
- ½ teaspoon salt
- 1 tablespoon butter, melted
- 5 to 8 teaspoons hot water

Oatcakes

Preheat the oven to 350°. Half a cup at a time, pulverize 1 cup of the oatmeal by blending at high speed in the jar of an electric blender. Combine the pulverized oatmeal, baking powder and salt in a bowl, and stir in the melted butter. When all the butter has been absorbed, add the hot water, a teaspoon at a time, stirring constantly, to make a smooth but firm paste.

Gather the mixture into a ball and place it on a board or table lightly sprinkled with ¼ cup of the remaining oatmeal. Roll the ball into the oatmeal until it is completely covered with the flakes. Spread another ¼ cup of oatmeal evenly over the board and, with a rolling pin, roll the ball out into an 8-inch circle about ⅛ inch thick. With a pastry wheel or sharp knife, cut the circle into 8 pie-shaped wedges. Scatter the remaining ¼ cup of oatmeal on a baking sheet and, with a large metal spatula, carefully transfer the wedges to the sheet.

Bake the cakes in the middle of the oven for about 15 minutes. When the wedges are light brown, turn off the heat and open the door of the oven. Leave the oatcakes in the oven for 4 or 5 minutes, or until they become firm and crisp. Serve at once.

In Scotland, oatcakes are traditionally buttered and served with herring or cheese, but they may be served, alternatively, with honey or jam.

To make about 2 dozen buns

- 2 packages or cakes of active dry or compressed yeast
- 2 tablespoons sugar
- ½ cup lukewarm milk (110° to 115°), plus 1 cup milk
- ½ teaspoon salt
- 1 teaspoon ground allspice
- 1 teaspoon ground cinnamon
- 2 eggs
- 4 tablespoons unsalted butter, softened
- ⅔ cup white raisins
- 1 lightly beaten egg combined with 1 tablespoon heavy cream

Hot Cross Buns

In a small shallow bowl, sprinkle the yeast and sugar over the lukewarm milk. Let the mixture stand for 2 or 3 minutes, then stir it to dissolve the yeast completely. Set the bowl in a warm, draft-free place, such as an unlighted oven, for 5 to 8 minutes, or until the yeast bubbles up and the mixture almost doubles in volume.

Sift 3½ cups of the flour, the salt, allspice and cinnamon into a deep mixing bowl. Make a well in the center and pour in the yeast mixture and the remaining cup of milk. Drop in the eggs and beat with a large spoon until the flour is absorbed. Beat in 3 tablespoons of the softened butter cut into bits, then add up to 1 cup more flour, a few tablespoons at a time, using only as much as necessary to make a dough that can be gathered into a soft ball. When the dough becomes too stiff to stir easily, work in the additional flour with your fingers.

On a lightly floured surface, knead the dough by folding it end to end, then pressing it down and pushing it forward several times with the heel of your hand. Sprinkle the dough with a little extra flour when necessary to prevent it from sticking to the board. Repeat for about 10 minutes, or until the dough is smooth and elastic.

Shape the dough into a ball and place it in a large, lightly buttered bowl. Dust the top of the ball with a little flour, drape a kitchen towel over the bowl, and set in a warm, draft-free spot for 45 minutes to an hour, until the dough doubles in bulk.

With a pastry brush, coat a large baking sheet with the remaining tablespoon of softened butter. Punch the dough down with a single blow of your fist, then transfer it to a lightly floured board and knead the raisins into it. Pull off a small handful of the dough and set it aside.

For each bun, roll a small piece of the dough between your palms into a ball about 1½ inches in diameter. Arrange the balls about 2 inches apart on the baking sheet and set them aside to rise in the warm, draft-free place for about 15 to 20 minutes, or until they double in volume. Meanwhile preheat the oven to 450°.

With a small knife, cut a cross ⅓ inch deep on the top of each bun. Shape the reserved handful of dough into one or two long ropes about ¼ inch in diameter and cut it into strips 1½ inches long. Press the strips into the crosses on the top of the buns.

Brush the buns lightly with the egg-and-cream mixture, and bake in the middle of the oven for about 15 minutes, or until the tops are a deep golden brown. Transfer the buns to a cake rack and let them cool for a few minutes before separating them.

NOTE: If you prefer, you may make the cross on top of the buns with thin strips of candied orange peel instead of the strips of dough.

Crumpets

To make about 10 crumpets

- 1 package or cake of active dry or compressed yeast
- ½ teaspoon sugar
- 2 tablespoons lukewarm water (110° to 115°)
- 1 cup all-purpose flour
- ¼ teaspoon salt
- ½ cup milk
- 1 egg
- 5 tablespoons butter cut into ¼-inch bits

NOTE: To make traditional English crumpets, you will need five or six 3-inch round flan rings or open-topped cookie cutters. Substitute molds easily can be made, if necessary, by removing the tops and bottoms from five or six tin cans that are 3 inches in diameter and 1 to 2 inches tall, such as ordinary tuna cans.

In a small, shallow bowl, sprinkle the yeast and sugar over the 2 tablespoons of lukewarm water and let them stand for 2 or 3 minutes. Then stir them together to dissolve the yeast completely. Set the bowl in a warm, draft-free place, such as an unlighted oven, for 4 or 5 minutes, or until the yeast bubbles up and the mixture almost doubles in volume.

Sift the flour and salt into a large mixing bowl and make a well in the center. Pour in the yeast mixture and the milk, and drop in the egg. Beat vigorously with a large spoon, then add 1 tablespoon of the butter and beat until a smooth soft batter is formed. Drape a towel loosely over the bowl and set it aside in a warm draft-free place for about 1 hour, or until the batter has doubled in volume.

In a small pan, clarify the remaining 4 tablespoons of butter by melting it slowly without letting it brown. Skim off the surface foam and spoon the clear butter into a bowl, discarding the milky solids at the bottom of the pan. With a pastry brush, coat the bottom of a heavy 10- to 12-inch skillet and the inside surfaces of the flan rings or cookie cutters or cans with about half the clarified butter.

Arrange the rings in the skillet and place the pan over moderate heat. For each crumpet, drop about 1 tablespoon of batter into each ring. The batter will immediately spread out and fill the ring. When the crumpets begin to bubble and their bottoms turn a light brown remove the rings. Turn the crumpets over with a wide spatula and cook for another minute or so to brown them on the other side. Transfer the crumpets to a heated serving plate and cover with foil to keep them warm while you coat the skillet and rings with the rest of the clarified butter and cook the remaining batter.

Crumpets are traditionally served at breakfast and at afternoon tea. Accompany them with unsalted butter, syrups and your choice of jams, jellies or marmalades.

III

Tea: Sustenance, Beverage and Ritual

With the tea silver polished and traditional cakes and sandwiches invitingly displayed on a table, a suburban hostess is ready to serve afternoon tea to a group of neighbor women in her home in Kent, a county south of London.

We buried the old colonel in style. Tradition was strictly observed, everyone wore something black, and even the weather conformed. A fine English rain drifted across the Gloucestershire churchyard, intensifying the early summer colors like varnish brushed over a painting. Blackbirds squabbled over their territorial claims in the dark yew trees, whose tiny, linear leaves glistened with an intense viridian. An aunt sniffed, and dabbed her eyes with a lace handkerchief of genteel Victorian proportions.

Later, at the colonel's home, emotions and opinions were freed over tea. "The old boy had a damn fine innings," said a cricketing uncle. "I hope I last as long." He turned and, lowering his voice, whispered, "Find out if there's any sherry; I'm not in the mood for tea."

The colonel's widow had prepared a suitably generous spread. There were sandwiches of many kinds and a bewildering variety of cakes with jam and thick cream. Occasion demanded the best tea service of Worcester Spode, a teapot with matching cups and saucers of blue on white, a wedding present from the colonel's regiment, the Somerset and Cornwall Light Infantry.

Such a funeral tea is common in many English homes, for in times of stress and sorrow (and in moments of joy, too), the Englishman turns almost automatically to his favorite beverage. Tea is to him a great comforter; it loosens tongues and encourages amity.

"Sarah looks so much *younger,* don't you agree?" And, "What a fine lad Tom has turned out to be, it must be ages since last I saw him." Sitting on the edge of a chair, and carefully balancing a plate of cake on her knee, a niece said, "That vicar does mumble so. I didn't understand one word he said—not one word." Maiden aunts brushed cake crumbs from their black crepe de Chine laps, and offered invitations not to be taken too seriously. "*Do* drop by next time you are round our way, we so rarely see each other."

Empty cups were proffered for a refill. Strong, hot tea blended with the milk in the cups. Silver sugar tongs selected lumps of sugar that dropped, with a plop, into the tea.

To the uninitiated, taking tea with the English may seem on a par with the tea ceremonies of the Japanese. An American friend of mine, invited out to tea in London and alarmed at the prospect of having to participate in a performance with which he was only vaguely familiar, asked an English lady friend for guidance.

"Isn't there some kind of tea ritual?"

"Heavens, no!"

"But don't you stand in front of a low table, and the lady of the house sits behind it, and there's lots of silver, and porcelain cups, and a special cake knife, and sugar tongs? And you're expected to talk about the weather, and how the garden is going, and doesn't she ask you whether you take milk or lemon with your tea?"

"Well, of course," came the reply, "but there's no ritual!"

Despite the lady's disclaimer, there is indeed ceremony and ritual surrounding the institution of tea—sometimes. For tea is more than simply a drink in England. It is that, of course, punctuating all hours of the day: as a bracing start to the morning, a welcome break in the work in offices and factories, an accompaniment for meals, and a pleasant cup at bedtime. But tea is also the name of a meal, or rather, several different kinds of meals. In rural areas, where dinner is eaten at midday, the evening meal that corresponds to an American country supper is called high tea, or meat tea. Among the gentry and the middle class, tea is a hospitable spread for guests, like those invited home after the colonel's funeral. In the cities, where dinner is served late in the evening, tea is a necessary afternoon snack. This afternoon tea becomes tea at its most ceremonious, an occasion for entertaining friends. It is an essentially female affair, and the conversation is as light and sweet as the cakes and breads that are taken with it, which the latter part of this chapter discusses. Afternoon tea is not the time for discussion of matters of state unless perhaps the vicar or the lone male who happens to be unoccupied in the afternoon wishes to deliver a weighty opinion or two; the talk is indeed of the garden or of the vicar's trouble in repainting the vestry.

The population of Britain purchases 475 million pounds of tea per annum, which comes to about six cups a day per head. There are elderly ladies in Bayswater and Bournemouth who drink so much strong tea that it causes a permanent flush on their cheeks. Such addiction to tea is by no means new in England. Like many another Briton, the 18th Century wit and lexicographer Doctor Samuel Johnson was a "hardened and shameless teadrinker who," he himself once admitted, "has for many years diluted his meals with only the infusion of this fascinating plant; whose kettle has scarcely time to cool; who with tea amuses the evening, with tea solaces the midnights, and with tea welcomes the morning."

It was a century before Dr. Johnson's time that tea was introduced into England by the Dutch, who had imported it from China. Its arrival was remarked by this advertisement in a London gazette: "That Excellent and by all Physitians approved *China* drink, called by the *Chineans Tcha,* by other Nations *Tay alias Tea,* is sold at the *Sultaness-Head,* a Cophee-house in *Sweetings* Rents by the Royal Exchange, *London.*"

When the new drink came to the attention of the 17th Century diarist Samuel Pepys, he "did send for a cup of *tee* (a China drink), of which I never had drank before. . . ." The "China drink" was taken in the Chinese manner—in bowls and without milk or sugar. It was regarded as a medicine, and that first shipment in the year 1658 went rather slowly; a bowl of tea was an expensive luxury. Tea had to become fashionable.

It did. In 1662 Charles II married Catherine of Braganza, a princess from Portugal, where tea had long been popular, and she introduced the Lisbon fashion of tea drinking to English court circles. Within 10 years imports had trebled, yet tea was still a comparative luxury, for demand now outweighed supply. The next hundred years saw a gradual increase in supplies—and a drop in price—until by the middle of the 18th Century, tea had become such a nationally popular drink that it had all but ousted beer. The government was quick to seize upon the demand as a source of revenue, and the high import duties that it levied gave rise to large-scale smuggling and the adulteration of cargo. Tea was mixed with all manner of unsavory things to increase its bulk. Smuggled tea was drunk by everyone from farm worker to top government executive. "Andrews the Smuggler brought me this night about 11 o'clock a bagg of Hyson Tea 6 Pd weight," recorded one diarist. "He frightened us a little by whistling under the Parlour Window just as we were going to bed. I gave him some Geneva [gin] and paid him for the tea [at the rate of 10 shillings and sixpence per pound]."

Not everyone approved of tea's popularity. "Your very Chambermaids have lost their bloom, I suppose by sipping tea," wrote a critic in 1757. "What an army has gin and tea destroyed!" Some doctors agreed that tea might be dangerous, advising the addition of milk. Such warnings went unheeded; by 1800 we British drank tea at the rate of two pounds per head each year. "Next to water tea is the Englishman's proper element," noted Erik Geijer, a young Swede who visited Britain in 1809. "All classes consume it, and if one is out on the London streets early in the morning, one may see in many places small tables set up under the open sky, round which coal-carters and workmen empty their cups of delicious beverage. . . ."

Until the 1830s, tea still came only from China. But the uncertainty of trade with that country and competition from American suppliers using their new, fast clipper ships forced the British to look elsewhere for supplies. The empire builders tried planting tea in Assam in what is now East Pakistan, where the wild tea plant grew. Tea planting then spread to Darjeeling, far up in the foothills of the Himalayas, and as far south as the island of Ceylon, for the market was broadening. In the early 19th Century the new railways enabled a steady supply of tea to be carried to the far corners of the British Isles. There, in the country villages, local dialect slowly evolved words to describe the all-important process of making tea. Thus in the north and the Midlands, teamaking is called "mashing." Although the term "brewing" is used all over England (soldiers talk of having a "brew-up"), the Scots still "mash." In Wessex and the southeast a pot of tea is a "wet."

As 4 o'clock approaches, mechanics in a London auto repair shop break for tea. Many factories, offices and shops have facilities for teamaking. Some supply the ingredients free to employees, and others have installed automatic vending machines.

Cornwall prefers "soak," and other counties of England "make," "scald," "damp," "draw" and "steep." I have no idea what the Welsh call teamaking, but it is bound to be something quite unpronounceable.

By the end of the 19th Century, kettles sang in every home in the land, and no family was complete without its teapot. The national tea consumption had shot up to more than four pounds per head. Tea firms, of course, were not content with that level of consumption. One, Nelson & Co., developed a scheme for ensuring loyalty among its customers by offering regular purchasers a 19th Century version of social security. One of its advertisements ran: "£20,000 in Gold [$100,000] has been deposited with the British Government as a guarantee for the payment of Nelson's Widows Pensions. ANY MARRIED WOMAN purchasing our tea is entitled to a weekly pension on becoming a widow. A quarter pound weekly entitles the purchaser to a pension of five shillings [$1.25] per week!"

Today, nearly half of the tea drunk in Britain still comes from India, with Ceylon and Africa furnishing most of the rest. Fully 99 per cent of this is black tea; the small remainder is green tea, most of which comes from China and Taiwan. Both varieties come from the same plant, *Camellia sinensis;* the difference between them lies in the preparation of the leaves. To make black tea, the leaves are partially crushed but not broken, liberating the juices within each leaf. The leaves are allowed to ferment, and then dried. To make green tea, the leaves are steamed and passed through rollers, but then dried before they ferment; they thus retain the leaf's natural color.

Green tea has a refreshing, delicate flavor, but most people today prefer black. Black tea is reddish in color, rich and full-bodied, and is a blessing indeed in a cold climate. Black tea provides the population of Britain with that extra courage required to get out of bed, especially on winter mornings. For them, the Teasmade, a bedside teamaking machine, was invented. A preset clock triggers a heater in a water container. The water boils and flows into a teapot that has been primed with tea leaves. All that one has to do is to reach over and pour tea into the cup, adding milk and sugar.

Such an automated method of making tea serves for the first cup of the day. But it is not in the grand old tradition. Everyone in Britain thinks he knows how to make a good cup of tea, and I am no exception. There is but one correct way: Put cold, fresh water into a kettle. Soft water is best. Put the water on to boil in the kettle. Just before it does, warm the teapot and put about four heaping teaspoonfuls of good-quality tea into the pot. The general rule is one spoonful for each cup and one for the pot, but if the water in your area is hard, use more. The water should reach a galloping boil, yet must not be allowed to boil too long. Now, take the pot to the kettle, never the other way about, and pour the water onto the tea leaves in the pot. There is logic behind this seeming British whimsy; to extract the desired fullness of flavor the water must be boiling rapidly when added to the pot. Allow the tea to stand for five minutes, and stir before pouring.

Now comes the great controversy. Which does one add first—the milk or the tea? In the correspondence column of *The Times* of London, that repository of great debate, an argument once raged for months between the two factions—those who put the milk in first and those who pour tea into the cup and then add the milk. Opinion remains divided. Everyone is certain about one thing, however. Whenever you put in the milk, make sure it's *cold*. Although I have had tea served with hot milk (in France), most Britons feel that only a rogue Martian would commit so heinous a crime, and my compatriots are correct. Hot milk ruins the flavor of tea.

When tea becomes more than a warming, stimulating liquid and takes up its role as a meal, the drink itself may be accompanied by almost anything from miniature cookies to sausages and salad, depending on the occasion and the place. The high tea of the rural north is a substantial meal, a combination of small cakes and of meat or fish. Cooked dishes are featured on most high-tea tables, with potted meat, fish, shrimp and shrimp paste (a combination of tiny shrimp, white fish and herbs that is a specialty of Yorkshire and a great favorite in the north), ham salad, salmon cakes and fruit. Afternoon tea is a much lighter affair. It comes about 4 p.m., when city-bred Britons wherever they are—at home, on a trip or at work—stop for a pot of tea usually buttressed by at least some cake or toast.

This refreshment may take the form of a "dainty afternoon tea," the feminine get-together that was reputedly made fashionable a century and a half ago by the Duchess of Bedford. In her circle, lunch had been getting earlier and dinner much later than ever before. An excellent opportunity for a snack between main meals was afforded by the new "afternoon tea," and delicious scandal was discreetly whispered across the silver tea service, above the plates of poundcake and strawberry jam. The tea society even drew comment from William Cobbett, a gruff radical of the time. "The gossip of the tea table," he said, "is no bad preparatory school for the brothel."

A manual of etiquette published for those about to make their debuts into afternoon tea circles warned: "Those who take sugar in their tea are advised to propel the spoon with a minimum of effort, and to remove it without fail before raising the cup." Furthermore, pouring tea that spilled into the saucer back into the cup, or worse, pouring it into the saucer to cool the tea, were the most frightful social blunders.

Today such blunders may be infrequently encountered, but the gossip is no less delicious and the food as delicately prepared as ever. A really elaborate spread for an afternoon tea entertainment might display sandwiches of shrimp paste, thinly sliced cucumber, tiny squares of white bread with a filling of sliced tomato and grated cheese, and a pile of rolls, some containing ham. There would be the Scottish teacakes known as scones, too *(Recipe Index)*, with jam and thick cream, chocolate cake, mocha cake and seedcake. Nearby the guest might find dishes piled with sausage rolls, ham sandwiches and slices of pork pie.

So much fancy food is laid on only for a very special occasion, and the 4 o'clock stop for tea may be a simple affair. British holidaymakers touring the country roads of Europe frequently carry with them a Primus stove, a kettle and a teapot. Teatime finds them having a brew-up by the side of the road. Local passersby are curious; here is the circumstantial evidence that confirms a fact known in Europe for centuries—the British are mad.

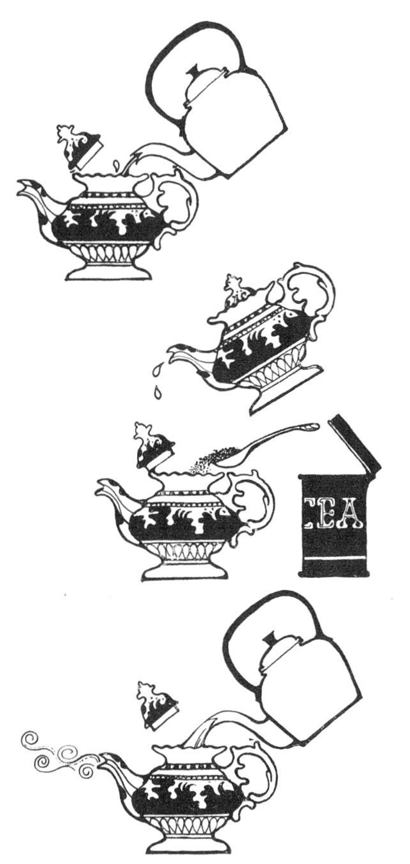

The proper method for making a proper cup of tea is illustrated above. Add a little boiling water to the pot to warm it *(top)*, and then pour off the water. Now add the tea to the pot, one teaspoon for each cup to be served, and one for the pot. Bring the water in the kettle to a galloping boil, add it to the pot, and let the tea steep for five minutes before serving.

On their home grounds, many Britons more sedately go out for tea. The English teashop is an example of a flourishing industry brought about by the national custom of the afternoon break for tea. Just a bit more than a century ago it was realized that the cup of tea, "the cup that cheered," had much more to offer than mere refreshment. There was a fortune in a teacup: Money was to be made from hot cups of tea. In 1862 a certain Dr. Dauglish invented aerated bread, raising the dough with carbon dioxide directly instead of indirectly with yeast, and began selling his bread in a shop close by the London Bridge railway station. He also tried selling cups of tea, and so the Aerated Bread Company's establishment may have been the first teashop in Britain. Business, like the bread, expanded rapidly.

In 1894, the ABC shops met competition when the first of the many white-fronted premises with the gold letters proclaiming "J. Lyons & Co." opened in Piccadilly, London. Known affectionately as "Joe Lyons," they spread across London and its neighboring counties like butter on hot toast. Lyons' cheerful waitresses, called "nippies" because of their speed with a smile and a cup, dispense tea and sympathy to tired shoppers and businessmen. And with the tea are snacks curiously English: canned baked beans on toast, canned spaghetti on toast, Welsh rabbit, meat pie, fried potatoes and a wide variety of buns and cakes, all at competitively low prices.

Millions of gallons of tea and millions of tons of potatoes and toast are yearly consumed in ABC's and in Lyons' neat, modern and efficient shops. Their décor varies from the glass-brass-zinc-linoleum style of the 1930s to the glass-plastic-neon-wood fashion of today.

In our cathedral cities, such as Winchester and St. Albans, where ancient houses cluster around the great cathedrals built centuries ago, the teashops follow a quite different tradition. "Chintzy, chintzy cheerfulness," as the poet John Betjeman called it. Many are fashioned in imitation Tudor or Elizabethan style: oak tables, surrounded by ornate, high-backed chairs. The windows are constructed of rhomboids of glass, small lozenges imprisoned in lattices of lead. Some of these glass diamonds are thick and green, like the bottom of a wine bottle.

Rosy-cheeked country girls and kindly old ladies in flower-decorated aprons serve the traditional fare: toasted teacakes and the flat, spongy bread-like cakes we call crumpets *(Recipe Index),* swimming in butter; chocolate rolls; and geometric Battenburg cake, squares of pink and yellow in a coat of marzipan. "Tea for two, please. Tea and cakes. . . ."

It is at a family tea at home, though, that one can best enjoy the warmth of this afternoon meal, and see how varied its foods may be.

I well remember the astonishment of a French friend who was invited to afternoon tea by my parents. My mother had prepared a spread of scones, home-made chocolate cake, sandwiches of cucumber, watercress and tomato, a pot of tea, a mound of bread and butter, and—celery.

"Celery?" said Jacques. "How strange."

My father broke a piece off, dipped it in salt, and munched it with a piece of the bread and butter.

"Celery," said my father, "is very popular in England. If you were to stand on a hill during any Sunday afternoon in winter and listen carefully you would hear a low, rustling, crunching sound. It is the entire English nation eating celery."

Celery, although not perhaps so popular as my father suggests, is indisputably a part of afternoon tea. More important, however, are the foods that are well woven into the fabric of the occasion—the baked sweets, breads, cakes and biscuits for which Britain is deservedly famous. Their history is so deeply rooted in folklore, festival and fable that the origins of many are obscure. But over the years every region of Britain has contributed to the specialties that make tea a respite to be looked forward to.

Cakes originally were a combination of bread and dough with currants and spices, and evolved in the areas of the southeast and the west of England where wheat was the main crop. The farm wives made batches of dough for bread, sometimes reserving a piece to which fruit and spice might be added. The words cake and bread became confused because of the similarity of the ingredients. A good white loaf of bread was often referred to as cake. Even biscuits were sometimes called "bisk-cakes"; Shrewsbury biscuits and Shrewsbury cakes are one and the same. Today in Britain, as in America, the word cake is usually reserved for something made of sweet dough or batter leavened by an agent other than yeast.

Before the introduction of chemical raising agents, cakemaking required a strong arm and a lot of time. Doughs and batters that were not raised by yeast had to have air introduced into the mixture, usually by beating egg whites to a stiff froth and adding them to the dough. You can imagine how long it took to beat 12 egg whites to that condition.

By the end of the 18th Century, bicarbonate of soda was being used as the raising agent in a number of cake recipes. Some Victorian recipes instructed the cook to add something called "volatile salts." Modern students of cooking tend to misinterpret volatile salts to mean bicarbonate of soda, when in fact *sal volatile*—ammonium bicarbonate—was the raising agent. It made the cakes very light and crisp, but the kitchen reeked of ammonia.

Cake recipes, most of which were invented when such new raising agents simplified cake baking, are legion today. Many are but variations of one another. The small Eccles cake *(Recipe Index)* that would just cover your palm is not unlike a Banbury cake. Eccles cakes are round and Banbury cakes are oval, but both are envelopes of pastry containing a filling of dried fruit and spices. Such cakes are found all over England, but the shape and content vary slightly according to the area: in Shropshire and Yorkshire mint leaves are sometimes added. The towns of Eccles and Banbury are more than 100 miles apart, but both might claim theirs to be the original cake.

The method of cooking often inspired the type of bread or cake. Bread and cakes in the north were cooked on a metal griddle or on a large, flat stone called a bakestone, the heat being supplied by peat, which provided a good, steady glow. Many homes in Ireland still cook on a griddle over a peat fire. This, the Irish believe, imparts a special flavor to Irish soda bread, a filling, biscuitlike loaf, although an excellent variety can be made in an oven *(Recipe Index)*.

In Scotland, oatcakes were made of oatmeal, salt, baking soda, water and fat, shaped into rounds, and cooked on the griddle. When cool, they were spread with fresh butter. Nowadays, the oven has replaced the old griddles

A bewildering array of teatime treats confronts patrons at the teashop of Manor Farm, in Ratlinghope, Shropshire. Deep in the countryside, the shop serves as a meeting place for the wives of local gentlemen. In the foreground are *(left to right)*: Dundee cake, cheese biscuits, raspberry shortbreads, and a coffeecake topped with walnuts.

and bakestones in the country cottages, and there is perhaps no one left in the whole of Britain who still makes the once-famous havercake of the West Riding district of Yorkshire. To make havercake required a knack born of long practice. A batter of fine oatmeal, yeast and water was prepared, and a quantity cast, with a dexterous flick of the wrist, onto the hot bakestone. The batter spread across the stone to form a thin sheet of oatcake.

In Wales the oatcake mixture was rolled out very thin on a board and then set to cook on the bakestone. Now the cake is usually made in a thick frying pan. Called *bara ceirch,* the cake is spread with butter and washed down with buttermilk. So were the buckwheat cakes known as "jannocks" or "anacks," made in Shropshire and fairly common along the Welsh Marches in the mid-18th Century.

Jannocks may have disappeared, but Northumbrian housewives have not forgotten how to make their own specialty, the "singing hinny." A hinny is a large, round cake made of a scone mixture and baked on a griddle where, as it cooks, it sings and fizzes. In parts of Northumberland they are known as "small-coal fizzers," since they cook over the small coals of the fire.

The men who come from the county of Northumberland, especially from along the River Tyne through Newcastle, are known as "Geordies," while hinny is a term of affection, perhaps because the cake is so well liked. Your friend is hinny. A folk song that reflects the grim, cramped conditions of lodginghouse life in the industrial northeast some 80 years ago, where several men were frequently forced to spend the night sleeping on the floor, pleads: "Keep your feet still Geordie hinny, / Lets be happy for the neet [night] / Fer Aa mayn't be se happy thro the day. / So give us that bit comfort, / Keep your feet still Geordie lad, / And divvent drive me bonny dreams away."

After a hard day's work on the coal barges of the Tyne, many a Geordie would return to his tiny, terrace house in Gateshead and sit naked in a tin bath in front of the parlor fire. His wife would wash the thick, black coal grime from his hair, while Geordie listened to the hinny singing on the griddle over the fire.

"What's to ate?"

"Well, there's some bacon and pease pudden, an a piece of sma'coal fizzer, if yer lake."

Yorkshire, too, has a cake with a rather endearing name, the "fat rascal." These are also known as turf cakes, cooked on a bakestone or a griddle above a peat, or turf, fire. Very similar to scones, and made with baking powder, currants and raisins, fat rascals came originally from the villages about the North Riding moors. One of the strangest cakes of all comes from the Isle of Man, a chip of land halfway between the Cumberland coast and Ireland's County Down. Dumb cake, as it is called, probably no longer affects the behavior of young island girls. Maidens would bake a flour cake in the ashes of a fire, and eat a piece while walking backward to bed. Folklore claimed that this ritual would help them to dream of their future husbands.

Scotland is particularly rich in the accouterments of tea. There are more varieties of cake in Scotland than there are whisky distilleries. Dundee cake, a rich fruitcake topped with toasted almonds, is famous all over Britain, yet black bun, also a fruitcake but encased in pastry, is rarely encountered south of the Scottish border. Gingerbread *(for all, see Recipe Index),* often baked in the shape of a man with currants for eyes and the buttons of his coat, is enjoyed both in Scotland and the North of England. The cakes are called "gingerbread husbands" and their origin is lost in antiquity (as we say when we do not know the reason for something). They were common in medieval times, when they were often richly decorated with gold leaf and gilded cloves. The ingredients included honey, flour and the hot, pungent spice called ginger, which was very popular in the Middle Ages.

Far to the south the counties of Wiltshire and Hampshire have their "lardy cakes." I wonder if they still sell them in the small Hampshire town where I went to school. Just the thing for hungry schoolboys: the plump, white dough cake, rich in fat and studded with currants. Lardy cake produced plump, white schoolboys, equally rich in fat. Not for us, the sophisticated éclairs and meringues of the grownups' teas, especially after an afternoon of cricket. Patient cricket! How I detested those languid hours of white, white flannel trousers and cotton shirts. The wooden "chop!" of bat hitting ball; the quarreling crows that squawked in the high elm trees. The only thing that made those afternoons bearable was the anticipation of the treats available at game's end.

Those long afternoons of summer created appetites that lardy cake was designed to assuage. Not all the supposed delicacies served up were delights,

A teataster for Walter Williams and Company, a London tea-blending firm, tries a mixture of some of the brews in the cups before him *(below, right)*. Each cup contains tea from the small pot behind it, every pot a brew made with leaves from one particular plantation. The taster pours from the individual-brew cups into his sampling cup, mixing and testing until he finds a combination with the desired flavor. Below, a sample of the blend he chose rests on a record-book page itemizing the sources of its ingredients.

however. Rock cakes, a sprinkling of currants held fast in a shapeless cake of dry dough, are a tribute to the stoicism of the English, and so to my mind are saffron buns. Both have a yeomanlike solidity that defies any but the strongest teeth and the stoutest hearts. Indeed, many schoolboys are of the opinion that the rock cake was designed primarily as a weapon.

Of all the teatime delicacies, buns seem most closely identified with their native localities. Chelsea buns, spirals of sweet dough crusted with sugar, originated in the borough of Chelsea in London. Somewhere else in the city originated the long, sweet buns covered with white icing that are known as London buns. Several towns in Britain make small, delectable tarts known as maids of honor *(Recipe Index)*, but none are so rich in flavor and therefore so famous as Richmond maids of honor, which come from Richmond, a suburb of London, and which are said to have been invented for the court of Henry VIII in the 16th Century.

One of the best known of England's buns is the Bath bun, which did indeed originate in the health-resort town of Bath. During the 18th Century the gouty, greedy and overindulgent society "took the waters" at Bath Spa, and Bath became the focal point of fashion. Bath, it was thought, produced the best of everything. A large bun, full of candied peel, caraway seeds and sometimes saffron, and strewn with crushed sugar, became popular: the Bath bun. London countered with the soon equally famous Chelsea bun. An establishment called Bun House opened at the end of Pimlico Road expressly for the purpose of selling Chelsea, hot cross and London buns.

Bath then returned fire with the Sally Lunn cake. Sally Lunn was said to have been a young Somerset lass who made and popularized this sweet, light cake of flour, eggs, yeast and cream, to which she gave her name. Some students of British cooking, notably the historian Dorothy Hartley, disagree. She claims that "Sally Lunn" is a corruption of the French *sol et lune,* a sun and moon cake. The origins of the cake are actually wrapped in a crisp crust of mystery. There is a French cake of Alsatian origin called a *solimeme,* and probably our own Sally Lunn is a derivation of this cake. Both are practically identical, both are split open and served with a topping—butter on the *solimeme,* whipped cream on the Sally Lunn. But how did a recipe from Alsace-Lorraine find its way to Bath, in 18th Century England?

Inevitably, some types of cake have disappeared forever. Others, the firm favorites, remain, resisting competition from packaged cake mixes and the mass production of multiple bakeries. British housewives continue to bake—using the simplest ingredients—many of the finest cakes and buns in the world. The treats they make are the delight of the tea lover. I remember overhearing two elderly gentlemen discussing the joy of that gentle hour in the afternoon when tea is served. For them, the pleasure of tea was intensified in autumn and winter, when the evenings drew in, and when one could impale a crumpet on a fork and toast it in the heat of a log fire.

"A pile of crumpets on a plate," mused one of the men, "and the crumpet at the bottom of the pile absolutely immersed in melted butter!"

"And chocolate cake," sighed the other, "decorated with walnuts."

Yet, of all the sentiments that tea has inspired, none is quite so heartfelt as that uttered by the 19th Century writer and clergyman, the Reverend Sydney Smith, who cried, "What would the world *do* without tea?"

CHAPTER III RECIPES

Swiss Roll with Lemon-Curd Filling

To make one 17-inch roll

2 tablespoons butter, softened
2 tablespoons all-purpose flour
6 tablespoons sugar
4 eggs
½ cup self-rising flour
Lemon curd *(below)*
2 tablespoons superfine sugar

Preheat the oven to 400°. Using a pastry brush, coat the bottom and sides of an 11-by-17-inch jelly-roll pan with 1 tablespoon of softened butter. Line the pan with a 22-inch-long strip of wax paper, and let the paper extend over the ends of the pan. Brush the remaining butter over the paper, and sprinkle 2 tablespoons of all-purpose flour over it, tipping the pan to spread the flour evenly. Invert the pan and rap it sharply to remove the excess.

With a whisk or a rotary or electric beater, beat the 6 tablespoons of sugar and the eggs together until the mixture is light and fluffy. A little at a time, sift the self-rising flour over the eggs, folding the mixture together gently but thoroughly with a rubber spatula. Do not overmix. Pour the batter into the jelly-roll pan and, with a spatula, spread it out evenly. Bake in the middle of the oven for 10 minutes, or until the top is a light golden color and the cake has begun to come away from the sides of the pan. Remove the cake from the oven and dust it evenly with the superfine sugar. Then turn it out on a sheet of wax paper and gently peel off the paper. Spread the top of the cake evenly with lemon curd and, starting at the long edge, roll it into a cylinder. Cool to room temperature. To serve, cut the cake into ½-inch slices and arrange the slices attractively on a plate.

Lemon Curd

To make about 1 cup

4 tablespoons unsalted butter
½ cup sugar
½ cup fresh lemon juice
4 egg yolks
1 tablespoon grated lemon peel

In a heavy 1½- to 2-quart saucepan, combine the butter, sugar, lemon juice and egg yolks. Cook over the lowest possible heat, stirring constantly, until the mixture thickens enough to heavily coat the back of a spoon. Do not let the mixture boil or the egg yolks will curdle. Pour the curd into a small bowl and stir in the lemon peel. Refrigerate until ready to use. Lemon curd is used as a filling for tarts and cakes such as Swiss roll *(above)*.

Chocolate Cake with Hazelnuts

To make one 8-inch round cake

8 ounces shelled hazelnuts
½ pound unsweetened baking chocolate, grated fine
1 teaspoon butter, softened
¾ cup plus 2 tablespoons flour
½ pound unsalted butter (2 sticks), softened
1 cup plus 2 tablespoons superfine sugar
1 teaspoon vanilla extract
7 egg yolks
7 egg whites
A pinch of salt

Preheat the oven to 400°. Spread the hazelnuts in a baking pan and toast for 15 minutes, turning them occasionally. Remove the pan from the oven and reduce the heat to 250°. While the hazelnuts are hot, rub them between kitchen towels to remove the skins. Chop 1 cup of the nuts fine and set them aside. Pulverize the rest in a blender or with a nut grinder or mortar and pestle. Stir them together with the grated unsweetened chocolate.

With a pastry brush and 1 teaspoon of softened butter, coat the bottom and sides of an 8-inch springform cake pan. Sprinkle the pan with 2 tablespoons of the flour and tip it from side to side to coat it evenly. Then invert the pan and rap it sharply to remove the excess flour. Set aside.

Cream the remaining ½ pound of butter, 1 cup of sugar and 1 teaspoon of the flour by mashing and beating them against the sides of the bowl with a large spoon. Then add the vanilla and beat in the egg yolks, one at a time. Combine the remaining flour with the nut-and-chocolate mixture, and beat in the butter-and-sugar mixture, a few tablespoons at a time. Continue to beat until the batter is smooth.

Place the egg whites and a pinch of salt in a separate bowl and beat with a whisk or a rotary or electric beater until they form firm unwavering peaks on the beater when it is lifted from the bowl. With a rubber spatula, gently but thoroughly fold the egg whites into the batter, using an over-under cutting motion rather than a stirring motion. Pour the batter into the cake pan and sprinkle the top evenly with the remaining 2 tablespoons of sugar. Bake in the middle of the 250° oven for 1 hour and 15 minutes, or until the sugar on top forms a crisp crust. Let the cake cool for 5 minutes. Then remove the sides of the pan and slide the cake off the base to a rack to cool completely.

To prepare the icing, combine 3/4 cup of sugar with the water, semisweet chocolate and coffee in a heavy 1- to 1 1/2-quart saucepan. Cook over moderate heat, stirring constantly, until the mixture is smooth. Do not let it boil. Set the icing aside to cool briefly. Then transfer the cake to a serving plate and immediately spread the top and sides with icing. While the icing is still soft, press the reserved chopped nuts into the sides of the cake.

ICING
3/4 cup sugar
1/3 cup water
7 ounces semisweet baking chocolate, cut into small pieces
1 tablespoon strong, freshly brewed coffee

Dundee Cake

To make one 8-inch round cake

1 tablespoon plus 1/2 pound butter, softened
2 tablespoons plus 2 1/2 cups all-purpose flour
1 cup sugar
5 eggs
3/4 cup dried currants
3/4 cup seedless raisins
3/4 cup coarsely chopped mixed candied fruit peel
8 candied cherries, cut in half
1/2 cup almonds, pulverized in a blender or with a nut grinder or mortar and pestle
2 tablespoons finely grated orange peel
A pinch of salt
1 teaspoon baking soda dissolved in 1 teaspoon milk
1/3 cup blanched almonds, split lengthwise into halves

Preheat the oven to 300°. Using a pastry brush, coat the bottom and sides of an 8-by-3-inch springform cake pan with 1 tablespoon of the softened butter. Sprinkle in 2 tablespoons of the flour, tipping the pan to spread the flour evenly. Invert the pan, and rap it sharply to remove the excess.

In a large mixing bowl, cream the remaining 1/2 pound of butter and the sugar together by mashing and beating them against the sides of the bowl with a spoon until they are light and fluffy. Beat in one of the eggs, then 1/2 cup of flour and so on alternately until all the eggs and the 2 1/2 cups of flour have been added. Beat in the currants, raisins, candied peel, cherries, pulverized almonds, grated peel and salt, and continue beating until well combined. Stir in the dissolved soda, pour the batter into the pan, and arrange the split almonds on top in concentric circles. Bake in the middle of the oven for 1 1/2 hours, or until a cake tester inserted in the center comes out clean. Let the cake cool in the pan for 4 or 5 minutes, then cool it thoroughly on a rack before serving.

Rich Tea Scones

To make about 12 scones

1 tablespoon butter, softened
2 1/2 cups self-rising flour
1 tablespoon sugar
1/2 teaspoon salt
3 tablespoons lard, cut into 1/4-inch bits and thoroughly chilled
1 egg
1/2 cup milk

Preheat the oven to 400°. Using a pastry brush, coat a large baking sheet with the softened butter and set it aside.

In a large chilled mixing bowl, combine the flour, sugar, salt and lard. With your fingertips, rub the flour and fat together until they look like flakes of coarse meal. Beat the egg with a whisk or fork until it froths and set 1 tablespoon of it aside in a small dish. Beat the milk into the remainder of the egg and pour over the flour mixture. With your hands or a large spoon toss together until the dough can be gathered into a compact ball. Dust lightly with flour and on a lightly floured surface roll the dough out into a 1/4-inch thick circle. With a cookie cutter or the rim of a glass, cut the dough into 2-inch rounds. Reroll and cut the scraps into similar rounds. Place the rounds about 1 inch apart on the baking sheet and brush the tops lightly with the reserved tablespoon of beaten egg. Bake in the middle of the oven for 15 minutes, or until light brown. Serve at once on a heated platter.

To make about 15 brandy snaps

- 8 tablespoons (1 stick) unsalted butter, softened
- 1/4 cup confectioners' sugar
- 2 tablespoons imported English golden syrup, or substitute 5 teaspoons light corn syrup combined with 1 teaspoon molasses
- 1/2 cup all-purpose flour
- 1/2 teaspoon ground ginger
- 1/4 cup brandy
- 2 teaspoons finely grated lemon peel

FILLING

- 1 1/2 cups heavy cream
- 1/4 cup confectioners' sugar
- 2 tablespoons brandy

Brandy Snaps

Preheat the oven to 350°. Use a pastry brush to coat a large baking sheet with 1 tablespoon of softened butter and then coat the handle of a long wooden spoon with another tablespoon of butter. Set aside.

In a heavy 10- to 12-inch skillet, bring 4 tablespoons of the butter, 1/4 cup of sugar and the syrup to a boil over moderate heat, stirring until the butter melts and the sugar dissolves. Remove the pan from the heat. With a large spoon gradually beat in the flour, ginger, brandy and lemon peel. Continue to beat until smooth. Drop the batter by the teaspoonful onto the baking sheet, spacing the cookies about 4 inches apart. Bake in the middle of the oven for 8 to 10 minutes, or until the cookies have spread into 3- to 4-inch rounds and have turned a golden brown. Turn off the heat and open the oven door, but leave the cookies in the oven to keep warm. If the cookies cool too much, they will harden and it will be difficult to shape them.

Working quickly, remove one cookie at a time with a metal spatula and roll it into a tube around the butter-coated handle of the spoon. Slide the tube off the handle onto a cake rack and proceed in the same fashion with the other cookies. Use the remaining 2 tablespoons of butter to keep the spoon handle well coated as you proceed.

Just before serving, beat the cream in a chilled bowl with a whisk or a rotary or electric beater until it thickens slightly. Add 1/4 cup of sugar and continue to beat until the cream forms stiff peaks on the beater when it is lifted out of the bowl. With a rubber spatula, gently but thoroughly fold in the brandy. Fill a pastry bag with the brandied cream and pipe it into the brandy snaps. Serve at once.

Make the batter for brandy snaps in a skillet, then spoon it onto a baking sheet. The snaps will spread, so space them 4 inches apart.

Shortbread

To make about 2 dozen triangles

1 tablespoon plus 1 pound (4 sticks) unsalted butter, softened
1 cup superfine sugar
5 cups all-purpose flour, sifted before measuring

Preheat the oven to 350°. Using a pastry brush, coat a large baking sheet with 1 tablespoon of the softened butter. Set aside.

With an electric mixer, beat the 1 pound of butter and the cup of sugar together at high speed until the mixture is light and fluffy. Then reduce the speed to medium and beat in the flour, a cup at a time; continue beating until the mixture is smooth. (To make the dough by hand, cream the 1 pound of butter and the sugar together by beating and mashing them against the sides of a mixing bowl with a large spoon until the mixture becomes fluffy. Add the flour, a cup at a time, beating well after each addition. If the dough becomes stiff to stir, knead in the remaining flour with your hands.)

On a lightly floured surface, roll the dough into a rectangle roughly 10 inches long by 8 inches wide and about ½ inch thick. With a ruler and a pastry wheel or a small, sharp knife, cut the rectangle lengthwise into four 2-inch-wide strips, and make crisscrossing diagonal cuts at 2½-inch intervals across them to form small triangles. Prick the pieces all over with the tines of a fork, making an even pattern of tiny holes on the surface. Arrange the triangles on the baking sheet and bake in the middle of the oven for 25 to 30 minutes, or until firm to the touch and delicately browned. With a wide metal spatula, transfer the triangles to cake racks to cool completely. Shortbread will keep for 2 or 3 weeks in tightly covered jars or tins.

NOTE: Shortbread dough may be baked in various shapes. Sometimes it is rolled and cut into rectangular cookies; sometimes it is rolled out into one large round cake and the surface marked with a knife tip so that it can be divided into individual wedges.

Roll each warm brandy snap around the handle of a wooden spoon to shape a tube. After they cool, pipe whipped cream inside each one.

Black Bun

To make one 8-inch cake

PASTRY

- 1/2 pound (2 sticks) unsalted butter, chilled and cut into 1/4-inch bits
- 2 1/2 cups all-purpose flour
- 6 to 8 tablespoons ice water
- 1 tablespoon butter, softened

FILLING

- 4 cups all-purpose flour
- 1/2 cup sugar
- 1 teaspoon baking soda
- 1 teaspoon ground cinnamon
- 1/2 teaspoon mace
- 1/8 teaspoon ground cloves
- 1/4 teaspoon salt
- 1/2 teaspoon freshly ground black pepper
- 6 cups seedless raisins (about 2 pounds)
- 6 cups white raisins (about 2 pounds)
- 2 cups coarsely chopped blanched almonds (about 12 ounces)
- 1 1/2 cups finely chopped, mixed candied fruit peel (about 8 ounces)
- 3 eggs
- 1/2 cup buttermilk
- 1 cup brandy

In a large, chilled bowl, combine the 1/2 pound of chilled butter and 2 1/2 cups of the flour and rub them together with your fingers until they look like flakes of coarse meal. Do not allow the mixture to become oily. Pour 6 tablespoons of ice water over the flour all at once; then shape the dough into a ball. If the dough crumbles, add more ice water by the teaspoonful until the particles adhere. Dust the pastry lightly with flour and wrap it in wax paper. Refrigerate for at least 2 hours.

Preheat the oven to 350°. With a pastry brush and 1 tablespoon of soft butter, coat the bottom and sides of a round baking dish about 8 inches in diameter and 3 inches deep.

To make the filling, sift 4 cups of the flour, the sugar, baking soda, cinnamon, mace, cloves, salt and pepper together into a mixing bowl. Add the seedless raisins, white raisins, almonds and candied peel a cup or so at a time, tossing them constantly with a spoon until the fruit and nuts are coated with the flour. Beat the eggs until frothy, stir in the buttermilk and brandy, and pour the mixture over the flour and fruit. Stir until all the ingredients are well combined.

Break off about two thirds of the chilled dough and place it on a lightly floured board. Pat it into a flat circle about 1 inch thick, and roll it out into a circle 15 to 16 inches in diameter and about 1/4 inch thick. Drape the pastry over the pin and unroll it loosely over the baking dish. Gently press it into the bottom and around the sides of the dish, being careful not to stretch it. With scissors or a sharp knife, trim off the excess dough around the rim, and spoon the filling into the dish. Then roll the remaining pastry into a circle 9 to 10 inches in diameter and unroll it over the top of the dish. Cut off the excess and seal the edges of the circle securely to the dish by crimping it with your fingers or by pressing it down firmly with the tines of a fork. With a fork, prick the pastry all over the surface and, with a small knife, cut two 1-inch-long parallel slits about 1/2 inch apart in the center.

Bake in the center of the oven for 1 1/2 hours, then reduce the heat to 275° and bake for another 1 1/2 hours, or until the top is golden brown. Cool and then cover tightly with foil or plastic wrap and let stand at room temperature for at least a week before serving. In Scotland this dish is traditionally served on New Year's Eve. (It will keep for 3 or 4 weeks.)

Seedcake

To make one 8-inch round cake

- 1/4 pound (1 stick) plus 1 tablespoon butter, softened
- 2 1/2 cups all-purpose flour
- 1 teaspoon double-acting baking powder
- A pinch of salt
- 3/4 cup sugar
- 1 tablespoon caraway seeds
- 1 egg
- 1/2 cup milk

Preheat the oven to 350°. With a pastry brush or paper towel coat the bottom and sides of an 8-inch round cake pan evenly with 1 tablespoon of the softened butter. Set the pan aside. Sift the flour, baking powder and salt together into a small bowl and set aside. In a large bowl, cream the 1/4 pound of softened butter and the sugar together by mashing and beating them against the sides of the bowl with a spoon until they are light and fluffy. Beat in the caraway seeds and then the egg. Add the flour mixture, 1/2 cup at a time, beating well after each addition. When the mixture is smooth, beat in the milk and pour the batter into the prepared pan. Smooth the top with a spatula and bake in the middle of the oven for 45 minutes, or until a cake tester inserted in the center comes out clean. Let the cake rest for 5 minutes in the pan, turn it out on a cake rack, and cool completely.

Maids of Honor

ALMOND TARTS

To make about 18 tarts

- 2 tablespoons butter, softened
- 5 tablespoons flour
- Short-crust pastry *(page 107)*
- 2 egg yolks
- ½ cup sugar
- ½ cup blanched almonds, pulverized in a blender or with a nut grinder or a mortar and pestle
- 1 tablespoon finely grated lemon peel
- 2 tablespoons heavy cream

Preheat the oven to 400°. With a pastry brush and the 2 tablespoons of softened butter, coat the inside surfaces of 2 medium-sized 12-cup muffin tins (each cup should be about 2½ inches across at the top). Sprinkle 4 tablespoons of the flour into the tins, tipping them to coat the bottoms and sides of the cups evenly. Then invert the tins and rap them sharply on a table to remove the excess flour.

On a lightly floured surface, roll the short-crust pastry into a circle about ¼ inch thick, and with a cookie cutter or the rim of a glass, cut it into 3-inch rounds. Gather the scraps together into a ball, roll it out into another circle, and cut out rounds as before. Gently fit the rounds into the cups of the muffin tins, pushing the pastry firmly into the sides. The pastry shells will be about 1 inch deep, and will not fill the cups completely.

In a mixing bowl, beat the egg yolks with a whisk to break them up. Then beat in the sugar, almonds, lemon peel and the remaining tablespoon of flour. Slowly add the cream and beat until the mixture is smooth. Ladle about 1 tablespoon of the mixture into each of the pastry shells, filling them to within ⅛ inch of the top.

Bake in the middle of the oven for 15 to 20 minutes, or until the filling is a light golden brown. Carefully remove the tarts from the tins and cool them to room temperature on cake racks. Maids of honor are traditionally served at afternoon tea.

NOTE: In some parts of England, jam or bread crumbs are added to the filling, and it is not uncommon to find the tarts topped with two crossed strips of the pastry.

Eccles Cakes

To make about 12 cakes

- 1 tablespoon butter, softened, plus 2 tablespoons butter, melted
- 3 tablespoons sugar
- ½ cup dried currants
- 1 tablespoon finely chopped mixed candied fruit peel
- ⅛ teaspoon ground allspice
- ⅛ teaspoon ground nutmeg
- Short-crust pastry *(page 107)*
- Superfine sugar

Preheat the oven to 475°. Using a pastry brush, coat a large baking sheet with 1 tablespoon of softened butter. Set aside. In a small bowl, combine the melted butter and the 3 tablespoons of sugar, and stir in the currants, candied fruit peel, allspice and nutmeg. Toss the fruit about with a spoon until it is evenly coated.

On a lightly floured board, roll the pastry into a circle about ¼ inch thick. With a cookie cutter or the rim of a glass, cut it into 3½-inch rounds. Gather the scraps together into a ball, roll it out into another circle, and cut out rounds as before.

Place a heaped tablespoon of the fruit mixture in the center of each round. Then bring up the outside edges of the pastry and twist together to enclose the filling. Turn over, and with the rolling pin press them gently but firmly into flat rounds. The currants should be just visible below the surface of the rounds. With the tip of a small, sharp knife make crisscrossing slits about 2 inches long in the center of each cake.

Place the cakes on the baking sheet and bake in the middle of the oven for about 15 minutes, or until they are golden brown. With a wide metal spatula, transfer the cakes to a rack to cool. Just before serving, sprinkle each cake generously with superfine sugar.

Eccles cakes are traditionally served at afternoon tea. They will keep for 1 to 2 weeks in a tightly covered jar or tin.

IV

A Nation of Beefeaters

Wearing the straw boater of his trade, a butcher displays lamb chops for inspection in a London shop. On his block are *(clockwise from the cleaver):* honeycomb tripe, saddle of lamb, crown of lamb, sausage and leg of pork. At the center are ribs of beef, while whole spring lambs hang in the background.

Consider that very personification of England—John Bull. He is dressed in the costume of a country squire, wearing a waistcoat made of the Union Jack, and a bulldog follows at his heels. He is fat, ruddy-cheeked, jovial and bibulous—what Uncle Sam might have looked like if he had let himself go. John Bull is merely a symbol, of course, but he is a symbol with a solid foundation of fact. He rose to prominence in the 18th Century, a period when upper-class Britons took consummate delight in the pleasures of the table, and his generous proportions are undoubtedly a result of his diet of roast beef and ale—how could John Bull possibly dine on anything other than beef, this most English of foods? (Of course, his bulldog got the scraps.) John Bull, symbol of squirearchy and Empire that he was, is of course somewhat out of fashion these days. But whatever else may have changed since his time, the roast beef of England was and is no myth or mere symbol. It remains today our most cherished national dish, its pride of place unchallenged for hundreds of years, the leading meat dish in a country in which meat, not bread, is so to speak the staff of life.

It is at Sunday dinner—called "lunch" in England, and served at midday—that we most frequently encounter roast beef. Usually it is Father who carves the meat, sharpening the carving knife to a keen edge on the steel; the blade moves surely through the crisp, brown skin of the roast, down to where the center is lean and pink and juicy. There are some of us around the table who prefer the outer slices, seared to a deep, dark brown.

While the joint is so carved, the Yorkshire pudding, that frothy cloud of batter that is the classic accompaniment to roast beef *(Recipe Index)*, rises to its completion in the oven's fierce blast. A high temperature is needed to cook a Yorkshire pudding; the roast was therefore removed before the heat was increased, and while the meat is being kept warm the pudding expands, rising up and out from the baking tin like a large yellow flower that opens, very slowly, with the sun's warmth. Yorkshire pudding cooks in the manner of a soufflé, and it is the diner who waits for the pudding, never the reverse. Mother, meanwhile, stirs the gravy and keeps an eye on the vegetables.

A joint of beef is usually roasted with its attendant circle of potatoes in the roasting pan, for roast potatoes, like Yorkshire pudding, are an integral part of the meal. So are the other accompaniments—mustard; snow-white and fluffy horseradish sauce; a boat of rich, brown, hot gravy. Green vegetables, and perhaps some carrots, add a splash of bright color to the harmony of pinks and browns on the plate. But few of us pause to admire the view. A fairly generous amount has been prepared, for second and third helpings are usually expected, in spite of the knowledge that a large and sugary plum pie must surely follow, crowned with thick cream. How formidable! How delicious!

It is indeed a delightful meal, and it is worth examining closely. For the Englishman's Sunday lunch offers important clues to his eating habits—and especially to his meat-eating habits. In part these habits developed chronologically; in part they were influenced by geographical considerations (note the Yorkshire pudding); to a degree they reflect the British cook's canny ability to find exactly the right partner for each dish in the nation's larder (the horseradish served with the beef).

Along with the figure of John Bull, the 18th Century propagated the attendant legend of Merrie England, the bucolic land of folk song, puddings, beer and beef. Landlords of inns in song and story, and often in fact, were perfect John Bull types, always depicted as bluff, genial Falstaffian men, their serving wenches rosy cheeked, generous, and liberal with their favors. The customers, like the landlords, were overfed gentlemen whose obesity threatened to split their attire.

So highly regarded were the pleasures of the table that society England fairly rang to the clash of cutlery and the chime of the wineglass. "I am convinced that character, talents, virtues and qualities are powerfully affected by beef, mutton, pie crust, and rich soups," said the clergyman and writer Sydney Smith. Hardly pausing for breath we English gobbled tons of boiled mutton, roast beef and pork. Puddings and pies were drenched in lashings of dark gravy. We quaffed countless gallons of ale, tucked into mountains of cheese. Visitors from Europe were staggered at our prandial voracity.

In London, denizens of the chophouse and dining room proudly bore the evidence of this voracity—obesity, surely encouraged by their insistence on consuming four bottles of port to round off a meal. Thus they created a legend that we have been trying to live up to ever since—that roast beef is the prerogative of all Englishmen, and our staple diet. In fact, this was only a half-truth, for the privileges dividing the rich from the poor were never more sharply defined than when it came to who got the meat. Fresh beef, mutton and pork were infrequent luxuries on the farm worker's table.

They worked hard, the countrymen of Britain, and lived frugally. For centuries they breakfasted at 5 in the morning on a slice of bread and a piece of bacon, or often merely bacon fat. Their lunch was cheese and beer or rough,

An orchard in Kent promises apples and pears and, from the Kentish sheep, some of the tenderest chops in the land.

biting cider. From the early Middle Ages until well after the "rich" years of the Victorian era the principal diet of the working classes, especially those in Scotland and Ireland, consisted of bacon and bread, cheese and beer. This simple fare was supplemented, as often as possible, by pothunting for rabbit, hare, badger and fresh-water fish; for centuries poaching was a necessity, not a pastime.

This unhappy situation was to pass, although not for several generations. An agricultural revolution was painfully emerging out of the land, encouraged by agrarian policies pursued by successive governments in the hope of producing more food. "Take away the peasants' strips of land around the villages; they are wasteful," went the general thinking behind this policy. "Let's amalgamate them into big fields, enclosed by hedges and ditches." There was enlightenment behind this policy; there was also avarice, and many a peasant lost his land as unscrupulous officials and large landowners took advantage of the government's decrees. Over a period of many years the government enclosed the peasants' strips of land, as well as wasteland and the common land on which the peasant was traditionally allowed to graze his livestock, for our expanding wool industry needed it for sheep grazing. Beginning in 1709, this series of Enclosure Acts forced many of the peasants whose land had been confiscated to find work in the expanding towns.

Keeping pace with this urban expansion was a steady increase in total population. Farming, still more or less primitive, accordingly faced pressures for greater productivity. Something had to be done, and quickly. Fortunately, into the history of agriculture in the early 1700s stepped Jethro Tull, a Berkshire farmer who vastly improved crop sowing with his invention, the machine drill, a mechanical sower whose efficiency enabled farmers to obtain greatly increased yields from their fields. His methods were supplemented by a statesman and Norfolk landowner, Lord Townshend. "Turnip Townshend," they called him. Townshend pushed the revolutionary idea of feeding cattle and pigs on turnips (which could now be grown in quantity) through the winter, instead of slaughtering the animals and salting the carcasses, as had been done as long as men could remember. Other farmers followed Townshend's progressive ideas, but cautiously. One innovator, more far-seeing than the rest, realized that the future of our agriculture depended on the improvement of the livestock. This was Robert Bakewell, who was a teenager when Lord Townshend died in 1738 and who grew up to become England's first commercial stockbreeder, developing such strains as the Leicestershire sheep and Dishley longhorn cattle.

All this—the improvement of breeds, the ability of stockmen to keep herds alive through the winter, the increasing availability of forage land for the growing herds—led to an enormous increase in productivity. While there were many people who could still not avail themselves of it, the expanding towns, especially London, began to receive meat in large quantities. Cattle from Scotland, sheep from Wales, and cows and pigs from Ireland were driven to London for sale at Smithfield market. Thousands of head of cattle made the trip across the Isle of Anglesey from the Irish cattle boats that docked at the port of Holyhead, and swam the half-mile Menai Straits, the channel that separates the island from the Welsh mainland. The distance from the coast to Barnet village on the outskirts of London, whence the cattle were

sent to Smithfield, was more than 200 miles—and the going was hard. During hot summers the cattle and drovers were maddened by clouds of dun-colored, biting flies. The roads dried and cracked; the ruts in some places were four feet deep. Many cattle died on the way; survivors often arrived at Barnet—where they were fattened for market—exhausted and diseased.

Beef, as a consequence of all this, was expensive and tough, and the meat was scarcely flavorsome. Yet even these shortcomings contributed to British cookery: spices and sauces were used in increasing amounts to enhance the flavor of beef. One cannot overestimate the importance of spices in the early British kitchen. Aside from helping out with flavor, they had an equally important function: the disguising of it. Meat was often "high," or tainted, in those days, and society considered it impolite to "smell at the meat while it was on the fork." Since Norman times we had used spices to mask the unpleasant taste of tainted meat, and to render salt meat more palatable. Often cooks put handfuls of strong-flavored marigold flowers in their soups and stews. Those who could afford the high prices purchased cloves, ginger, cinnamon, saffron and sugar (sugar being counted as a spice).

Britain's long association with India further educated the English palate to a taste for fiery flavors. Into our sauces and stews went coriander, chili, turmeric, cumin and cardamom. The East India Company's officers home on leave also introduced curries and *chatni*, the Hindustani word for strong, spicy condiments, later anglicized to "chutney." "China chilo" and "country captain" are other legacies of British India. China chilo is a combination of minced mutton with shredded lettuce, onions, peas and mushrooms, served together with boiled rice. Country captain is an Anglo-Indian term, meaning the captain of a foreign vessel, a ship from another country. It is also the

One of England's most valued inhabitants, Joy Erica of Slades, stands majestically beside the collection of show ribbons she has garnered. Two of the ribbons proclaim her champion of breed—Aberdeen Angus, the breed that provides much of England's best beef. Joy's calf Joyous Erica, at right, will be kept for breeding purposes, like her mother and many of her siblings, on this farm in Surrey.

name given to an onion-and-chicken curry flavored with cumin, turmeric, coriander and chili.

By the time refrigeration became available in the late 19th Century, so that meat from the Argentine, Australia and New Zealand could grace our tables, hot pickles, sauces and curries were very much to the English taste, and provided the occasional sharp accent to the quiet harmony of British cooking. Certain types of spice had become the principal ingredients in strongly flavored sauces, which have rarely been absent from British tables since their introduction in the 18th Century. Eventually, however, homemade bottled sauces superseded most spices in meat cookery.

Most of these sauces, in particular the famous Worcestershire sauce, contained powerful flavors such as anchovy essence, vinegar, soy, garlic and assorted spices. Worcestershire sauce is said to have originated in India, discovered there by Sir Marcus Sandys of Worcestershire, and it is a condiment very much in evidence today as a flavoring in soups, casseroles and stews.

In the big cities, where often both husband and wife go out to work, such time-consuming dishes as stews and casseroles have given way to quickly prepared meat dishes—steak, for example, and chops. This is partly because in the past 20 years steak has become widely available. Just after World War II and into the early 1950s sirloin steaks were luxuries that few could afford. The war years, food rationing, and the high price of meat put such cuts far above the average family purse. Now we can all, or mostly all, eat steak. The promise of the 18th Century and the legend of John Bull have become reality; there is indeed meat for all. Nearly every family can buy a joint of beef, pork or lamb for Sunday lunch.

This English Sunday lunch has been described by social psychologists as a symbol of security. The security of the home, and of parental affection, is symbolized in home cooking (Mother's cooking is always the best). Family ties continue to be powerful in England, perhaps partly because of Mother's wish that her family be well-fed, a desire that continues even when the children themselves are married. Many families never miss the Sunday lunch reunion, especially in farming communities where members of the same family live in fairly close proximity.

Sunday lunch satisfies the hearty appetites that have been aroused by pints of beer in the masculine retreat of the village pub a few steps from the church. For centuries, Englishmen have balanced Sunday morning piety against Sunday afternoon hedonism, and more often than not it was the morning preacher who set the noontime pace. An 18th Century Dorset farmer's wife and diarist named Ann Hughes was a bit put out to discover that her husband had invited a preacher named William Ellis to lunch on Sunday. The preacher "ate too much meat," she complained, and the cooking "gave her a lot of work." In her diary Ann tells us that she "boyled our biggest ham and cooked a saddle of mutton, three capons, and a round of spiced beef and a roast hare with his inside filled with herbs and bits, then some tarts and a pudding, some cheese and butter and bread, this with potatoes and greens and other trimmings should do very well, and there will be cyder and beer and sherry wine to drink, so we should have a good dinner."

Little of such a feast went to waste; what meat was left over would be served cold for Monday breakfast, eaten with bread and washed down with ale. For the period, this was a standard use of leftovers but hardly an inspired one; the inventive English cook could acquit herself far better than that. When the Victorians introduced lighter breakfasts, the cold cuts of meat left over from Sunday were saved for Monday lunch to make an entirely English dish called "bubble and squeak." A 19th Century recipe for bubble and squeak (the name is onomatopoeic, from the noise it makes when frying) calls for pieces of cold beef, covered with chopped cabbage and onion and then fried. Nowadays, the dish often is made with cold beef and cold cooked potato, mixed with either cold cabbage or brussels sprouts—the vegetable leftovers of the day before. Mashed together, the mixture is fried until brown and crisp on both sides, and then stirred with a fork until the crispy bits are incorporated within the whole. It is again fried on both sides until brown, mashed up with a fork, and so on, until the bubble and squeak is full of crispy brown bits.

Such thrifty re-use of leftovers has long shored up the larders of British kitchens, creating homely recipes like shepherd's pie and toad-in-the-hole. Shepherd's pie, also called cottage pie, is often made of minced cooked meat (usually mutton or lamb) covered with onions, topped with mashed potato, and baked in the oven until nicely browned. And toad-in-the-hole? This is a development of an old dish called froise (or fraise), consisting of slices of bacon coated in batter and deep-fried. Today any kind of meat can be used to make toad-in-the-hole *(Recipe Index)*. A thick batter is poured over pieces of the meat, and the dish is then transferred to the oven until the batter is cooked through. Most people use sausages when they make toad-in-the-hole, replacing the cold cuts of meat taken from Sunday's joint.

In a Cornish farmyard, a sow is besieged by one of her brood during an unplanned moment of privacy. Pigs are raised throughout the British Isles, but pork ranks third—well below beef and lamb—in meat consumption. Black-and-white saddlebacks, like those depicted on the Devonshire weathervane on the opposite page, are a common breed.

Dishes of this sort are simple but can attain distinction—and, in some cases, greatness—when accompanied by their traditional complements. The British have always been masters at putting together superb culinary combinations. Our country ancestors did what came naturally, and left us, among other wonderful legacies, roast pork with its crisp, crackling skin—and adjunct of applesauce. They served mutton or lamb with jelly. Nobody questions the right of Yorkshire pudding to appear together with roast beef and horseradish sauce; they have proved classic partners over the centuries. Boiled beef also has its traditional accompaniments. The cherished dish of London's East-End Cockneys, boiled beef goes with carrots, pease pudding and dumplings. Today's dumplings are invariably made of flour and prepared beef suet, worked to a stiff dough and boiled in the meat broth. Originally, most dumplings were made from bread dough. An extra quantity of dough would be made on baking day, and small pieces the size of walnuts would be dropped into the broth or stew and boiled until they swelled up.

Many of these combinations are, of necessity, seasonal. When the hoarfrost hardens the soil, we dine on tripe and onions seethed for hours in milk with a bay leaf for added flavor, oxtail soup, Scotch broth, Irish stew, boiled beef and dumplings, rabbit pie, salted pork. Pig's trotters were boiled and served cold in their own thick jelly with a vinaigrette sauce, or grilled and served hot with parsley sauce.

When the month of March blew winter away, the farmer's family looked forward to roast leg of veal stuffed with sage leaves, to boiled calf's head with boiled bacon (not to my taste), and roast lamb. Now they also could enjoy calf's liver, fried with rashers of bacon and crisp onion rings, and make veal-and-ham pies, with their fine decorative crust of hot-water pastry, and grill lamb chops with sprigs of evergreen rosemary from the herb garden.

The raw materials—excellent meat, cereal and dairy products—combined to create the dishes that became the mainstay of the population. In Ireland, lamb or kid married with potatoes became Irish stew. This same combination with variations is called hot pot in Lancashire and Yorkshire. Almost everywhere along the Pennine chain that runs down the center of England you will find hot pot *(Recipe Index)*, made with the scrag-end or the neck chops of the Pennine sheep, together with onions, potatoes and an oyster or two. Cooked in an earthenware pot, and served with pickled red cabbage (as is Irish stew), hot pot was elevated to national recognition. The addition of oysters may seem curious, but it must be remembered that hot pot was created by the Lancashire millworkers at a time when oysters were cheap.

Over the Lancashire border in the port of Liverpool there is a famous dish called lobscouse. The abbreviation "scouse" is the name given to a Liverpool dialect, and the city's inhabitants are sometimes known as "Scousers." Lobscouse is presumed to be of nautical origin. It is a mutton-and-vegetable stew, similar to hot pot, but with the addition of ship's biscuits or barley, and the omission of oysters. Some people are of the opinion that lobscouse was introduced into Liverpool by the Irish, as a kind of expatriate Irish stew, but most Scousers assert that lobscouse is indigenous to Liverpool. The origin remains obscure, but the Liverpool lobscouse was undoubtedly sired by expediency in poverty.

Eighteenth Century England, as we have noted, had a great reputation for

Some of Britain's finest meat, game and poultry is sold in the shops of Leadenhall Market, described once as "the vaulted ventricle in the heart of the City"—the financial district of London. The Victorian arcade that shelters the market dates from 1881, but the site was apparently used as a public poultry market as long ago as 1321. Today hundreds of bowler-hatted brokers on their way to commuter trains pause at Leadenhall each evening to pick up the family meat supply.

MARKET
ERECTED

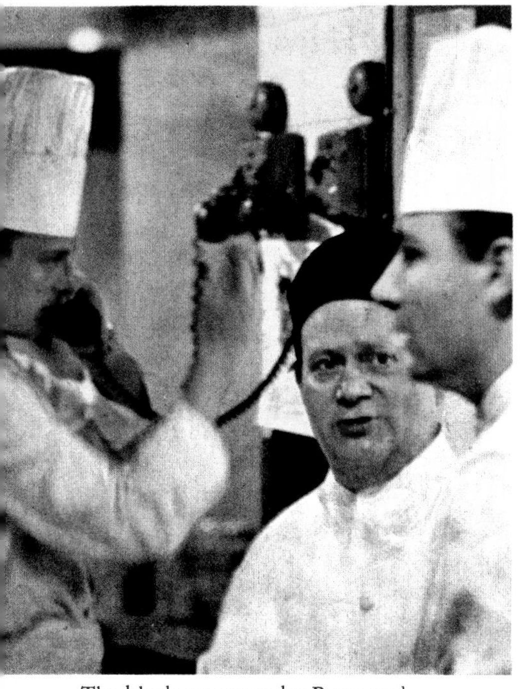

The black cap worn by Raymond Gower is the traditional badge of office of the master cook of the Savoy kitchens, which serve the Savoy Grill and Simpson's-in-the-Strand, two of London's greatest restaurants. The saddles of lamb and ribs of beef at right are ready for transfer to carvers' trolleys.

good food. It has often been said that this reputation suffered a sharp decline when we began to roast our meat in the oven, instead of roasting it on a spit, and perhaps there is something to the argument.

A fine piece of meat is at its simplest and best when roasted over an open fire. Sometime in prehistory man discovered the advantages of roasting his catch. Compared to raw meat it was firmer, easier to chew and had a pleasant aroma. The roasting also enhanced the flavor. Spit roasting was invented when some sharp Neolithic mind realized that when meat was cooked on a stick, pieces of charred wood or coals no longer adhered to the food. In the big manor houses of the Middle Ages there was always a boy or two employed to turn the spit, upon which the carcass of an ox or sheep crackled, spluttered and browned, while the dripping fat and juices dropped into a pan below. In smaller houses the spit was operated by a large drum about the diameter of a cartwheel, turned by a running dog inside it. While the spit revolved, the cook basted the joint with its drippings, and occasionally turned the potatoes that baked by the fire.

In those days, meat was appraised on its qualities of freshness, flavor, tenderness and leanness—in that order. Freshness presents no problems today, and we judge our meat by its tenderness and leanness, regrettably putting

A rare roast of beef yields to the knife of a carver in Simpson's. This section of the restaurant is one of the few spots left in London still adhering to the Victorian custom of barring women from places of serious eating. Famous for its beef, Simpson's is frequented by affluent British businessmen and by senior journalists from Fleet Street, center of the British newspaper world.

strength of flavor last. This is one of the reasons for the disappearance of strong-flavored mutton from butchers' shops, for everyone demands lamb, the flavor of which is relatively mild compared to mutton.

The lack of interest in strong flavor is one factor in the disappearance of some of our domestic breeds. Of the many varieties of cattle, sheep and pigs that grazed the countryside a century ago, few have survived. There are not many farmers who are prepared to support flocks of Southdown sheep when they can increase production with the Dorset Horn, which produces lambs twice a year. Yet the flocks that once drifted like white clouds across the chalk South Downs of Sussex and Hampshire were the most famous breed in England. These Southdown sheep that grazed the Neolithic fort of Devil's Dyke, high above the town of Brighton, were much prized for their flavor—derived, it was said, from the wild thyme, marjoram and basil herbs that grew along the downs.

Today, Devil's Dyke is inhabited by picnickers, not sheep, and botanists looking for thyme and marjoram will have a long day's search. Much has changed, and will continue to change. But in that hopefully far-distant future when a man's meal may consist of a compressed and nutritious pill, who will dare to remain obstinately, defiantly carnivorous? Why, the British.

CHAPTER IV RECIPES

Roast Beef

To serve 6 to 8

An 8-pound standing 3-rib roast

Preheat the oven to 450° (it will take about 15 minutes for most ovens to reach this temperature). For the most predictable results, insert a meat thermometer into the thickest part of the beef, being careful not to let the tip of the thermometer touch any fat or bone.

Place the beef, fat side up, in a large shallow roasting pan. (It is unnecessary to use a rack, since the ribs of the roast form a natural rack.)

Roast the beef undisturbed in the middle of the oven for 20 minutes. Reduce the heat to 325° and continue to roast, without basting, for about 90 minutes, or until the beef is cooked to your taste. A meat thermometer will register 130° to 140° when the beef is rare, 150° to 160° when medium, and 160° to 170° when it is well done. If you are not using a thermometer, start timing the roast after you reduce the heat to 325°. You can estimate approximately 12 minutes per pound for rare beef, 15 minutes per pound for medium, and 20 minutes per pound for well done.

Transfer the beef to a heated platter and let it rest for at least 15 minutes for easier carving. If you plan to accompany the beef with Yorkshire pudding *(below)*, increase the oven heat to 400° as soon as the beef is cooked. Transfer the roast from the oven to a heated platter, drape foil loosely over it, and set aside in a warm place while the pudding bakes. If you have two ovens, time the pudding to finish cooking during the 15 minutes that the roast rests.

To carve, first remove a thin slice of beef from the large end of the roast so that it will stand firmly on this end. Insert a large fork below the top rib and carve slices of beef from the top, separating each slice from the bone as you proceed. Traditionally, roast beef is served with its own juices and with a horseradish sauce *(opposite)*.

NOTE: Bringing meat to room temperature before cooking it is unnecessary. Roasts may go directly from the refrigerator to the oven.

Yorkshire Pudding

To serve 6 to 8

2 eggs
½ teaspoon salt
1 cup all-purpose flour
1 cup milk
2 tablespoons roast beef drippings, or substitute 2 tablespoons lard

To make the batter in a blender, combine the eggs, salt, flour and milk in the blender jar, and blend at high speed for 2 or 3 seconds. Turn off the machine, scrape down the sides of the jar, and blend again for 40 seconds. (To make the batter by hand, beat the eggs and salt with a whisk or a rotary or electric beater until frothy. Slowly add the flour, beating constantly. Then pour in the milk in a thin stream and beat until the mixture is smooth and creamy.) Refrigerate for at least 1 hour.

Preheat the oven to 400°. In a 10-by-15-by-2½-inch roasting pan, heat the fat over moderate heat until it splutters. Briefly beat the batter again and pour it into the pan. Bake in the middle of the oven for 15 minutes, reduce the heat to 375°, and bake for 15 minutes longer, or until the pudding has risen over the top of the pan and is crisp and brown. With a sharp knife, divide the pudding into portions, and serve immediately.

Yorkshire pudding is always served with roast beef *(above)*. The same batter is used to make toad-in-the-hole *(page 75)*.

Horseradish Sauce

To make about 1 cup

1/4 cup bottled horseradish, drained and squeezed dry in a kitchen towel
1 tablespoon white wine vinegar
1 teaspoon sugar
1/4 teaspoon dry English mustard
1/2 teaspoon salt
1/2 teaspoon white pepper
1/2 cup chilled heavy cream

In a small bowl, stir the horseradish, vinegar, sugar, mustard, salt and white pepper together until well blended. Beat the cream with a whisk or a rotary or electric beater until stiff enough to form unwavering peaks on the beater when it is lifted from the bowl. Pour the horseradish mixture over the cream and, with a rubber spatula, fold together lightly but thoroughly. Taste for seasoning. Serve the sauce from a sauceboat as an accompaniment to roast beef *(opposite)* or to such fish as smoked trout, smoked eel and grilled salmon.

Boiled Beef and Carrots with Dumplings

To serve 6

MEAT
A 3- to 3 1/2-pound lean corned beef brisket, rolled and tied
18 peeled white onions, about 1 inch in diameter (about 1 pound)
12 small scraped carrots

DUMPLINGS
1 cup all-purpose flour
1/2 teaspoon double-acting baking powder
1/2 teaspoon salt
1 1/2 ounces fresh beef suet, finely chopped and thoroughly chilled (about 3 tablespoons)
1/3 cup milk

Place the brisket in a 5- to 6-quart casserole, and add enough water to cover it by at least 1/2 inch. Bring to a boil over high heat, meanwhile skimming off the scum and foam as they rise to the surface. Reduce the heat, partially cover the casserole, and simmer for 2 1/2 hours. Then add the onions and carrots, and cook partially covered for another 30 minutes, or until the vegetables are tender and the meat shows no resistance when pierced with a fork.

Meanwhile, preheat the oven to 250° and make the dumpling mixture. Sift the flour, baking powder and salt into a large bowl. Add the suet and, working quickly, rub the flour and fat together with your fingertips until they look like flakes of coarse meal. Pour the milk over the mixture, toss together lightly, and gather the dough into a ball. If the dough crumbles, add up to 2 more tablespoons of milk, a drop or two at a time, until the particles adhere. With lightly floured hands, shape the dough into 1-inch balls.

With a slotted spoon, remove the meat and vegetables from the stock, and arrange them on a large heated platter. Cover and keep them warm in the oven. Drop the dumplings into the stock remaining in the casserole, stirring gently once or twice. Cook uncovered over moderate heat for 15 minutes, or until the dumplings rise to the surface. Transfer the dumplings to the platter of beef and vegetables, and serve at once, accompanied if you like by pease pudding *(Recipe Index)*.

Oxtail Stew

To serve 6

3 1/2 to 4 pounds oxtail, cut into 2-inch lengths
1 1/2 teaspoons salt
Freshly ground black pepper
1 cup flour
6 tablespoons rendered bacon fat or lard
1 medium-sized carrot, scraped and coarsely chopped
1 medium-sized turnip, scraped and coarsely chopped
1 small celery stalk, coarsely chopped
1 large onion, coarsely chopped
3 cups beef stock, fresh or canned
1 small bay leaf
1/4 teaspoon thyme
3 sprigs fresh parsley

Preheat the oven to 325°. Wipe the pieces of oxtail with a dampened towel, then sprinkle them with salt and a few grindings of pepper. Dip the pieces in flour and shake them vigorously to remove any excess. In a heavy 12-inch skillet, melt the fat or lard over high heat until it splutters. Add the oxtail (in two batches if necessary) and cook, turning frequently, until the pieces are brown on all sides, regulating the heat so that they color quickly and evenly without burning. With tongs, transfer the meat to a heavy 5- to 6-quart casserole or Dutch oven.

Add the carrot, turnip, celery and onion to the fat remaining in the skillet, and cook over moderate heat, stirring frequently, for 8 to 10 minutes, or until the vegetables are soft and light brown. Spread the vegetables over the oxtail. Then pour in the stock and add the bay leaf, thyme and parsley. Bring to a boil over high heat, cover, and bake in the middle of the oven for 2 1/2 hours, or until the meat can easily be pulled away from the bone with a fork. With a large spoon, skim as much fat from the surface of the cooking juices as you can. Taste for seasoning and serve directly from the casserole.

"Boiled Beef and Carrots" is the title of a merry little ditty originated by the Cockneys of London. It expresses their glad mood when that satisfying dish, which includes onions and dumplings, is on the menu. For their boiled beef and carrots the English use either brisket or the cut of beef shown here, known as silverside, taken from the round. The British beef is cured for several days in a saltpeter brine before it is sold, a process that produces characteristic streaks of purplish red. Such cured beef is not obtainable in the United States, but a close approximation of the dish may be made *(Recipe Index)* by using American corned beef brisket.

Potted Pork

To make about 1½ cups

- ¾ pound lean boneless pork, cut into ½-inch cubes
- ¼ pound fresh pork fat, cut into ¼-inch cubes
- ½ teaspoon salt
- Freshly ground black pepper
- ½ cup water
- 1 large bay leaf
- 2 whole cloves

Preheat the oven to 275°. In a heavy 2- to 3-quart casserole, toss together the pork, pork fat, salt and a few grindings of pepper. Pour in the water, add the bay leaf and cloves, and cover tightly. Bake in the middle of the oven for 4 hours, or until most of the liquid has evaporated and the pork is tender enough to be mashed against the side of the casserole with a spoon. Do not let the pork brown. Check the casserole occasionally and, if the liquid seems to be cooking away, add more water a tablespoon or so at a time.

With a slotted spoon, transfer the pork to a shallow bowl. Discard the bay leaf and cloves, and reserve all the fat and cooking juices. Cut away any bits of gristle and shred the pork as fine as possible with a fork. Stir in the reserved fat and juices, then pack the mixture tightly into a 2-cup mold, a terrine or an earthenware crock. Cover with a lid or foil, and refrigerate for at least 24 hours before serving. Potted pork is traditionally served with hot toast as a first course or at teatime.

Pease Pudding

PURÉED PEAS

To serve 6 to 8

- 2 cups dry green split peas (1 pound)
- 2 cups water
- 1 teaspoon salt
- 4 tablespoons butter
- ¼ teaspoon white pepper

Wash the split peas thoroughly under cold running water and continue to wash until the draining water runs clear. Pick over the peas and discard any discolored ones. In a heavy 3- to 4-quart saucepan, bring the 2 cups of water to a boil and drop in the peas slowly so that the water continues to boil. Reduce the heat and simmer partially covered for 1½ hours, or until the peas can be easily mashed against the side of the pan with a spoon. Drain the peas in a colander and purée them in a food mill or force them through a fine sieve set over a large bowl. Return the peas to the pan and cook over low heat, stirring constantly, until the purée is heated through. Stir in the salt, butter and pepper, and taste for seasoning. Serve at once from a heated vegetable dish. Pease pudding is the traditional accompaniment to boiled beef and carrots with dumplings *(Recipe Index)*.

Irish Stew

To serve 4 to 6

- 6 medium-sized peeled potatoes (about 2 pounds), cut crosswise into ¼-inch slices
- 4 large onions (about 1½ pounds), peeled and cut into ¼-inch slices
- 3 pounds lean boneless lamb neck or shoulder, trimmed of all fat and cut into 1-inch cubes
- 1 teaspoon salt
- Freshly ground black pepper
- ¼ teaspoon thyme
- Cold water

Spread half the potatoes on the bottom of a heavy 4- to 5-quart casserole or Dutch oven, and cover them with half the onion slices and then all the lamb. Sprinkle with ½ teaspoon of the salt, a few grindings of pepper and the thyme. Arrange the rest of the onions over the meat and spread the remaining potatoes on top. Sprinkle with ½ teaspoon of salt and a few grindings of pepper, then pour in enough cold water just to cover the potatoes.

Bring the stew to a boil over high heat, reduce the heat to its lowest possible point, and cover the casserole tightly. Simmer for 1½ hours. Check from time to time and add boiling water, a tablespoon or two at a time, if the liquid seems to be cooking away.

Serve the stew directly from the casserole or Dutch oven, ladling it into heated deep individual serving plates. Traditionally, Irish stew is accompanied by pickled red cabbage *(Recipe Index)*.

NOTE: If you prefer, you may cook the stew in a preheated 350° oven instead of on top of the stove. In that event, bring the casserole to a boil on top of the stove before placing it in the lower third of the oven.

Toad-in-the-Hole

SAUSAGES BAKED IN BATTER

To serve 4

1 cup all-purpose flour
2 eggs
1 cup milk
½ teaspoon salt
Freshly ground black pepper
1 pound small, fresh pork sausages

To make the batter in a blender, combine the flour, eggs, milk, salt and a few grindings of pepper in the blender jar, and blend at high speed for 2 or 3 seconds. Turn off the machine, scrape down the sides of the jar, and blend again for 40 seconds. (To make the batter by hand, beat the eggs and salt with a whisk or a rotary or electric beater until frothy. Slowly add the flour, beating constantly. Then pour in the milk in a thin stream and beat until the mixture is smooth and creamy.) Refrigerate the batter for at least 1 hour.

Preheat the oven to 400°. Place the sausages side by side in a heavy 10- to 12-inch skillet, and prick them once or twice with the tines of a fork. Sprinkle them with 2 tablespoons of water, cover the pan tightly, and cook over low heat for 3 minutes. Then remove the cover, increase the heat to moderate, and continue to cook, turning the sausages frequently with tongs or a spatula, until the water has completely evaporated and the sausages have begun to brown in their own fat.

Arrange the sausages in a single layer in a baking tin or dish about 6 by 10 inches and 2 inches deep, and moisten them with 2 tablespoons of their drippings. Keep them at least an inch apart. Then pour the batter over them and bake in the middle of the oven for 30 minutes, or until the pudding has risen over the top of the pan and is crisp and brown. Serve at once.

Pork-and-Apple Pie

To serve 8 to 10

6 tablespoons butter, softened, plus 2 tablespoons butter, melted
2 cups finely chopped onions
1 teaspoon crumbled dried sage leaves
1 teaspoon salt
Freshly ground black pepper
4 pounds lean boneless pork, trimmed of all fat and cut into ½-inch dice
4 medium-sized tart cooking apples (about 1½ pounds), peeled, cored and cut into ¼-inch slices
½ cup water
6 medium-sized boiling potatoes (about 2 pounds), peeled and cut into quarters
½ to ¾ cup milk

Preheat the oven to 325°. Using a pastry brush, coat the bottom and sides of a heavy 5- to 6-quart casserole with 2 tablespoons of the softened butter. In a small bowl, combine the chopped onions, sage, salt and a few grindings of pepper, and toss them about with a spoon until well mixed. Spread about one third of the diced pork in the casserole, strew with ½ cup of the onion mixture, top with half the apple slices, and sprinkle with another ½ cup of the onions. Repeat with layers of pork, onions and apples, and top with the remaining pork. Pour in the water, and bring to a boil on top of the stove. Cover the casserole tightly, and bake in the middle of the oven for 1½ hours, or until the pork is tender and shows no resistance when pierced with the tip of a small, sharp knife.

Meanwhile, drop the potatoes into enough lightly salted boiling water to cover them completely. Boil briskly, uncovered, until tender, then drain and return the potatoes to the pan. Shake over low heat until the potatoes are dry and mealy. Then mash them to a smooth purée with a fork, a potato ricer or an electric mixer. Beat in the remaining 4 tablespoons of softened butter and ½ cup of the milk, 2 tablespoons at a time. Use up to ¼ cup more milk if necessary to make a purée thick enough to hold its shape in a spoon. Beat in ½ teaspoon of salt and a few grindings of black pepper, taste for seasoning, and set aside.

When the pork is done, spread the mashed potatoes evenly over it with a spatula. Make an attractive pattern on the potatoes with the tines of a fork, and brush liberally with the melted butter. Bake in the upper third of the oven for about 10 minutes, or until the top of the pie has begun to brown. Slide under the broiler for a few seconds to give the potatoes a deeper color, and serve at once, directly from the casserole.

Lancashire hot pot, a workingman's stew of lamb and potatoes, contains a noble surprise of oysters and mushrooms.

Lancashire Hot Pot

LAMB-CHOP CASSEROLE WITH KIDNEYS AND OYSTERS

To serve 6

- 1 tablespoon butter, softened, plus 1 tablespoon butter, cut into 1/4-inch bits
- 6 medium-sized potatoes, peeled and cut crosswise into 1/4-inch slices
- 6 lean shoulder lamb chops, cut about 1 inch thick and trimmed of fat
- 1 teaspoon salt
- Freshly ground black pepper
- 6 lamb kidneys, membranes removed, trimmed of all fat, and cut crosswise into 1/4-inch slices
- 6 shucked oysters (optional)
- 1/2 pound fresh mushrooms, including stems, cut lengthwise into 1/4-inch slices
- 3 medium-sized onions, peeled and cut into 1/8-inch slices
- 2 cups water
- 1 tablespoon finely chopped parsley

Preheat the oven to 350°. Using a pastry brush, coat the bottom and sides of a 4- to 5-quart casserole at least 6 inches deep with the 1 tablespoon of softened butter. Spread about one third of the potato slices evenly over the bottom of the casserole, and place 3 lamb chops side by side on top. Sprinkle the chops with 1/2 teaspoon of the salt and a few grindings of pepper. Add half the kidneys, 3 oysters, half the mushrooms and half the onions, and cover with another third of the potatoes. Place the 3 remaining chops on the potatoes and sprinkle them with the remaining salt and a few grindings of pepper. Add the remaining kidneys, oysters, mushrooms and onions, and spread the rest of the potatoes evenly over the top. Pour in the water. Dot with the bits of butter. Cover and bake in the middle of the oven for 1 1/2 hours. Remove the cover and bake for 30 minutes longer, or until the top is brown. Sprinkle with parsley and serve directly from the casserole.

Beef Roll

To serve 4 to 6

- 1 pound lean top round, chuck or shin of beef, coarsely ground
- 1/2 pound raw ham, coarsely ground
- 1 cup fresh soft crumbs, made from homemade-type white bread, pulverized in a blender or shredded with a fork
- 1/4 teaspoon ground nutmeg
- 1 1/2 teaspoons salt
- 1/4 teaspoon freshly ground pepper
- 1 egg, lightly beaten

In a large bowl, combine the beef, ham, crumbs, nutmeg, salt and pepper. Add the egg and beat vigorously with a spoon until the ingredients are well blended. Do not overbeat; the texture should be somewhat coarse. Spoon the meat mixture into a 4- to 6-cup pudding mold, or any other plain mold, packing it down firmly. Cover the mold with its lid or a sheet of buttered foil.

Place the mold in a deep pot and pour in enough cold water to come halfway up the sides of the mold. Bring to a boil over high heat, reduce the heat to low, cover the pot tightly, and simmer for 2 hours. Replenish the water in the pot with more boiling water when necessary.

Remove the mold from the pot, remove the cover or foil, and cover the beef roll with fresh foil. Place a plate over the top of the mold, and weight it with a heavy pan or casserole weighing about 3 or 4 pounds. Cool to room temperature, then refrigerate, with the weight still in place, for 4 to 5 hours, or until the roll is thoroughly chilled. Unmold the beef roll in the following fashion: Run a sharp knife around the sides of the mold, and dip the bottom in hot water for a few seconds. Wipe the outside of the mold dry, place an inverted serving plate over the mold and, grasping both plate and mold together firmly, turn them over. Rap the plate on a table and the beef roll should slide out easily. Traditionally, beef roll is served with mustard and accompanied by freshly baked bread and butter.

Scotch Broth

To serve 6 to 8

- 2 pounds lamb neck or shoulder with bones, cut into 6 pieces
- 2 quarts cold water
- 2 tablespoons barley
- 2 teaspoons salt
- 1/8 teaspoon freshly ground black pepper
- 1/2 cup finely chopped carrots
- 1/2 cup finely chopped turnips
- 1/2 cup finely chopped onions
- 1/2 cup finely chopped leeks
- 1/2 cup finely chopped celery
- 1 tablespoon finely chopped parsley

Place the lamb in a heavy 4- to 5-quart casserole and add the water. Bring to a boil over high heat, meanwhile skimming off the foam and scum as they rise to the surface. Add the barley, salt and pepper, reduce the heat to low, and simmer partially covered for 1 hour. Add the carrots, turnips, onions, leeks and celery, partially cover again, and cook for 1 hour more. With a slotted spoon, transfer the lamb to a plate and pull or cut the meat away from the bones. Discard the bones, fat and gristle, and cut the meat into 1/2-inch cubes. Return the meat to the soup and simmer for 2 or 3 minutes to heat it through. Taste for seasoning. Sprinkle with parsley before serving.

A SWEET-SOUR MINT SAUCE GOES BEST WITH LAMB.

Roast Leg of Lamb with Mint Sauce

To serve 6 to 8

MINT SAUCE
- 1/4 cup water
- 1 tablespoon sugar
- 1/4 cup finely chopped fresh mint leaves
- 1/2 cup malt vinegar

MEAT
- 2 tablespoons salt
- 1 teaspoon finely ground black pepper
- 1 tablespoon finely cut fresh rosemary or 2 teaspoons dried crushed rosemary
- A 5- to 6-pound leg of lamb, trimmed of excess fat, but with the fell (the parchmentlike covering) left on

Make the mint sauce in advance. Combine the water and sugar in a 1- to 1 1/2-quart saucepan, and bring to a boil over high heat, stirring until the sugar dissolves completely.

Remove the pan from the heat, and stir in the mint leaves and vinegar. Taste and add up to 1 more tablespoon of sugar if desired. Set aside at room temperature for 2 or 3 hours.

Preheat the oven to 500° (it will take about 15 minutes for most ovens to reach this temperature). Combine the salt, pepper and rosemary in a small bowl, and with your fingers press the mixture firmly into the lamb, coating the entire surface as evenly as possible. For the most predictable results, insert a meat thermometer into the thickest part of the leg, being careful not to touch a bone.

Place the leg, fat side up, on a rack in a shallow roasting pan, and roast it uncovered in the middle of the oven for 20 minutes. Reduce the heat to 375° and roast for another 40 to 60 minutes, or until the lamb is cooked to your taste (basting is unnecessary). A meat thermometer will register 130° to 140° when the lamb is rare, 140° to 150° when medium, and 150° to 160° when well done.

Transfer the lamb to a heated platter, and let the roast rest for 15 minutes for easier carving. Stir the mint sauce once or twice, pour it into a sauceboat and serve it separately with the lamb.

Caper Sauce

To make about 1 cup sauce

- 1 tablespoon butter
- 1 tablespoon flour
- 1 cup lamb, beef or fish stock, depending on the food with which it is to be served
- 1 tablespoon capers, drained and cut into halves
- 2 teaspoons malt vinegar
- 1/4 teaspoon salt
- Freshly ground black pepper

In a heavy 8- to 10-inch skillet, melt the butter over moderate heat. When the foam begins to subside, stir in the flour and mix thoroughly. Pour in the stock and, stirring constantly with a whisk, cook over high heat until the sauce thickens and comes to a boil.

Reduce the heat to low and simmer the sauce for about 3 minutes to remove any taste of raw flour. Then stir in the capers, vinegar, salt and a few grindings of pepper. Taste for seasoning and serve hot from a small bowl or a sauceboat.

When made with the lamb stock, caper sauce traditionally accompanies boiled lamb. The beef-stock version would accompany boiled beef *(Recipe Index)* and other versions of this sauce, made with fish stock or even bottled clam juice, are served with boiled or poached fish, such as poached haddock *(Recipe Index)*.

Brawn

JELLED PIGS' FEET AND BEEF

To serve 4 to 6

6 fresh pigs' feet (about 3½ to 4 pounds)
1 pound boneless beef shin
1 tablespoon salt plus 1½ teaspoons salt
1 cup coarsely chopped onions
4 whole cloves, coarsely crushed with a mortar and pestle or wrapped in a towel and crushed with a rolling pin
Freshly ground black pepper

Wash the pigs' feet thoroughly under cold running water, then place them with the beef in an 8- to 10-quart pot. Pour in enough cold water to cover the meats by about 1 inch. Add 1 tablespoon of the salt, and bring to a boil over high heat, meanwhile skimming off the scum and foam that rise to the surface. Then add the chopped onions and cloves, and reduce the heat to low. Simmer partially covered for about 2 hours, or until the meats are tender and show no resistance when pierced with the tines of a fork. Transfer the meats to a platter and strain the cooking liquid through a fine sieve set over a bowl.

While the pigs' feet are still hot, remove their skin and bones, and discard them. Coarsely chop the meat from the feet and the beef shin and place it in a mixing bowl. Add 1 cup of the strained cooking liquid, 1½ teaspoons of salt and a few grindings of pepper, and mix thoroughly. Then pour the entire contents of the bowl into a 1-pint loaf pan or mold. Cover the top with wax paper or foil and weight it with a heavy pan or casserole weighing 3 or 4 pounds. Cool to room temperature, then refrigerate the brawn, with the weight still in place, for at least 6 hours or until it jellies.

To unmold and serve the brawn, run a sharp knife around the side of the pan and dip the bottom in hot water for a few seconds. Wipe the pan dry, place a chilled serving plate over it and, grasping pan and plate firmly together, quickly turn them over. Rap them sharply on a table and the brawn should slide out easily. Cut the brawn into ¼-inch crosswise slices and arrange the slices attractively on a chilled serving plate, overlapping them slightly. Brawn may be served as a first course or as a light luncheon dish. Accompany it with fresh bread and pickled onions *(Recipe Index)*.

Deviled Beef Bones

SHORT RIBS IN A SPICY SAUCE

To serve 3 to 4

6 tablespoons butter, softened
1 tablespoon Worcestershire sauce
1 teaspoon dry English mustard
1 teaspoon curry powder (preferably imported Madras curry powder)
Freshly ground black pepper
¼ teaspoon cayenne pepper
1 teaspoon salt
2½ to 3 pounds lean short ribs of beef, each 4 to 5 inches long
½ cup flour

Preheat the oven to 450°. With a pastry brush and 2 tablespoons of the softened butter, coat the bottom and sides of a shallow roasting pan large enough to hold the short ribs in one layer. In a small bowl, cream the remaining 4 tablespoons of softened butter by beating and mashing it against the sides of the bowl with a large spoon until it is light and fluffy. Then beat in the Worcestershire sauce, mustard, curry powder, 1 teaspoon of black pepper, cayenne pepper and ½ teaspoon of the salt. Set aside.

With a small, sharp knife, make ¼-inch-deep crisscrossing cuts about 1 inch apart on the meaty surface of the ribs. Then coat them with the flour and shake them vigorously to remove any excess. Sprinkle the ribs with the remaining ½ teaspoon of salt and a few grindings of pepper and arrange them fat side up in a single layer in the roasting pan. Roast in the middle of the oven for 10 minutes. Using a pastry brush coat the ribs evenly with the seasoned butter, reduce the heat to 400°, and roast for 1 hour and 15 minutes, or until the meat is tender and shows no resistance when pierced with the tip of a fork. Arrange the ribs on a large platter and serve at once.

NOTE: Traditionally, the bones deviled were those left over from a standing rib roast. They were simply spread with the seasoned butter and broiled until brown and crusty.

V

A Royal Collection of Rural Cheeses

A wedge of Stilton, the king of the blue cheeses, served with crackers and port, stands supreme as a dessert or snack. Seventeen gallons of milk and four months of care go into the making of each prime 15-pound Stilton.

Ben Gunn, the marooned pirate in Robert Louis Stevenson's *Treasure Island*, spent three lonely years dreaming of toasted cheese. The cheese, I think, must have been Cheshire—the oldest and in many ways the most distinctive of the delectable variety of English cheeses. Mellow with a hint of sharpness, firm but slightly crumbly, it has been for centuries the prime cheese of England, the cheese of the rich and the poor, the king and the peasant, the sailor and the soldier. When the Romans came in the First Century and built the garrison town of Chester in the lush Dee Valley, the men of the 20th Legion stuck pieces of Cheshire on the points of their short swords and toasted them on an open fire, discovering what the inhabitants of the area already knew—that toasting increased the already rich flavor. The men of Offa, the Eighth Century King of Mercia, probably lunched on Cheshire cheese, roast meat and wild berries as they built their 70-mile defensive embankment along the border between Mercia and Wales to mark the limits of Offa's realm. Quartermasters of the British regiments in Scotland during the 17th Century Civil War ordered 300 tons of Cheshire sent up by stage wagon, for the British quartermasters knew, as perhaps did their Roman and Mercian counterparts before them, that protein-rich cheese, the oldest manmade food, can be a complete meal in itself.

Today, however, it might be difficult to feed an army on Cheshire, for far less of it is made than was produced a century ago. And, alas, the same lamentable fact applies to our other great English cheeses—Cheddar and Stilton, to name the finest examples, and such lesser breeds as Wensleydale, Caerphilly and Gloucester. There was a time when nearly every farm and cottage in England made cheese, including many that attained the noble stature called "blue," of which we will speak more below. The farmers made cheeses in such variety that there must have been thousands of different types. Today there are no more than a dozen. The first train that puffed slowly past cud-chewing cows changed the ways of the countryside and the lives of farmers forever, for it is much easier to send milk in bulk by road and rail to a creamery or cheese factory than it is to use it to make cheese yourself. In 1900 there were almost 2,000 farmers in Cheshire who produced the county's most famous product; today there are only 30. There are, of course, commercial cheesemakers who make fine Cheshire.

A good Cheshire possesses these qualities: a bright color (some makers color their cheeses orange, others leave them the natural yellowish-white), a nutty flavor, an open, silky texture and a hint of saltiness. Like Scotch whisky, which cannot be successfully produced outside Scotland, Cheshire cannot be copied, as many who have tried will testify: "If it isn't made in Cheshire, then it simply isn't Cheshire cheese."

The basic reason for this is that the county of Cheshire contains some of the finest grazing land in England, a result of the fact that the sea a very, very long time ago covered that area now known as the Cheshire plain and, on receding, left behind rich sedimentary deposits. Bronze Age men milked the goats that grazed on the herbs and wild grasses of the plain, and with the milk made small cheeses, the first Cheshires. By Roman times, the cheese was made of cows' rather than goats' milk and was known as Chester, after the Romans' word for a garrison town.

Through the centuries the name changed to Cheshire, and the cheese itself varied widely in quality and in character. In 1854, the writer George Borrow visited Chester and reported: "We put up at an old-fashioned inn in Northgate Street, to which we had been recommended; my wife and daughter ordered tea and its accompaniments, and I ordered ale, and that which always should accompany it, cheese." Chester ale, according to Borrow, was possessed of a "villainous character" and he expected it to be bad, "but I shall have a treat in the cheese, Cheshire cheese has always been reckoned excellent, and now that I am in the capital of the cheese country, of course I shall have some of the very prime."

To his horror the cheese when served had "the appearance of soap," and Borrow accordingly threw it out of the window. The ale, being as bad as he expected, was promptly thrown out after the cheese. "Well!" said Borrow, "if I have been deceived in the cheese, I have at any rate not been deceived in the ale, which I expected to find execrable. Patience! I shall not fall into a passion. . . . Wife! I will trouble you for a cup of tea. Henrietta! Have the kindness to cut me a slice of bread and butter."

For Henrietta's sake, we may hope that the bread and butter were satisfactory, but in an age of government regulation of dairy products Borrow today would have difficulty finding a bad Cheshire. The product is now so good that Cheshire's fame has spread even to France, which is really something, considering that the French—understandably, I suppose—refuse to recognize any cheese that isn't French. Yet they have a sneaking regard for Cheshire, which they call *"le Chester,"* even to the point of composing disrespectful couplets:

Dans le Chester sec et rose,
A longues dents l'Anglaise mord.
(Into the Chester, dry and pink,
The long teeth of the English sink.)

Whatever the length of teeth, the best way to enjoy the full richness of Cheshire is to toast it first. And there are other English cheeses that, like Cheshire, respond to toasting and that spread evenly. Cheddar is one. The best-known cheese in the world, it has a fine, rich, strong flavor, the characteristic Cheddar taste that has given the cheese its eminence, and that is brought out by toasting even better than that of Cheshire.

Cheddar can of course also be taken without toasting. In the country, and I don't mean the garden counties around London, but in the West Country, in Somerset, Devon and Hereford—in fact all over rural England—the pubs serve one of the finest lunches ever devised, incredibly simple, rustic and plain, yet a meal that can be memorable given the right conditions. Called a "ploughman's lunch," it consists of a cut of Cheddar, a home-baked bread roll, pickled onions and a pint of beer—English beer, mind, not the light amber and insipid continental stuff, but the strong dark ale, full of malt and hops, beer that is the natural accompaniment to such a feast.

A Stilton cheese, here shown with accompaniments of port and walnuts, should always be sliced into wedges from the top. It should never be scooped out with a spoon.

Cheddar was once called the "Somerset cheese," for it was first made in the farms around Wells and the villages in Somerset's Mendip Hills. The farmers produced it, as some still do today, only during the months from May through September, when the cattle were grazing on the rich grass of summer; now such is the demand that commercial creameries make it all year round. We also consume a good deal of imported Cheddar, for the "cheddaring" process by which the cheese is made—a matter of chopping the curd very fine and removing the moisture by squeezing it out in a mechanical press—travels well.

Cheddars today are usually made in standard sizes, the average being about 65 pounds, but monster Cheddars have been made both in England and the U.S. One such cheese was presented to Queen Victoria as a wedding present. Some people have odd ideas about wedding presents. Who would think of giving the happy couple a gigantic cheese? The farmers of the Cheddar district did, back in 1840; they got together and produced—or rather built—a huge Cheddar weighing about 1,100 pounds. It took the milk of 750 cows and measured almost 10 feet in circumference; the Queen graciously accepted the gift, and the farmers requested that it might be exhibited. "Yes," said Queen Victoria, who was no doubt glad to get rid of it. When the farmers tried to return the cheese after the exhibition, the Queen refused to take it back and the farmers quarreled among themselves over its ownership. The argument was protracted, the cheese was placed in legal custody, and was never heard of again. It simply disappeared!

Regardless of size, a Cheddar in full maturity—that is, some six months after the pressing process—should be completely uniform in color, with a smooth texture and no white veining. The use of contaminated milk—a result of cows' drinking from polluted pools—can cause gas holes to form in a cheese. Invasion by the wrong kind of bacteria is a constant hazard. That is why scrupulous cleanliness must be observed at all times during cheesemaking. Cheesemakers say, "If the milk is poor, the cheese will find it out."

Sometimes, although very rarely, cracks will develop in a Cheddar if the acidity is a bit too high; spores will enter and the cheese will "blue," a condition much to be desired in some cheeses though not in Cheddar.

The bluing process can perhaps best be described by analogy. Spores of fungi, ever present in the air, find bread a perfect place on which to live and develop. If we find a long-forgotten piece of bread at the bottom of the bread box it will most certainly be covered by a delicate coat of blue fur, and so we throw it away. The mold that grows on bread is the same one that is found on many cheeses, and a blue cheese is a positive citadel of rapidly multiplying fungi. Yet we are prepared to pay a high price for a ripe Stilton, a fine Roquefort or a rich Gorgonzola.

There is good reason for this apparent anomaly. Cheshire is perhaps the best example of a cheese that sometimes turns blue by happy accident, changing the open-textured, crumbly cheese into something quite different. The flavor alters from the normal nutty, silky taste to the pungent flavor characteristic of the blue mold—a flavor sharp on the tongue yet bland in the mouth, with a fugitive hint of ammoniac decay. The texture becomes softer, buttery and smooth, for the mold penetrates the structure of the cheese, breaking it down. Blue Cheshire is prized by many connoisseurs, who maintain that it is the finest blue cheese in the world. Unhappily, Cheshires will not turn blue on demand; "old blue," as the blue is also called, is an accident caused by several factors: higher acidity than usual in a particular Cheshire, coupled with more moisture and a more open texture than normal.

Cheesemakers select a cheese with these properties in the hope that it may eventually turn blue, testing nearly every cheese produced in Cheshire in their search for one with the right qualities. All attempts to make a blue Cheshire artificially have failed; the only thing we can do is to select a likely cheese and aerate it by piercing it with long, stainless-steel needles so that spores can enter and grow in the cheese.

At Hutchinson's of Whitchurch, Shropshire, the only firm in the world to select and mature blue Cheshire, the big handsome cheeses await their chance in cellars beneath the street. The damp atmosphere is heavy with the smell of ripening cheese. Here the cheeses are regularly pierced with an instrument called a cheese iron, a semitubular knife. The iron is withdrawn and, every once in a while, there at the very tip of the plug of cheese is the faintest blessing of blue, just a mere discoloration that shows the invasion of mold. In a week or so the character will have changed entirely from that of an ordinary Cheshire into that of a great and noble blue, and it will fetch a high price in London, especially in the gentlemen's clubs around St. James's where, after his lunch of roast beef and claret, the stout old colonel will say to the waiter, "A glass of Cockburn, please, Phillips." And, lowering his voice to a husky whisper, "Any chance of a bit of blue Cheshire?"

Since all semihard cheeses possess the potential of turning blue under certain conditions, Cheshire is of course not the only blue we make, although the number of blues produced, like the number of all cheeses, has dwindled over the years. Wensleydale was long made from a Norman recipe by the monks of Jervaulx and Fountains Abbey in the county of Wensleydale; after the dissolution of the Roman Catholic monasteries when the Anglican Church was established in the 16th Century, the local farmers' wives carried on the tradition and blue Wensleydale is still available in the county in small quantities. From Cottenham near Cambridge came blue Cottenham but, like many local cheeses, it has probably disappeared forever. The traveler in England nowadays who discovers a local blue cheese in some remote village store has made a rare and wonderful find.

Of all the blue cheeses the finest is Stilton. It stands beside Roquefort, bleu de Bresse, Gorgonzola and Cheshire as one of the world's great. It is a white cheese, tinted with yellow and richly marbled with greenish blue. The crust is dark and wrinkled and the flavor subtly mellow, yet rich.

Stilton, almost everyone agrees, was named after the tiny Huntingdonshire village of Stilton, once a principal coaching stop for travelers on the Great North Road between London and York, but a great controversy rages over whether Stilton was ever actually made at Stilton. Proponents of the Stilton-origin theory maintain that the cheese was first sold by one Cooper Thornhill, landlord of the Bell Inn at Stilton during the 1730s, having been invented by Thornhill's sister, Mrs. Paulet, housekeeper to Lady Beaumont at nearby Quenby Hall. So the cheese became known as Mrs. Paulet's cheese, or Lady Beaumont's cheese, or Quenby cheese. Nonsense, say others; it was also known as Mrs. Orton's cheese and Dalby cheese, proof that it was invented by a Mrs. Orton in Little Dalby, which lies near Melton Mowbray, some 30 miles from Stilton. There is also a school that leaves Mrs. Orton out altogether, contending that the cheese originated in Melton Mowbray.

It must be said that those who favor the story of landlord Thornhill of Stilton and his inventive sister have a high hurdle to get over: the great English writer and traveler Daniel Defoe visited the village in 1720 and "partook of a cheese called Stilton"—and Thornhill, the anti-Thornhill partisans point out triumphantly, did not take over as landlord of the Bell Inn until after 1730! In any event, it's a great cheese, and it probably simply evolved in the farm houses around Stilton.

Stiltons, usually made in either 10- or 16-pound sizes, are covered by a thick crust peculiar to the individual manufacturer and easily recognizable by him. No two manufacturers ever produce an identical crust. Two of them once told me a story about a lunch they had in one of London's most famous restaurants. After the roast beef and Yorkshire pudding had been washed down with ale, the two men ordered Stilton. A half Stilton, wrapped in a napkin, was borne to their table by the waiter. They peered at the crust. "Looks like one of yours, John," said one.

"Ay, it does," replied the other, tasting it. "But it's not Stilton."

The first helped himself to a piece of the cheese on a cracker, and agreed: "By God, you're right, John. It's Danish blue." The chicanery was simply explained. Diners in restaurants usually help themselves to the cheese with a silver scoop, starting at the center and working outward, so that when the cheese is gone the crust remains. The unscrupulous proprietor had filled an emptied Stilton crust with the much-cheaper Danish blue.

Aside from what it says about the perfidy of this particular proprietor, this story contains a moral: A Stilton should never be scooped out with a spoon. Instead, thin wedges should be cut with a knife. In a prime Stilton the soft-textured blue marbling is concentrated at the center, the mold gradually thinning out toward the crust. Although this blue heart is the most desirable portion of the cheese, spooning it out causes the part toward the crust to dry and crumble, whereas slicing ensures that the cheese does not go dry and that the texture remains constant all the way down.

Scooping is not, however, the only barbarous practice followed with Stilton; to counteract dryness, some people pour port wine into the scooped-out cavity, making an otherwise perfect cheese soggy, purple-hued and horrible. Port with it, but not in it, should be the rule. A good Burgundy also goes well with Stilton, as do crackers and bread. Or try the Yorkshire habit of combining Stilton or a blue Wensleydale with a slice of apple pie.

If Stilton and some of the other great cheeses are a bit difficult to obtain nowadays, there are still others of considerable repute that are even more difficult to find—blue vinny, also called blue Dorset, for example, a hard, fat-deprived cheese made from hand-skimmed milk. It is perhaps the last of England's rare, local cheeses. If you possess the pioneering spirit of Vasco da Gama, have the scientific tenacity of Louis Pasteur and the deductive capacity of Inspector Maigret, you might, only *might,* get to taste some.

"Dorset," I was told, "is where you will find blue vinny. Try Sherborne, or try Dorchester."

I went to Sherborne. "Blue vinny? Well, sir, you might find someone as sells it, but not here. If I were you, I'd go to Dorchester."

"Blue vinny?" they said in Dorchester. "Place to go for that is Puddletown, Tolpuddle or Piddlehinton. That's where they make blue vinny."

At Piddlehinton a villager said: "Bloo vunny? Ar. I'd goo over t' Cerne Abbas. Ask they in the pub." "Ar," exclaimed other villagers, and they exchanged little secretive smiles.

At Cerne Abbas I went into the pub. "Yes," said the landlord, "I can get you some blue vinny, but I can't tell you where, it's a secret, see. They won't even tell me, because I am not a local. I'm Lancashire, so I have to go and contact a middleman."

"Why," I asked, "won't they tell you, and why does blue vinny have to be such a damned great secret?"

"I don't know," said the landlord, "maybe it's because so little is made that they will only supply it to folk who live in the area, or maybe the way that it's made has to be kept secret. Who knows?" The landlord climbed into a white MGB sports car and accelerated up the village street on his errand of mercy and mystery to the unknown destination and the source of blue vinny cheese. He returned some 10 minutes later bearing a 10-pound cheese wrapped in newspaper.

"That's a blue vinny?" I inquired.

"It is," he said. "And I'm afraid that you will have to buy the whole cheese. They refuse to cut it up."

I asked him if it was a good one.

"I have no idea, but you could always try asking them at the Cheese Grading Centre in Wells. It's about forty miles away."

I didn't have much time left, but I went to Wells anyway. At the government's Grading Centre I showed my cheese to one of the graders.

"I have here a blue vinny," I said.

"Have you now," said the grader, "it's a long time since I've seen a blue vinny." He had the flat accent of someone from the Midlands, Nottingham perhaps, or maybe Leicester. Reverently he unwrapped the cheese from the newspaper. He went away and returned a few minutes later with a cheese iron, which he thrust into the side of the cheese, extracting a long plug of white, blue-veined cheese. He broke a piece off and rubbed it between his fingers. Then he took a piece and tasted it. "The word vinny," he said, "comes from the old English word 'vinew,' which means mold."

"Is it what a blue vinny should taste like?" I asked. "Is it a blue vinny?"

The grader gazed at the cheese iron, then at me.

"No," he said. "No."

"What do you mean, no?"

"No, it isn't what a blue vinny should taste like, because it isn't a blue vinny at all—it's a substandard Stilton." He pronounced "substandard" so that it sounded like "substundud." I began to feel at the end of a very long, drawn-out joke, in which the whole of Dorset, the landlord and the cheese-grader had played their parts to a carefully written script.

"It would appear," continued the grader in grave tones, "that there is a smuggling route of second-rate Stiltons from Melton Mowbray to Dorset. I am afraid you've been had." Now I knew what all the secrecy was about. "Blue vinny cheese," said the grader, "was never worth much anyway. It's a poor, deprived cheese that they made from skimmed milk. Bournemouth used to be a butter-making area, and they skimmed all the fat from the milk by hand. What was left went to make blue vinny. It was dead white and would turn as hard as a rock. You had to eat it soon after the mold had taken. I remember an old man here in Dorset who told me, 'You can do a hard day's work on a lump of Cheddar cheese, bread and beer, but nobody ever did a day's work on a lump of blue vinny.'

"You see," the grader went on, "everything's too clean these days, and vinny used to be made from inferior, fatless milk, dirty milk even. Some people used to start their cheese with an old leather harness that was never washed, but hung in the shed, gathering mildew. When the cheese started to shrink, it cracked and let in the mold—that's why it turned blue."

I have never been back to Dorset, because I cannot spare the time. But one day I shall renew my search for blue vinny cheese. I don't care if it is hard, fat-deprived and poor, I want to try some for myself, even if I roll Dorset up like an old carpet and blue vinny cheeses drop out at both ends.

Other cheeses are not quite so difficult to find today but, if they do not possess the mystery of a blue vinny or the greatness of a Stilton, some are still worthy of remark. Caerphilly, a soft, gentle, unripened cheese, is popular all over England. A relatively modern cheese not more than 150 years old, it is easy to digest and thus useful to men working in cramped conditions. It originated in Wales as a miner's food but today is made in the West Country, in Somerset and in Wiltshire. Very little is made in Caerphilly in Wales, one of those contradictions common in a land whose cheeses are made almost everywhere but their place of origin. "Cheese," people claim, "is the best way of preserving milk." So light in texture is Caerphilly, so moist and mild, that it is perhaps the nearest thing to milk that can be achieved.

Another distinctive cheese is Derby, a product of Derbyshire. White in color, with a buttery, open texture, it sometimes comes in a form called sage Derby, which looks like a spongecake with a green filling. The vivid green streak is produced by flavoring and coloring the cheese with the juice from crushed sage leaves. Sage cheese is a Christmastime specialty. We also have

Opposite:
The nine most popular British cheeses are shown in several of their guises in this group portrait, arranged in a Shropshire warehouse. All bear names—Leicester, Derby, Stilton, Gloucester, Lancashire, Cheddar, Cheshire and Wensleydale in England; Caerphilly in Wales —of places where they achieved their reputations when they were still being made in country farmhouses. Differences in climate, soil, grass and maturity gave each variety its distinctive flavor and texture.

1 Farmhouse Cheshire
2 Wensleydale
3 Red Farmhouse Cheshire
4 Caerphilly
5 Leicester
6 Blue Cheshire
7 Double Gloucester
8 Cheddar
9 Blue Stilton
10 Lancashire
11 Cheshire (also in the background, maturing in the warehouse)
12 Farmhouse Cheddar
13 Sage Derby
14 White Farmhouse Cheshire

a really bright, startling orange cheese called Leicester. It is made in Melton Mowbray, the home of Stilton and pork pies. Leicester is not a great English cheese, but its flamboyant color comes in handy when the cheese is used for cooking, giving a touch of extravagance to Welsh rabbit *(Recipe Index)* and cheese sauces. It is creamy and tangy, with a high moisture content that does not allow prolonged keeping. Lancashire also produces a notable cheese long known as "Leigh toaster"; it can be spread like butter and is therefore ideal as a toasting cheese, as the old name implies.

Many of these cheeses have altered in character over the decades. Double Gloucester from Gloucestershire, for example, a hard but buttery cheese with a full, mellow flavor, once enjoyed a reputation as a rival in quality to Cheshire. But its excellence owed much to the Gloucester cow, a black breed that gave particularly rich milk but that has now died out. With the breed's passing, and the move of the cheese from farmhouse to factory manufacture, double Gloucester's reputation faded. While still a noteworthy cheese, nobody compares it to Cheshire.

The only English country cheeses that have survived, remaining more or less the same as they were hundreds of years ago, are cream cheese and cottage cheese. Country people still make them. Cream cheese cannot be made with homogenized milk, but a fine, rich and creamy cottage cheese can, and it's easy to make, for you don't need a cheese press. Ordinary kitchen utensils will serve. Scotland has a cottage cheese of considerable antiquity—crowdie *(Recipe Index),* which the Scots produce by taking warm milk straight from the cow and adding a few drops of rennet. When the curd forms, it is separated from the whey and left in a colander to drain. A good dollop of double cream is added, and salt to taste. Crowdie, served with oatcakes *(Recipe Index)* and butter, is a Scottish teatime favorite.

Scotland's principal contribution to cheeselovers, however, is Dunlop, which, although milder, resembles Cheddar in flavor. Soft and creamy, it is usually eaten quite young before it has had a chance to mature. It is said to be of Irish ancestry. The story goes that a Protestant refugee from the religious troubles at the time of James II, a lady named Barbara Gilmour, fled from Ireland to Scotland and in 1688 or thereabouts established in Ayrshire the Dunlop cheese that she had brought with her. If this is accurate, then Dunlop is the only cheese of any credit ever produced in Ireland. There is a cheese called "Blarney" from County Cork, described by one authority as "a make-believe Swiss. . . . It is well named, for its looks are cheerful and its ways deceiving." The Irish also make Cheddar, which they export, and I quite recently was told that they had started the production of Camembert, leaving the way open for the French to brew Guinness.

Some of our cheeses, to sum up, are memorable, others not. Some *might* have been memorable, given the chance; when the English stepped reluctantly into the 20th Century we brought with us many of our 19th Century ways but left a lot of cheese behind. We left the Bath cheeses, the Newmarket, the Daventry and the Lincoln, the Oxford and the York. We left the Essex and Suffolk cheeses behind—a just decision, for "Hunger will break through stone walls and anything except a Suffolk cheese." The same might be said for the Essex. But of the cheeses that remain, you can be certain that the great three—Cheddar, Cheshire and Stilton—are here to stay.

6
7
7
5
8
9
4
10
4
CAERPHILLY
WELSH CHEESE
10
11
12
8
2
13
3
14
2
1

VI

Riches in Gardens and Hedgerows

Vegetables for mixed salad, a dish perennially popular with the British, lie between rows of tomato plants in the Surrey greenhouse where they were grown. The long green vegetable on the spring onions is a typically shaped British cucumber. A greenhouse, big or little, is a feature of most British gardens, down to the smallest.

Britain is a large, flourishing garden cultivated by a nation of gardeners. Virtually everyone has a garden. It may be expansive and expensive, a sweep of velvety lawn and rows of roses and poplars and yews tended by the staff of the manor. Or it may be much smaller but no less fussed over, one of many plots lined up behind the modest dwellings of a suburban development. Even city apartments have their gardens, in plots and window boxes, or perhaps in a miniature herbarium in a sunny room.

Wherever there is a patch of earth you will see solicitously tended grass, seemingly greener and smoother in cool, moist Britain than anywhere in the world. The kaleidoscope of colors of daffodils, dahlias and hollyhocks brightens towns and countryside across the land. But there is more than visual delight to be harvested from the gardens of Britain. Near the flowers and vines and alongside the lawns grow the fruit, berries, herbs and vegetables that provide distinctively British treats for the table. Here are tart gooseberries and sweet raspberries to fill delicate tarts, currants and crab apples for the jellies that make teatime so special, and blackberries and apples for that glory of the English kitchen, a rich, sweet pie *(Recipe Index)* baked under a short pastry crust and served with custard sauce or thick dollops of cream. No exotic import can compare with the English carrot, small, sweet and crisp. Few tropic fruits can match the wonderful fat rosy-hued Victoria plum. And the juicy crispness of a Cox's Orange Pippin apple is unique, savored best when you pluck the apple fresh from a tree in the orchards of Kent.

The garden I remember best was no formal plot, soft, green, neat and orderly, but the one on my grandfather's farm in Hertfordshire, north of

London, overgrown, mysterious and perfumed. It had a wall around it, an old wall of thin orange bricks held together by crumbling yellow mortar. Roses, honeysuckle and ivy clambered over the top in a tangle of confusion. Fat bumblebees, their flight encumbered by the burden of pollen, trailed from flower to flower. A clump of peonies with huge pink blossoms had held their ground against an invasion of wild flowers: bindweed, meadowsweet, enchanter's nightshade, cow parsley and white bryony.

By the time the old-fashioned cabbage roses had accumulated heat from the sun, they were the favorite resort of peacock butterflies. At dusk the roses' heady perfume seemed to attract moths—the elegant plume moth and the six-spot burnet. While the midges danced in columns above the wall, bats dropped from their secret places high in the eaves of the black barn and wheeled silently in the heavy, still air.

I explored my grandfather's garden and orchard with a child's curiosity. At the age of 10 I had no need to search far for adventure—it was all around. I knew where the gray rat had made a path through the long grass in the orchard, and to my everlasting shame I killed it with a stick one day. From a high window in the farmhouse I watched the rabbits creep in from the meadow to eat the lettuces and to nibble the tops off the radishes in the vegetable plot. Throughout one soft summer I searched and found. There were foxes, partridges and rabbits in the meadow, and countless birds' nests to be found in the hedgerows.

The hedgerows might be called Britain's wild gardens. Today they are almost the last refuge of wildlife in much of the countryside, for the farmers cultivate every foot of their ground, right up to where the hedges form the property boundaries. Rabbits and birds have fled the tractor and the harvester to the safety of the hedge. It is a haven not only for them but for much varied plant life—yellow celandine, the shrouded arum and the clinging goose grass, as well as berries prized for their delicate wild flavors.

The bounty of the hedgerows is less used now that fruit is easily available from commercial sources. But for many years, country people found in the hedgerows the fruit that made summer desserts a delight and, preserved, provided delicacies in winter. The higher the bushes grew, the greater the challenge to the pickers. They stood on tiptoe for the wild blackberry, whose sharp thorns provided no defense for the fruit it bore, the apple and the cherry, but bent their backs in search of the whortleberry and the wild strawberry. They picked rose hips, the reddish-orange fruit of the wild rose, which became fragrant rose-hip jelly, and bunches of the tiny purplish-black berries of the elder—from ancient times considered a tree vested with magical and mysterious properties but more mundanely used to make wine and jelly. They picked the hazelnut, the crab apple and, more rarely, the wild raspberry. They took, also, the small sloe that flavors gin, and other wild plums like the bullace. Once I found a bullace tree by the hedge that bordered the road. I thought that I knew every inch of ground encompassed by the boundaries of the farm, yet I had never noticed the bullace tree before, although it must have stood there for more than 40 years. The tree is a relative of the cultivated damson. The fruit of each can be eaten raw, but most palates prefer it cooked. Most bullace trees bear dark purple plums, others pale yellow. The fruit may be used for the same purposes as damsons—to make jam or a very English thing called a bullace or a damson cheese.

To make a damson cheese, the fruit should be baked at moderate heat (traditionally, in a stone jar) until the juice runs freely and the stones are loose. Then the fruit is stirred and rubbed through a sieve. A few of the stones left in the sieve may be cracked, and their kernels added to the fruit. Since the fruit is extremely sour, an equal weight of sugar is added to the pulp. The mixture is then boiled until it forms a very thick paste, which is sealed in jars and aged for anywhere from six months to two years. Fruit cheeses are of cheeselike consistency, hence the name. They have a special piquancy; even though the cheese is sweetened by the sugar, the tart flavor of the plums comes through, and a fruit cheese makes a delightful dessert or a splendid spread for teacakes.

Green gooseberries are another treasure of ancient lineage. For centuries cooks collected them to bake in earthenware pots with sugar or with honey. They beat the hot fruit to a purée and, when it cooled, folded the pulp into an equal quantity of thick cream to make a fool. A delicate and delicious summer sweet *(Recipe Index)*, fool is today made with custard rather than cream, and raspberries or apricots are frequently substituted for the original gooseberries. The name? The word fool was at one time synonymous with the word trifle, meaning something that was trifling—a thing of little consequence. Evidently a fruit purée, mixed with cream, was considered by the cooks of years gone by to be foolish—a mere trifle.

A gooseberry fool, piled high in a glass, slightly chilled, faintly greenish-yellow in color, is really a sublime dessert. We also have a dish, fussy and rather elaborate, called a trifle. No one can say whether the term "trifle" or "fool" came first. A trifle is a pudding encountered year round, made of split spongecake spread with raspberry jam, liberally doused with sherry, in a dish to which raspberries are sometimes added. The whole is then imprisoned in a thick custard and covered with whipped cream, decorated with blanched almonds, glazed cherries and candied angelica. It might be called a comforting dish; children love it for its heady sweetness, and adults are enamored of its alcoholic flavor—some perhaps inordinately so: there are countless but undoubtedly apocryphal stories of old ladies' getting themselves a bit tipsy after one too many servings of trifle.

The raspberry jam that gives a tang to trifle is most often homemade, for every fruit season housewives all over Britain make jams, jellies and marmalade. They are right to do so; the best English preserves are still homemade. For all the excellence of many commercial jams, the fresh fruits of the English countryside lend themselves well to time-honored preserving techniques.

When the fruit in the gardens and orchards is ripe, country cooks go out with buckets and baskets in preparation for jam- and jelly-making. Soon the fruit pulp is bubbling away in huge pots on the stove, and the kitchens are filled with the heady scent of hot red currants and raspberries. Jam-making is one of the most rewarding tasks that can be performed in the entire repertory of cooking. (Specific directions for making various preserves are contained in the recipe section following this chapter.)

Marmalade for breakfast, jam for tea is the general rule, and no tea is worth considering without one or more varieties of jam. We use jam for puddings, for tarts and for filling cakes. Strawberry is the favorite, I suppose, with raspberry a close second, but the choice is bewildering. There is apri-

Continued on page 96

BLACKBERRIES

HAWTHORN

Delicacies from Living Fences

Hedgerows, living fences of natural vegetation, carve the English countryside into a patchwork of plots *(opposite)*. They were left to serve as boundaries when the land was cleared long ago. Unlike most manmade fences, hedgerows may wind in sinuous lines, as does the one at far right in this view of the rolling Shropshire countryside, or assume graceful arcs, as does the one at the center, which encloses a cow pasture.

Composed of a number of trees, shrubs and bushes, hedgerows form barriers that are almost impenetrable by livestock, and they offer a culinary bounty as well. From summer through early fall, hedgerows are a treasure trove of wild fruits, nuts and berries. Wild blackberries, crab apples and hazelnuts are the hedgerow products that are put to the most varied uses. Some connoisseurs make wine from the elderberries, brandy from hawthorn, and jelly from the rose hips. The blackthorn's fruits, called sloes, are used to give a distinctive taste and color to gin.

SLOES

ROSE HIPS

CRAB APPLES

ELDERBERRIES

An old Kentish housewife carefully places a strawberry in its proper box, ready for the greengrocer's shelf. She is picking berries on a 55-acre patch owned by Hugh Lowe, who has short-cut the usual sorting and grading processes by hiring housewives on whom he can depend to sort and grade as they pick. The stony loam of Kent is ideal soil for the growing of strawberries.

cot, often containing blanched almonds held in suspension. There are also tart greengage and gooseberry jams, rich black currant, bright cherry and sweet plum. Among the rarer breeds are mulberry, tomato, vegetable marrow and carrot jams, and mixtures such as rhubarb jam flavored with ginger, whortleberry or blackberry.

Unlike jams, which are used exclusively as sweet spreads, jellies also are used to garnish roasted meats. The difference between the two preserves lies in the fact that jam is made by cooking the fruit with sugar; a jelly is made by straining the cooked pulp to make juice, which is then cooked with sugar. A jelly shimmers with colorful clarity, and is as pleasing to the eye as to the palate. To make a particularly fine jelly, one might gather a crop of tiny red and yellow crab apples. Their jelly, a delicate, scented, slightly tart preserve that has been made in English cottages for centuries, was for years a complement to a roast of pork. Red currant jelly, also extremely popular, goes well with roast mutton, lamb or venison.

Such fruits grew in profusion and confusion in my grandfather's garden and in his orchard. This was no carefully planned and well-ordered plot, for things just grew—and how they grew! During particularly good summers, we would have a superabundance of fruits all at the same time, an embarrassment of riches as the berries hung heavy from their branches—black currants, red currants and a few bushes of the rarer white currants. The strawberries were still in season and grew thick on the ground, or climbed over the edge of the old rain barrel in which they had been planted, and hung fat and glistening in the sun. Raspberries grew ripe on the canes and were ready for picking two weeks before the end of the strawberry season.

Chickens clucked and scratched under a Victoria plum tree whose branches threatened to break under the weight of the crop, so that they had to be supported by stout wooden props. Sometimes we ate the fruit straight from the tree, but much was made into sweet, succulent puddings. In the late summer we collected countless bushels of apples and pears, which were carefully stored on straw or on the slatted shelves in the barn; the fruity, heavy perfume from a barn full of stored apples is an intoxicating memory—as perhaps it should be, for the apples of England are among the prides of the land, as excellent to bite into fresh as to cook into pies, tarts and fools.

Apple trees existed in England even before the Romans came. Wild specimens grew in the forests when our ancestors wore animal skins and stained themselves blue with the leaves of the yellow-flowered woad. Among the earliest cultivated varieties on record are the pearmain and the costard. Costards, sold in the streets by "costardmongers," fetched a shilling a hundred in 1296. It could have been a costard that set Sir Isaac Newton to meditating about gravity when, as the story goes, an apple fell in front of him in his orchard at Woolsthorpe in 1666. There can be no doubt that even then there were a number of varieties. Thomas Tusser, a 16th Century East Anglian chronicler, records the existence of apple trees "of all sorts," and by 1800 many new varieties, both cooking and dessert apples, had been developed. But the best were yet to come. About 1815 professional growers discovered the Blenheim Orange apple, fruit of a long-overlooked tree in an orchard at Woodstock near Blenheim Palace in Oxfordshire. Curiously, the Blenheim was not the result of a plant breeder's effort, but a fortuitous mutation, producing a handsome large apple—sweet, crisp, juicy and pleasantly acid.

There can be no question, however, that the most famous of all English apples is that known as Cox's Orange Pippin, a variety first produced about 1830 by Richard Cox, a retired brewer, in the little village of Colnbrook, not far from London. The original Orange Pippin tree was blown down in 1911, but not before it had established a line producing what many connoisseurs consider the finest dessert apple in the world—smooth to the touch, with a yellowish tender flesh and a fine perfume.

The British way with apples is usually simple but always effective. We make a rich and filling dessert, one version of apple charlotte, by first stewing the apples with sugar and spice and then baking them in the oven with a topping of bread crumbs. Around the edge of the dish the apples become caramelized and the bread crumbs turn crisp and brown. If instead of bread crumbs you use a mixture of flour, butter and sugar, worked with the tips of the fingers until it resembles fine crumbs, you will produce apple crumble. Both dishes are excellent either hot or cold, served with thick cream. So is apple pudding, made of sliced apples and sugar in a suet crust boiled in a basin, or apple snow, a mixture of cooked, sweetened apple pulp and white of egg whipped to a froth. Apple sponge is similar to apple crumble, except that the topping is made of sponge batter. Another favorite, perhaps the sim-

Continued on page 100

Planted and tended with expert care, an English garden flourishes in the summer sunshine at Upton House, an estate some 75 miles northwest of London. Cultivated to supply the fruits, vegetables and flowers used by the main house *(background)*, this garden is an elaborate version of the backyard plots that are found all over the British Isles. These are called kitchen gardens, and every householder with a little land plants one.

The beauty of the landscaping in this garden is utilitarian rather than esthetic. The walls, for example, were built to provide warmth and shelter for fruit trees like the plums against the middle wall, whose branches have been cut in a fanlike fashion to permit them to receive a maximum amount of sun, a process called espaliering. The garden itself is oriented to catch sun winter and summer, so that it produces almost year round.

The ordinary kitchen garden is a family operation, but a staff of three tends this one. According to season, they plant rows of spinach, carrots, parsnips, peas, beans, cabbages, onions and potatoes in the section between the pond and the middle wall. Cutting flowers are grown in the section at right.

plest of all, is baked apple: Remove the core from an unpeeled apple and fill the cavity with sugar or honey, raisins and cinnamon or cloves, and bake until soft in a moderate oven. Equally good hot or cold, a baked apple becomes a luxury when served with cream.

To our gardens and hedgerows we owe more than dessert. The herbs, flowers and other condiments that the country people have long used to enhance the flavor of dishes lend distinction to the simple dishes of British cooking. On the heaths and moors grew the juniper, the cloudberry, and the whortleberry, which some cooks used to flavor wild-game roasts and stews. There were fennel for fish, and chives for salads. So subtly mixed did herbs become with our cooking that they found their way into folk poetry, as witness this anonymous rhyme: "Can you make me a cambric shirt,/Parsley, sage, rosemary and thyme,/Without any seam or needlework?/And you shall be a true lover of mine."

In that period far more herbs were in common use than there are today; Thomas Tusser, the chronicler, wrote in 1557 that no kitchen garden was complete unless it produced more than 40 different herbs. The decline in the use of herbs is greatly to be regretted, for they lend a special piquancy to many dishes. To take only the four in the aforementioned bit of folk poetry: Parsley, which so many Americans consider only a decorative accent on a plate, is excellent in sauces, and will similarly do much in casseroles, soups and stews. Sage enhances stuffings for poultry, particularly duck, and it gives added interest to pork and meat puddings. It is, however, a very strongly flavored herb, and should be used sparingly and with caution. Rosemary, also a strong herb, will bring added flavor to lamb and mutton, if chopped and sprinkled over the meat before roasting; again, only small quantities should be used. Thyme, lastly, is an extremely versatile herb, also excellent in stuffings for chicken, goose and turkey. In addition, it greatly enhances beef stews and hearty soups.

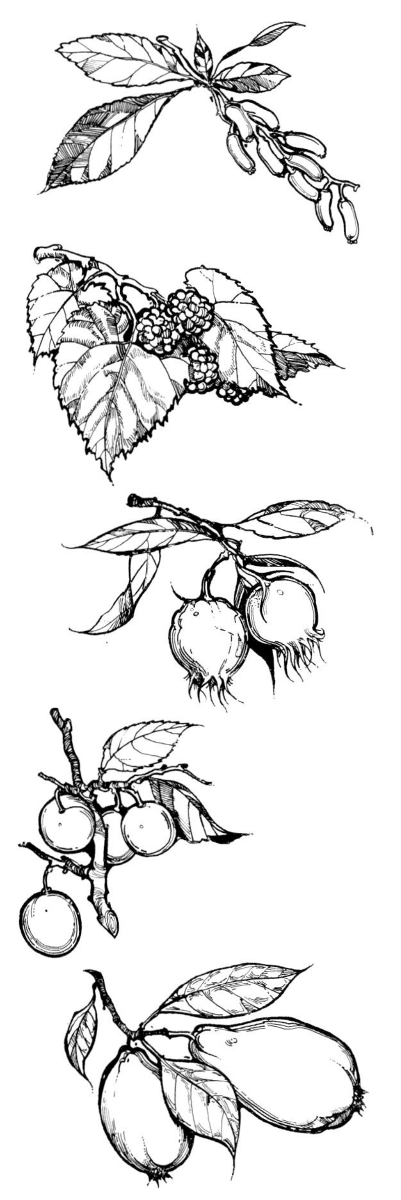

Glories of English gardens and hedgerows, these fruits used to be popular during the 17th and 18th Centuries. From the top are barberry, mulberry, medlar, bullace and quince. All were used—as some are today—to make jams and jellies, but some were also eaten cooked or raw.

Herbs and similar flavorings have been found in these isles for a very long time; but not all, of course, of the fresh delicacies grown today in British gardens—particularly vegetables—are indigenously British. In the heady days when the tall wooden ships of England ruled the waves, they returned with all manner of strange foodstuffs. "Turkeys, carp, hops and beer/Came to England all in one year," went one wildly inaccurate ditty. The cooks of the wealthy experimented with oranges, with an exotic vegetable called asparagus, and with a mysterious root brought back from the New World, one more floury than the boring parsnip that had long been a staple of the countryside—the potato.

This new arrival, which rapidly became the basic foodstuff of Ireland, did not become widely popular in England until the latter part of the 18th Century, when its properties as a "filler" came to be recognized. In the cool, moist climate and friable soil of Ireland, potatoes thrived. Everyone planted them, and soon everyone depended on them. In Ireland and also in many parts of England, the West Country in particular, potatoes threatened to replace bread, much to the disgust of William Cobbett, the journalist and reformer. According to him, "In whatever proportion the cultivation of potatoes prevails. . . . in that same proportion the working people are wretched." The working people apparently disagreed, for they found many simple ways to make potatoes a pleasurable dish. Potatoes could be dug out of the black soil, as they are today, washed, and cooked in their skins, a method that preserves the flavor and the essential vitamins that lie under the skin. They were boiled, baked, roasted and fried. Cut in lengths when raw, and fried in smoking fat, they became chips. Chips with everything: bacon and egg with chips, fish and chips, steak and chips, even chip sandwiches. Potato suppers are an annual tradition in parts of the North of England. After the crop has been harvested, the workers, many of whom are Irish, enjoy a supper of boiled potatoes with lots of fresh farm butter and milk.

The protean potato became the basic ingredient in a variety of recipes including potato soup, potato-apple cake, potato bread and potato pie. They form the main ingredient in the Irish pancakes known as boxty, for which the "praties" are grated raw, mixed with flour, salt and milk, and fried into crisp, thin cakes *(Recipe Index)*. Hot, mashed potatoes, mixed with chopped scallions and served with a generous portion of fresh farm butter, into which each mouthful is dipped, make a main meal known as champ in some places and in others as thump or stelk. In Scotland, potatoes are peeled and put into a pot with a little water and either butter or meat drippings. Stovies, they are called, because they cook for a long time on the gentle heat of the stove. Some cooks prefer to slice the potatoes, others cook them whole with beef or mutton bones or leftover meats or vegetables in the pan.

Such simple procedures are very sound; the dishes are hardly *grande cuisine* but they please the palate as well as they satisfy hunger. Regrettably we do not always show the same respect for vegetables other than potatoes. Vegetables are best enjoyed when prepared as simply as possible—long, broad beans boiled in a little water and flavored with the herb called savory; tiny carrots cooked whole with a spoonful of sugar and then tossed in butter. Elaborate preparation is generally frowned upon by frugal country people, who disapprove of dishes that have been "messed around with," suspecting that such extravagance and frivolity are bound to cloak some foreign perfidy. Yet many are guilty of overcooking vegetables, and masking their crime with some sort of sauce. We still continue the tradition of besieging our meat with heaps of overcooked vegetables, "well pepper'd and salted," as one 17th Century visitor noted, and when criticized, continue stoutly to defend the indefensible.

Witness our treatment of the cauliflower, which is frequently grossly overboiled. Cauliflower au gratin is an example, an English dish in spite of its French-sounding name. Here, a cauliflower is overcooked in salted water, and often served coated with a thick blanket of cheese-flavored white sauce of butter, flour and milk. We make a similar mistake with cabbage. Unhappy cabbage! Regarded by schoolboys as a form of punishment and by adults as a last resort when other vegetables are not available, it is a splendid vegetable when properly cared for. Cooked briefly in a little salted water, it should remain crisp, and be dressed simply with melted butter, salt and lots of black pepper. Or it might be boiled with vegetables, chopped, and mixed with mashed potato, when it becomes colcannon *(Recipe Index)*.

Colcannon is a delightful treat, and writing about it brings back a memory. My grandmother used to make a similar dish of finely chopped carrots and turnips, moistened with a dab or two of margarine (butter was too expen-

Following an age-old custom, a Cornish vicar offers thanks for a fruitful harvest that will be distributed to the needy.

sive) and well seasoned with pepper and salt. Big, floury boiled potatoes would be served separately, and there would be thick slices of meat and lots of gravy. Although the family was poor, there was always plenty of well-cooked, if simple, food. We would eat it in front of the big coal fire and its bright, shiny polished brass fittings, in a little kitchen full of steam and savory smells. It was warm and it was cozy then, more than 30 years ago, in the days before we purchased our vegetables frozen and in packets.

Canned food was rarely bought, partly because it was considered "artificial," a last resort when fresh produce was not readily available. In my grandfather's family we rarely had more than one fruit or vegetable (other than potatoes) at any one meal, but there was variety through the week: potatoes with cabbage, with carrots, onions, beans, peas, cauliflower, "greens" (as spring cabbage is called), parsnips and brussels sprouts, the latter being among the most popular vegetables in Britain. Picking sprouts is back-breaking finger-freezing work, for they are a winter vegetable, at their best in December and January. Huge areas of Bedfordshire are devoted to the raising of brussels sprouts; in the early-morning mist the bent, huddled figures of the sprout pickers move from row to row across the field, stripping the hard, icy buds that sprout from the plant stems.

Everyone eats sprouts, but alas, not everyone knows how to cook them. Sprouts should be tiny, no larger than a thumbnail, boiled for a few minutes in salted water, and eaten while still crisp. They should be slightly undercooked—never overcooked—and then tossed in melted butter.

Knowing—or believing—that the produce of our own fields is vastly superior to that of other nations, a British housewife will always choose home-grown food in preference to imported (you never know where it's been!), and she has inherited a deep-rooted respect for all that is meant by "home cooking" and "home grown." The fruits and vegetables from the gardens and orchards of Britain well reward her allegiance; they are to be enjoyed for their fresh and honest flavor, and are not mere supports to main dishes. An English apple can be savored as one might savor a good wine. A dish of garden peas, cooked with a sprig of mint, is at the very heart of English cooking; such things are simple—and the simple can be sublime.

Hot Mustard Pickle

To make about 3 quarts

1 medium-sized cauliflower (about 1 pound), trimmed and separated into individual flowerets with approximately 1-inch stems
2 small green (unripe) tomatoes (about ½ pound), cut into 1-inch chunks
1 pound small white onions, about 1 inch in diameter, peeled
2 medium-sized yellow onions (about ½ pound), peeled and cut into ¼-inch slices
1 cup plus 1 teaspoon salt
2 small cucumbers (about 1 pound), peeled and cut into ¼-inch slices
1 tablespoon capers, drained and rinsed in cold water
½ teaspoon celery seed
¼ pound butter
¼ cup all-purpose flour
2 cups malt vinegar
½ cup sugar
1 tablespoon turmeric
¼ cup dry English mustard

In a 10- to 12-quart enameled or stainless-steel pot, combine the cauliflower, green tomatoes, white onions and sliced yellow onions. Dissolve 1 cup of the salt in 4 quarts of water, pour it over the vegetables, and stir until they are thoroughly moistened. Set aside in a cool place (not the refrigerator) for 12 to 18 hours.

Drain off the liquid, and add the cucumbers, capers, celery seed, the remaining teaspoon of salt and 1 quart of fresh water to the pot. Bring to a boil over high heat, stirring occasionally. Then reduce the heat to moderate and cook, uncovered, for about 10 minutes, or until the vegetables are tender but still slightly resistant when pierced with the tip of a small knife. Drain through a colander, discard the liquid and place the vegetables in a large stainless-steel, glass or enameled bowl.

Melt the butter in a heavy 1½- to 2-quart saucepan over moderate heat. When the foam begins to subside, stir in the flour, and mix thoroughly. Pour in the vinegar and cook, stirring constantly, until the sauce thickens and comes to a boil. Reduce the heat to low and simmer for about 3 minutes, then beat in the sugar, turmeric and mustard. Pour half the sauce over the vegetables, turning them about to coat them evenly. Set the remaining sauce aside, covered with plastic wrap. (Do not refrigerate.) Marinate the vegetables at room temperature for 24 hours, then stir in the reserved mustard sauce. The pickles may be served at once, or packed into jars and stored, tightly covered, in the refrigerator for up to 3 months. Mustard pickle is traditionally served with cold meats or bread and cheese.

Pickled Cabbage

To make about 4 pints

2 medium-sized red cabbages (about 6 pounds)
6 tablespoons coarse (kosher) salt
1 quart malt vinegar
¼ cup sugar
2 tablespoons mixed pickling spice
1 teaspoon whole black peppercorns

Wash the cabbages under cold running water, remove the tough outer leaves, and cut each head into quarters. Shred the cabbage by first cutting out the cores and then slicing the quarters crosswise into ⅛-inch-thick strips. In a large stainless-steel or enameled bowl or pot, arrange the cabbage in 3 layers, sprinkling 2 tablespoons of coarse salt evenly over each layer. Let the cabbage stand in a cool place for 2 days, turning it about and lifting it up from the bottom of the bowl with a large wooden spoon several times each day.

On the third day, combine the vinegar, sugar, pickling spice and peppercorns in a 2- to 3-quart saucepan, and bring to a boil over high heat, stirring until the sugar dissolves. Boil briskly, uncovered, for 5 minutes, then remove the pan from the heat and cool to room temperature. Meanwhile drain the cabbage in a large colander. Squeeze it as dry as possible, a handful at a time, and return it to the bowl or pot. Strain the vinegar mixture over it, turning the cabbage about with a fork to moisten it thoroughly.

Cover, refrigerate, and let the cabbage marinate for at least 3 days before serving. Stir it occasionally. Covered tightly and refrigerated, it will keep for about 2 weeks.

Mustard, peppercorns, vinegar and spices can transform many fresh fruits and vegetables into pickles or relishes ("chutneys" to the British) to accompany meats. The canning jars on the opposite page contain, from left, pickled red cabbage, hot mustard pickle and apple chutney.

Colcannon

MASHED POTATOES WITH CABBAGE AND SCALLIONS

To serve 4 to 6

- 6 medium-sized boiling potatoes (about 2 pounds), peeled and quartered
- 4 cups finely shredded green cabbage (about 1 pound)
- 4 tablespoons butter
- 1 cup lukewarm milk
- 6 medium-sized scallions, including 2 inches of the green tops, cut lengthwise in half and crosswise into 1/8-inch slices
- 1 teaspoon salt
- Freshly ground black pepper
- 1 tablespoon finely chopped fresh parsley

Drop the quartered potatoes into enough lightly salted boiling water to cover them by 2 inches, and boil briskly until they are tender but not falling apart. Meanwhile, place the cabbage in a separate pot, pour in enough water to cover it completely, and bring to a boil. Boil rapidly, uncovered, for 10 minutes, then drain thoroughly in a colander. Melt 2 tablespoons of the butter over moderate heat in a heavy 8- to 10-inch skillet. When the foam begins to subside, add the cabbage, and cook, stirring constantly, for a minute or two. Cover the skillet and set aside off the heat.

Drain the potatoes and return them to the pan. Shake over low heat until they are dry and mealy. Then mash them to a smooth purée with a fork, a potato ricer or an electric mixer. Beat into them the remaining 2 tablespoons of butter and then 1/2 cup of the milk, 2 tablespoons at a time. Use up to 1/2 cup more milk if necessary to make a purée thick enough to hold its shape in a spoon. Stir in the cooked cabbage and the scallions, and add the salt and a few grindings of pepper. Taste for seasoning. Then transfer the colcannon to a heated serving bowl, sprinkle with parsley, and serve at once.

Blackberry-and-Apple Pie

To serve 6 to 8

- 3 medium-sized tart cooking apples (about 1 pound), peeled, cored and cut into 1/4-inch-thick slices
- 1/2 cup plus 3 tablespoons sugar
- 2 tablespoons butter, melted
- 3 pints ripe blackberries (about 2 1/4 pounds), washed and thoroughly drained
- Short-crust pastry *(opposite)*
- 1 tablespoon superfine sugar

Preheat the oven to 425°. In a heavy 8- to 10-inch skillet, combine the apples, 3 tablespoons of the sugar and the butter, and cook uncovered over moderate heat, stirring frequently, for 5 minutes, or until the apples are tender but not falling apart. Remove the pan from the heat and let the apples cool to room temperature.

Pack the blackberries snugly into the bottom of a round, deep pie dish about 7 1/2 inches in diameter and 2 1/2 inches deep, preferably a dish with a 1/2-inch-wide rim. Sprinkle the berries with 1/4 cup of the sugar, adding up to 1/4 cup of additional sugar to taste, and spread the cooled apple slices evenly over the top.

On a lightly floured surface, roll the pastry into a rough circle at least 10 inches in diameter and 1/8 inch thick. From the edge cut two strips about 12 inches long and 1/2 inch wide. Moisten the edge of the pie dish with a pastry brush or your finger dipped in cold water and lay the strips of pastry around it, overlapping the ends to secure them and pressing the strips firmly against the edge of the dish. Moisten the tops of the strips, then drape the remaining pastry over the rolling pin and unroll it over the dish. Press it gently in place. With scissors or a knife, trim the pastry to within 1/2 inch of the dish and fold the border into a roll around the rim. Press the tines of a fork all around the edges of the pastry to secure it to the dish. With a small, sharp knife, cut three 1-inch-long parallel slits about 1/2 inch apart in the center of the pie. Brush the top lightly with cold water and sprinkle it evenly with 1 tablespoon of superfine sugar. Bake in the middle of the oven for 25 minutes, or until the crust is golden brown. Serve the pie at once, directly from its baking dish, or let it cool to room temperature before serving. Blackberry-and-apple pie is traditionally accompanied by custard sauce *(Recipe Index)* or heavy cream.

NOTE: Like all English fruit pies, blackberry-and-apple has no pastry bottom and is very moist; it is eaten with a dessert spoon rather than a fork.

Short-Crust Pastry

In a large, chilled bowl, combine the butter, lard, flour, salt and sugar. With your fingertips rub the flour and fat together until they look like coarse meal. Do not let the mixture become oily. Pour 3 tablespoons of ice water over the mixture all at once, toss together lightly, and gather the dough into a ball. If the dough crumbles, add up to 1 tablespoon more ice water by drops until the particles adhere. Dust the pastry with a little flour and wrap it in wax paper. Refrigerate for at least 1 hour before using.

NOTE: If you are not making a sweet pastry, substitute ½ teaspoon salt for the ¼ teaspoon salt and the 1 tablespoon sugar in the recipe above.

6 tablespoons unsalted butter, chilled and cut into ¼-inch bits
2 tablespoons lard, chilled and cut into ¼-inch bits
1½ cups all-purpose flour
¼ teaspoon salt
1 tablespoon sugar
3 to 4 tablespoons ice water

Pickled Onions

To make 2 pints

To peel the onions easily, first drop them into a pot of boiling water and let them boil briskly for a minute or so. Then drain at once, pour cold water over them, and carefully remove their skins with the aid of a small, sharp knife. Place the onions in a large bowl, sprinkle them with ½ cup of salt, and turn them about with a spoon to coat them evenly. Cover the bowl and set aside in a cool place for at least 12 hours.

Drain the onions, wash them under cold running water, and pat them dry with paper towels. In a heavy 4- to 5-quart saucepan, bring the vinegar, sugar, pickling spice, cloves and peppercorns to a boil over high heat, stirring until the sugar dissolves. Boil briskly for 5 minutes, then add the onions. The liquid should cover the onions by ½ inch; if necessary add more water. Return to a boil, and cook briskly, uncovered, for 10 minutes, or until the onions show only slight resistance when pierced with the tip of a small, sharp knife. Do not overcook. With a slotted spoon, transfer the onions to hot sterilized jars, following the directions for canning and sealing on page 34. Pour the vinegar-and-spice mixture over them, filling the jars to within ¼ inch of the top. Seal at once and process with a water bath, described on page 11 of the Recipe Booklet.

2 pounds white onions, each about 1 inch in diameter
½ cup salt
1 quart malt vinegar
½ cup sugar
2 tablespoons mixed pickling spice
5 whole cloves
10 whole black peppercorns

Boxty Pancakes

IRISH POTATO PANCAKES

To make about 10 pancakes

Peel the potatoes and drop them into a bowl of cold water to prevent their discoloring. In a large bowl, stir together the flour, salt and milk, and optional caraway seeds. One at a time, pat the potatoes dry and grate them coarsely into a sieve or colander. As you proceed, press each potato firmly down into the sieve with the back of a large spoon to remove its moisture, then immediately stir the gratings into the flour-and-milk mixture.

In a heavy 8- to 10-inch skillet, melt 2 tablespoons of the butter or fat over moderate heat. When the foam begins to subside, pour in about 1 tablespoon of batter for each pancake. Cook 3 or 4 pancakes at a time, leaving enough space between them so that they can spread into 3½- to 4-inch cakes. Fry them for about 3 minutes on each side, or until they are golden brown and crisp around the edges. Transfer the finished pancakes to a heated plate and drape foil over them to keep them warm while you cook the remaining cakes, adding fat to the pan when necessary. Serve the pancakes as soon as they are all cooked, accompanied if you wish by crisp bacon.

3 medium-sized potatoes (about 1 pound), preferably baking potatoes
½ cup flour
½ teaspoon salt
¼ cup milk
½ teaspoon caraway seeds (optional)
3 to 4 tablespoons butter or rendered bacon fat
Crisp fried bacon (optional)

Green-Tomato Chutney

To make about 4 pints

- 9 cups coarsely diced unpeeled green tomatoes (about 3 pounds)
- 6 cups coarsely diced, peeled and cored green cooking apples (about 2 pounds)
- 4½ cups coarsely chopped onions (about 1½ pounds)
- 2 cups coarsely diced celery, trimmed of all leaves (about ½ pound)
- ¾ cup seedless raisins
- ½ cup candied or preserved ginger (about 4 ounces), cut into ¼-inch dice
- 2 cups dark-brown sugar
- 1½ cups malt vinegar
- 1 tablespoon salt

In a heavy 6- to 8-quart enameled or stainless-steel pot, combine the green tomatoes, apples, onions, celery, raisins, ginger, brown sugar, vinegar and salt. Bring the mixture to a boil over high heat, stirring occasionally. Then reduce the heat to low. Simmer uncovered for 3 hours, or until most of the liquid has cooked away and the mixture is thick enough to hold its shape in a spoon. Stir it frequently as it begins to thicken, to prevent the chutney from sticking to the bottom and sides of the pan.

Remove the pot from the heat. With a large spoon, ladle the chutney immediately into hot sterilized jars, filling them to within ⅛ inch of the top and following the directions for canning and sealing on page 34.

Bramble Jelly

To make about 2 pints

- 2 quarts fresh, ripe blackberries (about 3 pounds)
- 2 cups water
- 2½ cups sugar

Pick over the berries carefully, removing any stems and discarding fruit that is badly bruised or shows signs of mold. Do not discard any underripe berries; although tarter than ripe ones, they contain more pectin (the substance that jells the fruit), and a few will help ensure a firm jelly. Wash the berries in a colander under cold running water and drop them into an 8- to 10-quart pot. Add the 2 cups of water and bring to a boil over high heat. Reduce the heat to low and simmer uncovered for 1 hour, crushing the berries from time to time against the sides of the pot with a large spoon until the fruit becomes a coarse purée.

Line a colander or a sieve with protruding handles with 4 layers of dampened cheesecloth, and set it in another large pot. Pour in the berry purée. Allow the juice to drain through into the pot without disturbing it; squeezing the cheesecloth will make the final jelly cloudy.

When the juice has drained through completely, discard the berries and bring the juice to a boil over high heat. Boil the juice briskly, uncovered, until it is reduced to 3 cups, then add the sugar and cook, stirring until the sugar dissolves. Boil uncovered, without stirring, until the jelly reaches a temperature of 220° (or 8° above the boiling point of water in your locality) on a jelly, candy or deep-frying thermometer.

Remove the pot from the heat and carefully skim off all of the surface foam with a large spoon. Ladle the jelly immediately into hot sterilized jars or jelly glasses, filling them according to the directions for canning and sealing on page 34.

Apple Chutney

To make 3 pints

- 8 cups coarsely diced, peeled and cored green cooking apples (about 3 pounds)
- 2 cups coarsely chopped onions (about 1 pound)
- 2 cups white seedless raisins
- 2 cups dark-brown sugar
- 1½ cups malt vinegar
- 1 tablespoon mustard seeds, crushed with a mortar and pestle or wrapped in a towel and crushed with a rolling pin
- 1½ teaspoons mixed pickling spice, tied in cheesecloth
- ½ teaspoon ground ginger
- ½ teaspoon cayenne pepper

In a heavy 6- to 8-quart enameled or stainless-steel pot, combine the apples, onions, raisins, brown sugar, vinegar, mustard seeds, pickling spice, ginger and cayenne pepper. Bring the mixture to a boil, stirring occasionally, then reduce the heat to low and simmer uncovered for 2 hours, or until most of the liquid has cooked away and the mixture is thick enough to hold its shape in a spoon. Stir it frequently as it begins to thicken, to prevent the chutney from sticking to the bottom and sides of the pan.

Remove the pot from the heat. With a large spoon, ladle the chutney immediately into hot sterilized jars, filling them to within ⅛ inch of the top and following the directions for canning and sealing on page 34.

Bittersweet in flavor thanks to the plum-pit kernels, plum jam is easily preserved.

Plum Jam

To make about 1 quart

4 pounds firm, ripe blue or red plums
4 pounds sugar (10 cups)

Wash the plums under cold running water and pat them dry with paper towels. Then cut them in half and pry out the pits. With a nutcracker or the tip of a knife, break open 12 of the pits and remove their kernels. Combine the plum halves and the 12 kernels in a 6- to 8-quart pot. Stir in the sugar.

Let the mixture rest at room temperature for 30 minutes, then set the pot over low heat and cook, stirring constantly with a wooden spoon, until the sugar dissolves. Bring to a boil over high heat, reduce the heat to moderate, and cook, stirring occasionally, for 45 minutes, or until the jam thickens and reaches a temperature of 221° (or 9° above the boiling point of water in your locality) on a jelly, candy or deep-frying thermometer. Remove from the heat. With a large spoon, carefully skim off the foam from the surface and ladle the jam into hot sterilized jars or jelly glasses, following the directions for canning and sealing on page 34.

VII

Fish: "For Anglers and Honest Men"

The picture of the "compleat" angler, a fisherman awaits a bite on the upper Thames. His gear includes a light, flexible rod, a fast-action spinning reel, and a "keep" net into which his catch can be dropped to be kept alive under water. The green umbrella marks him as a member of one of the workingmen's clubs that charter buses for a day's relaxation by Britain's well-stocked rivers.

Ah, the roast beef of Old England, the romantics murmur, secure in their belief that roast beef, rampant on a field of Yorkshire pudding, is emblazoned on the coat of arms of every family in the land, just as they are certain of the culinary habits of others. The Americans eat hamburgers and apple pie, people say; the French eat all manner of things in sauces—even, it is darkly hinted, frog's legs and snails; the Germans eat sauerkraut and sausages, the Scandinavians—all of them—eat cold sandwiches. Such generalizations have, of course, more than a grain of truth. The English do eat roast beef, rarely without Yorkshire pudding, and *always* on Sunday. Every other day of the week they eat fish and chips—deep-fried fish with the potatoes known to Americans as French fries.

Fish and chips, often slurred into "fishnchips," now wrestles for supremacy with roast beef as the National Dish of England. Britain, once a forest of trees, is today a forest of fish-and-chips shops and, like the trees they replaced, no two are alike. The fish-and-chips shops are a legacy of the Industrial Revolution that came to England in the 18th Century. Factory workers needed cheap, quick and nourishing food. Shops that specialized in hot pies and peas, eels and mash (mashed potatoes), sausages and mash, and fish and chips grew steadily with the demand.

The fish-and-chips shop, in particular, supplied hot nourishment that could be eaten in the shop where it was sold, or could be wrapped and eaten on the street, or taken home. The development of the deep-sea trawler, improvements in refrigeration and the expansion of the railways meant that fresh fish could be shipped to inland cities and towns. Now that fish were readily available and potatoes were already abundant all over the British Isles, the combination came together as naturally as a pair of lovers. England, a maritime nation, was a small island in a sea of fish.

Many of our northern towns still preserve their old industrial architecture. Tiny houses where the coal miners and the cotton-mill workers live. Row houses, red-brick, with slate roofs, and front doors that open right onto the street. Each house adorned with a telly aerial, but the street still lit by gas lamps, the road still cobbled, the pavement still chalked for hopscotch. Along the street all the curtains drawn so the neighbors can't look in; wouldn't matter if they could, for the family's in the back parlor watching the telly. Soon Mum will say, "Gan doon the corner, young Alfie, an' get four pieces of haddock an two shilluns' chips." Alfie runs down the rain-wet, shiny street, passing a spruce, well-dressed miner taking his whippet for a walk. The bright, cheerful little fish-and-chips shop on the corner emits an aroma of frying fish, an aroma both seductive and compelling, holding out a promise of comfort to the hungry.

Alfie joins the queue. A notice on the window says FRYING TONIGHT and then gives the choice of fish: plaice, haddock, hake. No cod. There is always a queue, those at the end irritable and impatient with the ones up front. "Why can't they move faster? Why have they run out of cod?" From the door to the end of the shop runs a counter, chest high, with a Formica top. On this counter stands a large, battered aluminum salt shaker. Next to it is a bottle of vinegar. Pickled onions, pickled gherkins and bottles of sauce wait to be sold. Heinz tomato ketchup. Dad's Sauce. H.P. sauce. O.K. sauce. TAKE A BOTTLE HOME WITH YOU, says the sign. Behind the counter is a bank of fryers, tanks of bubbling, spitting fat into which wire baskets of chips are plunged. When the chips are introduced the fat foams and rises almost to the edge of the tank.

The design of many fish-and-chips shops, like that of the one young Alfie is visiting, is left over from the 1930s. An 8-foot fan of green-and-white opaque glass, edged in polished aluminum, with a central mirror and a clock above it, decorates the wall behind the fryers. The walls are tongue-and-groove wood planks, once painted white, but now yellow with age, fat and smoke. The fish shop is a family concern: the wife serves the customers and takes the money, the husband fries the fish. Next to each fryer is a flat tin containing a batter made of milk, eggs and flour. Into it the fillet of fish is dipped and straightway goes into the fat, emerging as a delicate, delicious morsel dressed in a crisp, golden jacket of batter. Fish and chips are wrapped in newspaper. This is traditional, and one feels that without newspaper fish and chips would not taste quite the same. (A recipe, without a recommended newspaper, can be found on page 122.)

The queue shuffles forward. Those leaving with an armful of warm newspaper packets squeeze past the waiting line. Someone leaving sees a mate at the end of the queue: "Yo gannin doon t' club tonate, Jack?" (He means the workingmen's club, red-brick, erected 1881.) "Naw," comes the reply. "Naw, Hinnie, I'm gwan with the missus t' bingo."

Alfie is at the front of the queue; the counter is chest high, but not Alfie's chest. He stands on tiptoe: "Four haddock an' two shilluns' chips." The four pieces of sizzling golden fish are piled on the center page of the *North-*

The reason why fish-and-chips shops thrive can be read in the faces of these young patrons in Richmond, Surrey.

A young Cornish fisherman rigs a hoist to lift baskets of fish from the hold of his boat, just back from a trip out of the town of Newlyn. The fleet of Cornwall is small compared to those of regions like Yorkshire and Aberdeen, but it helps supply the London market with such renowned seafood as mackerel, cod, plaice, sole and turbot. *Opposite:* On a calm day, a fishing boat sets out to sea from the Cornish coast.

Western Evening Mail, dated yesterday. The chips are piled around and over the fish on the same paper.

"Salt and vinegar, Alfie?"

The parcel of fish and chips is handed over the counter, a 10-shilling note ($1.20) is taken, and there won't be any change.

Now it's your turn, and while you wait you read upside-down headlines from the *Daily Mirror,* the *News of the World* or the *Greyhound Express.* At one side, its corners torn, is an oil-spattered copy of the *Fish Friers' Review,* price one shilling. "Salt, luv?" you are asked.

You shake salt over the fish and chips in their nest of newsprint and douse them with vinegar. Outside the shop, on the corner, you stand and eat hot fish with your mates. Two hours of drinking beer in the pub has given you a mighty appetite, and there is nothing in the world that can appease your hunger in the way fish and chips can.

Fish have been appeasing British appetites for hundreds of years. The physician and author Andrew Boorde wrote in 1542, "Of all nations and countries, England is best served of fish . . . and of all manner of sorts of salt-fish." So abundant were salted herring that the scholar Desiderius Erasmus of Rotterdam thought it worth recording that the people were "wonderfully fond" of them. Probably an inaccurate observation, for the 16th Century British housewife was certainly bored stiff with the monotony of the salt-fish diet, tired of hearing her family complain, "What! Salt fish again?" and envious of those who could afford the luxury of fresh fish and meat. In spite of the fact that fresh fish were plentiful, fish were also expensive, as one observer from abroad reported. "Fish," said he, "in proportion is dearer than any other belly-timber at London." The fish were sold at Billingsgate, the oldest market in Britain, where hucksters filled their barrows with cod, haddock, mackerel and herring, as well as oysters and lobster, then pushed their wares up steep Fish Street Hill and "cried" them in the streets. Fish are of course no longer so dear in Britain, and are in consequence featured on British tables at least once a week. We are still "best served of fish," and the marble slabs in our fish shops glisten with a tumbling cornucopia of shiny fish amid blocks of dripping ice.

Here are such salt-water produce as stiff, rainbow-hued mackerel with bright eyes, red zodiac crabs, whiting, cod, hake and haddock. On its own block of ice reposes a pink Scottish salmon—expensive, yet in great demand. Here too are Dover sole; plaice, the flatfish with the orange spots; the fat turbot; and the immense halibut, firm of flesh and rich in oil. Smoked fish flank one side of the display: haddock, chrome yellow, unbelievably yellow; deep-dark kippers, the color of old varnish; and bloaters with their skins of gold. Many fish shops sell fresh-water fish: the roach, the chub, the carp, the speckled trout with the down-turned mouth, and that wolf of our rivers, the voracious pike—a muscular torpedo with sharp teeth.

In London in particular there are, in addition to the customary fish shops, modern counterparts of the medieval fish barrows where seafood is sold to be eaten on the spot. These shellfish stalls offer a variety of shellfish and also jellied eels for sale on street corners. They don't really compete with the fish-and-chips shops, which are found in London too, for shellfish stalls merely provide an appetizer, not a meal. At any time of the day, right up to midnight (trade is particularly brisk around 10:30 or 11 p.m., in keeping with pub-closing time), the stalls are busy. They are usually flat-topped barrows on two wheels, each illuminated at night by an overhead lamp that casts a pool of brilliant white light around the stall. Enameled bowls containing jellied eels, bowls of shrimp, mussels, cockles that resemble tiny clams, fat whelks and winkles in their snaillike shells (you fish them out with a pin) are displayed. For a few pence you are handed a small china dish and a generous portion of shellfish, over which you may sprinkle chili-flavored vinegar from the bottle provided. You eat with a spoon. If jellied eels are your fancy, you will be served them in a bowl, with a spoon and a thick slice of white bread called a doorstep. You spit the bones out on the pavement. Unhappily, there are far fewer of the shellfish stalls nowadays, and many seem to be relics of Victorian gaslight times. They are a remnant of the real old-fashioned Cockney London, in keeping with the music halls and the now extinct muffin man who walked along the streets ringing a hand bell, a tray of muffins on his head.

Disappearing, too, are the eel-and-pie shops that once dotted London, where one could buy jellied or stewed eels and meat pies (a curious combination), either to eat on the premises or to take away. A few remain, however. There is still such a shop on the Tower Bridge Road, South London. I'll bet it hasn't changed in a hundred years. You sit in pews, as in a church, and eat from a scrubbed pine table. Clean sawdust is spread over the floor twice a day, and here you can make a meal of hot stewed eels in parsley sauce with mashed potatoes, or of jellied eels with bread and a mug of fresh tea *(Recipe Index)*. Everything is made right on the premises, and the eels are kept alive in tanks, so they can be cooked fresh. We have, indeed, an abundance of eels, as we do of other fish, though perhaps there were even more of them a century or so ago. In the year 1801 a writer recorded that "great quantities of eels were caught after heavy storms of rain. Eels were fried and boiled." He didn't seem very surprised. If I got caught out in an eel storm I would talk about it forever.

One of the greatest of eel dishes is eel pie, a piquant mixture of the fish with lemon, parsley and shallots, covered with a puff pastry. So famous was this dish that it gave its name to a small island, Eel Pie Island, which lies in the Thames just upriver from London, opposite the suburb of Twickenham, where I once lived. That whole stretch of the river, from Kingston to Richmond, was noted for its yield of Thames eels during the season, and the recipe that we give in this book *(Recipe Index)* comes from Richmond, but there is no reason to suppose that Richmond's pie is in any way inferior to the Eel Pie Island one. There is good eel eating even on the other side of Britain. In Gloucester on the Severn, one can buy the young eels known as elvers during the season when they swim up the river and are caught by the bucketful. Elvers are boiled in the water in which they are collected, or they are washed, dusted with flour and deep-fried. If they are not quite dry, or if they are too floury, they turn into inedible lumps of floury paste. Properly prepared, however, they are a great delicacy, frequently compared to whitebait, which are a great delicacy indeed—tiny, almost boneless, also fried in deep fat, and eaten whole, hot from the griddle.

Whitebait used to be found in great quantity in the Thames. They swam up the river in huge shoals and were caught at Greenwich, a London borough that, apart from setting the right time for the world, is a center of maritime tradition and British history. Henry VIII was born there, as was Elizabeth I. The architect Christopher Wren designed a magnificent hospital for seamen in Greenwich. After the battle of Trafalgar, Lord Nelson's body was brought there to lie in state. Whitebait was still a noted delicacy in Greenwich a century ago, for it figured in some lines of doggerel celebrating the rivalry between two of Queen Victoria's most famous ministers: "Gladstone at Greenwich / Ate his whitebait gaily / Then ordered tea and shrimps / And sent for Disraeli. / Benjamin Disraeli sent back word to say / 'I'm wanted in the city, / It's Lord Mayor's Day.' "

Disraeli did not go hungry because he missed whitebait at Greenwich with Gladstone; as Prime Minister on Lord Mayor's Day it was his duty to attend the annual banquet in London celebrating the installation of the new Lord Mayor of the City. But he did miss something of a treat; the fish were cooked by first flouring them and then deep-frying them in smoking-hot fat in a copper caldron over a charcoal fire. "At table," wrote one delighted epicure, "lemon juice is squeezed over them and they are seasoned with cayenne pepper; brown bread and butter is substituted for plain bread and they are eaten with iced champagne or punch."

Unhappily, whitebait have not been seen in the Thames as far up as Greenwich for 50 years or more, on account of the river traffic and the pollution. The river is, however, getting cleaner, and so some of the species of fish that used to frequent it are returning. Perhaps the whitebait may once more shoal at Greenwich, though the possibility is hard to believe if you look out over the old river port from the bow window of the Trafalgar Tavern's banqueting room. Behind you in the room is the past recalled in a painting of Nelson and a group of his captains. In front of you, across the wide canvas of the river, is the present of some 30 factory chimneys and a dense forest of dockyard cranes. One may still enjoy whitebait at the Trafalgar Tavern, but they don't come from the Thames.

Fresh fish like whitebait have always been delicacies. The staples of the British table are smoked fish, especially haddock and kippers—split and salted herring. Now a kipper, if you have never tried one, is something to look forward to. Ask a Scot about kippers, and he will describe them with an eloquence he usually reserves for the praise of his favorite whisky. The finest kippers and haddock come from Scotland's east coast, from tiny fishing villages like Arbroath in Angus, and Findon in Kincardine.

Findon haddock ("Finnan haddie," as the Scots say) is a haddock that has been split and smoked, and if you happen to catch a haddock some day and want to smoke it, this is what you do: Clean the fish, split it, remove the gut and take off the head. Rub it inside and out with salt, and let it stand overnight. Now hang your fish in the open air for three hours to dry. Next you will need a container such as a a 10-gallon can with the bottom cut out and a replaceable top. A few holes should be punched in the top. The idea is to suspend the fish over a concentrated source of heat and smoke. Stand the container on end over a fire of peat, oak chips, hardwood sawdust or fir cones. Then place a metal rod or a stick of wood strong enough to support the fish over the upper end of the drum and hang your fish on it by the tail, securing it with a piece of string or wire; the fish should be at least a foot above the fire. The top should be replaced and the heat must be evenly maintained throughout the period of smoking, which should take nine to 12 hours. At the end the fish will have taken on a rich, saffron-yellow color.

Trout may be smoked by the same method, but there's no need to split them—just take out the gut but leave the head on. Smoked trout are delicious, as are smoked eels and salmon. Unfortunately, the procedure for smoking salmon is impractical on a small scale. If I ever caught a salmon I would poach it gently with a sprig of fennel or lemon thyme, serve it with a butter sauce, and leave the smoking to the commercial experts.

A simple method of smoking freshly caught fish is illustrated in the cross section above. The smoke chamber is simply a steel drum with a removable lid into which holes have been punched and from which the bottom has been removed. The drum is set on bricks enclosing a fire of oak chips, and the fish are suspended inside it from a stick.

Each part of the British Isles, from Scotland to Ireland to the Channel ports, has its fish specialty. Scotland is the place for salmon; I never have, before or since, tasted any like that I had in Grantown, only hours after it had been caught in the Spey River. For shrimp, it's the Yorkshire coast of the North Sea. But for oysters you have to go to the Channel, perhaps to the port of Whitstable, where the little black boats are anchored a mile out and dredge the shells up from the ocean bed—*that's* the place to eat oysters. Or drive down the coast during the month of September and buy from the fishermen as they land their catch, and if you just happen to have a loaf of brown bread, some butter and a bottle of Guiness stout in the car with you—words are inadequate.

Two salmon fishermen toss part of their catch to children welcoming them on their return from drift-netting, a technique in which fish are netted as they drift along with the tide, in the estuary of the River Barrow on the south coast of Ireland.

Not all of us are fortunate enough to live by the sea, and therefore some may never know what a really fresh ocean fish can taste like. I once lived among the wild green hills on the Ring of Kerry in Ireland, where peace, as the poet William Butler Yeats said, "comes dropping slow." The water that gushed down from the mountains every time it rained was golden, colored by the thick layers of peat. In the Bay of Kenmare I caught mackerel, and had them in a smoking-hot frying pan within 20 minutes after the fish had taken the hook. Cooked in this manner and dusted with oatmeal and salt, mackerel and herring (the herring should be served with mustard sauce) are every bit as excellent as fresh salmon or trout.

Those Irish mackerel! We fried them, successfully soused them in a marinade *(Recipe Index)*, baked them, grilled them and boiled them (a mistake), and we lived on fresh mackerel for weeks. Now and then we were offered lobster and salmon by fishermen who dropped into Moriarty's Bar for a glass of stout. More often than not the lobster was poached by someone from someone else's pots, while a mile from the village, down the Kenmare River, local men illegally fished for salmon with a stick of dynamite. Quite recently, skindivers started to fish for lobster along the Kerry coast, and made such a haul that they shipped them by the thousands to France and the United States from Shannon Airport. An Irish friend told me that the government moved so fast that the divers never had a second chance. "It was the quickest law they ever passed," he said. "They won't let anyone dive for lobsters; you have to catch them in a lobster pot." There is a brisk trade in lobster from Ireland; whatever the price, there is always someone willing to buy them in Paris or London.

The Irish are very sensible about serving lobster. "Why," they argue, "dress a lobster in fancy sauces [they mean thermidor, Américaine, Mornay, etc.], when all you need to do is grill, boil or bake it and serve it with fresh whole-meal soda bread and butter?" In Irish coastal areas they sometimes wrap a lobster in clay, or a flour-and-water crust, and bake it on an open fire for about half an hour in the fashion of the gypsylike, wandering tinkers still seen in the countryside, whose culinary techniques in their kitchens-under-the-sky preserve the true natural flavor of everything that they cook. Next time you have a holiday by the sea, and are clever enough to catch a lobster, try the tinkers' method of cooking it. You will find the flavor delicate, and beautifully fresh, like that of the famous prawns of Dublin Bay, which are a small variety of lobster.

The Irish claim that their prawns are pinker and more delectable than those found in the North Sea and the Mediterranean, and it would be a brave man who would dispute that statement to their faces. Italians call the Mediterranean prawns *scampi,* a word since adopted by the English, who often mistakenly serve the smaller, common prawn under that name. Dublin Bay prawns are in such demand all over Europe that it is small wonder they rarely appear on Irish tables.

In waters far to the south of Dublin Bay is caught still another British delicacy—Dover sole. Dover, that conglomerate of white chalk cliffs on the English Channel that has been for centuries the first landmark for travelers bound to England from the Continent, has given its name to Dover sole, most delicate of all flatfish, not because the Dover waters are superabundant in sole, but because fishmongers thus distinguish them from the inferior lemon sole that inhabits the North Sea. The two fish are similar in appearance, but what a difference in the flavor! Using lemon sole, I once tried to cook *sole à la normande*—a French dish in which the fish are poached in white wine and served with a rich, creamy sauce—hoping that the preparation might lift the lemon sole to the level of Dover sole. But the ensuing failure proved only that you cannot imitate the real thing. The excellence of Dover sole is such that it should, like lobster, be prepared in the simplest manner possible, just steamed or grilled and accompanied by herb butter and perhaps a crisp green salad. (This is making me hungry.)

There are, of course, many English fish dishes requiring lengthier preparation. Cod's head and shoulders, a longtime favorite in the big fishing ports along England's northeast coast, is one of these and calls for a deft hand with the boning knife. Many cooks bone the head and stuff it with the cooked cod roe, onion and parsley. The distinguished 19th Century British cookbook writer, Mrs. Isabella Beeton, advised a preliminary salting, then poaching in water flavored with herbs, and serving with an oyster or caper sauce. Other cooks suggest dredging, or dipping, the head in bread crumbs and roasting it while basting with the drippings from the fish. Why not combine the two recipes? Clean the head and rub with salt, leaving it for an hour or two before poaching in water flavored with fennel, bay and parsley. The water should just cover the head and must simmer very gently for half an hour, or until the meat is tender. Take out the head and drain it; when it has cooled a little, you can begin taking out the bones, starting from the underside. The lower jaw, the gills, the skull and the eyes should be removed, and the space filled with the stuffing of roe, chopped onion and parsley. Dredge in

Three children who waited for the small boats to come in *(opposite)* set out for home with their trophies. Most of the salmon are sold to local dealers who call at the fishermen's homes to make purchases each evening during the season.

bread crumbs or oatmeal that you have mixed with freshly ground black pepper, and bake the head in a hot oven for 10 minutes, until it is nicely browned. The cheeks of the fish are esteemed as great delicacies. Serve with a shrimp sauce.

There is, I believe, a similar recipe for cod's head from New England, but far richer in that wine-and-mushroom sauce is an essential ingredient. There are some delicious recipes for red mullet *(Recipe Index),* and very hearty Scots ones for fish pie *(Recipe Index).* And there are a few very odd ones, too, the oddest of which must be "stargazey pie" from Cornwall, using pilchard or herring under a blanket of pastry. The fish are laid whole on a plate, their tails in the center and their heads at the edge, so that they lie like spokes in a cartwheel. There is a sheet of pastry under them, cut to the shape of the plate, and a crust of pastry over them, trimmed just short of the edge, so that the heads of the fish gaze out from underneath the top sheet. Sometimes a single fish will be stuffed and tightly wrapped in an overcoat of shortcrust pastry, the idea being to preserve the oils and juices within the fish while it is being cooked.

But most of England's fish recipes involve no such complexities. They are very simple for the good reason that they come from the coastal villages, where the natural flavor of fish straight off the boat can best be savored. Hake, turbot, halibut and haddock are served with simple sauces such as shrimp and oyster, fennel or parsley, horseradish or mustard *(Recipe Index).* We sometimes serve mackerel with gooseberry sauce, and accompany cold salmon with cucumber.

The necessity for simplicity of preparation was well understood by Izaak Walton, that immortal of English literature, whose *The Compleat Angler* is

In Mousehole, Cornwall, the local vicar, the Rev. R. H. Cadman, asks a blessing on food to be sold for the benefit of the needy in the Ship Inn pub. Seafood, the principal harvest in many coastal towns, is sometimes included in the gifts contributed at harvest festival time.

still read by anglers (and English majors). Walton's expertness with the rod is somewhat questionable, but his culinary advice remains sound. "These kinds of Fish," said Walton in 1653, "a trout especially, if he is not eaten within four or five hours after he is taken, is worth nothing." I quote from Walton because not to do so would be to ignore the most important factor of cooking fresh-water fish—as soon as possible. Run home if necessary or, better still, cook your catch on the riverbank, as Walton often did. But remember this: Fish from ponds and the lower reaches of rivers are inclined to taste muddy unless you are careful in the handling. Do not disturb the scales, and do not wash the fish, but merely wrap it in clay or a flour-and-water paste and roast or grill quickly. The crust can be broken off and the skin will come away, leaving the flesh clean tasting.

I have caught carp and perch that I unwisely washed, scaled and fried in butter; they tasted rather muddy but I ate them anyway, because I had caught them. If you don't wish to eat your catch, throw it back; if you take it home, then be sure you know how to prepare it. Fish from fast-running streams need only be gutted, salted and rubbed with a little butter, dusted with oatmeal or flour, and cooked on a very hot grill. If you have a few herbs at hand, such as sweet cicely, fennel or wild thyme, stuff a small bunch into the fish, for the delicacy of wild herbs complements the flavor. Pike may need to be stuffed. We have included a recipe for stuffed pike *(Recipe Index)*, somewhat different from Izaak Walton's, that may serve for any large river fish—except of course salmon, which must be prepared as simply as the trout when really fresh. Followed carefully, you will find, as Walton did, that: "This dish of meat is too good for any but Anglers, or honest men: and I trust, you will prove both. . . ."

After the vicar has blessed the food *(opposite)*, a crab contributed by a fisherman is auctioned off. The proceeds of the auction will provide two bags of coal for every old-age pensioner in the Cornish village; leftover profits from the sale are distributed through charities.

CHAPTER VII RECIPES

Fish and Chips

DEEP-FRIED FISH AND POTATOES

To serve 4

BATTER
1 cup flour
1 egg yolk
4 tablespoons beer
1/4 teaspoon salt
6 tablespoons milk combined with 6 tablespoons cold water
2 egg whites

CHIPS
Vegetable oil or shortening for deep-fat frying
2 pounds baking potatoes, sliced lengthwise into strips 1/2 inch thick and 1/2 inch wide

FISH
2 pounds fresh, firm white fish fillets such as haddock, sole, flounder or cod, skinned and cut into 3-by-5-inch serving pieces

To prepare the batter, pour the flour into a large mixing bowl, make a well in the center and add the egg yolk, beer and salt. Stir the ingredients together until they are well mixed, then gradually pour in the combined milk and water, and continue to stir until the batter is smooth.

For a light texture, let the batter rest at room temperature for at least 30 minutes, although if necessary it may be used at once. In either case, beat the egg whites until they form unwavering peaks on the beater when it is lifted from the bowl. Then gently but thoroughly fold them into the batter.

To cook the chips and fish, heat 4 to 5 inches of oil or shortening in a deep-fat fryer to a temperature of 375° on a deep-fat-frying thermometer. Preheat the oven to 250°, and line a large shallow roasting pan with paper towels.

Dry the potatoes thoroughly and deep-fry them in 3 or 4 batches until they are crisp and light brown. Transfer them to the lined pan to drain and place them in the oven to keep warm.

Wash the pieces of fish under cold running water and pat them completely dry with paper towels. Drop 2 or 3 pieces of fish at a time into the batter and, when they are well coated, plunge them into the hot fat. Fry for 4 or 5 minutes, or until golden brown, turning the pieces occasionally with a spoon to prevent them from sticking together or to the pan.

To serve, heap the fish in the center of a large heated platter and arrange the chips around them. Traditionally, fish and chips are served sprinkled with malt vinegar and salt.

Baked Stuffed Pike

To serve 4 to 6

3 tablespoons butter plus 2 tablespoons butter, softened
1/2 cup finely chopped onions
1 1/2 cups fresh soft crumbs, made from homemade-type white bread, pulverized in a blender or shredded with a fork
2 tablespoons finely chopped parsley
2 tablespoons milk
2 flat anchovy fillets, thoroughly drained and finely chopped
1/2 teaspoon finely grated lemon peel
1 teaspoon crumbled dried sage leaves
Salt
Freshly ground black pepper
1 large garlic clove, peeled and bruised with the flat side of a heavy knife
A 3-pound whole pike, cleaned and scaled but with head and tail left on, or substitute any other whole 3-pound firm white fish
1 cup red Bordeaux or other dry red wine combined with 1/3 cup fresh orange juice

In a heavy 6- to 8-inch skillet, melt the 3 tablespoons of butter over moderate heat, add the onions and cook, stirring constantly, for 5 minutes, or until they are soft and transparent but not brown. With a rubber spatula, transfer them to a large mixing bowl, and stir in the bread crumbs, parsley, 2 tablespoons of milk, anchovy fillets, lemon peel, sage, 1/4 teaspoon of salt and a few grindings of pepper. Taste for seasoning and set aside.

Preheat the oven to 350°. Rub the bruised garlic over the bottom and sides of a shallow baking-and-serving dish just large enough to hold the fish comfortably. Then with a pastry brush or paper towel, coat the bottom of the dish with 1 tablespoon of the softened butter.

Wash the fish inside and out under cold running water, and dry it thoroughly with paper towels. Loosely fill the cavity of the fish with the stuffing, then close the opening with small skewers, crisscrossing them with kitchen cord as if lacing a turkey. Brush the fish with the remaining tablespoon of softened butter and sprinkle it with salt and a few grindings of pepper. Place the fish in the baking dish, and pour in the combined wine and orange juice. Bake uncovered in the middle of the oven for 30 to 40 minutes, basting every 10 minutes with the pan liquid. The fish is done when its flesh is firm to the touch. Serve at once directly from the baking dish, moistening each serving with a little of the sauce.

Resting on the usual fish-and-chips wrapping, fried haddock and potatoes will be seasoned with salt and vinegar.

Soused Mackerel

To serve 6

3 one-pound mackerel, eviscerated, with heads removed but tails left on
2 medium-sized onions, thinly sliced and separated into rings
1/4 cup finely chopped parsley
2 small bay leaves
1/8 teaspoon thyme
12 whole black peppercorns
1 1/2 teaspoons salt
1 cup malt or white wine vinegar
1 cup cold water
2 tablespoons fresh lemon juice
Parsley sprigs

Preheat the oven to 325°. Wash the mackerel inside and out under cold running water and pat them dry with paper towels. Lay the fish side by side in a shallow flameproof ceramic, stainless-steel or enameled baking pan just large enough to hold them comfortably. Strew the onion rings, chopped parsley and bay leaves evenly over the fish and sprinkle them with the thyme, peppercorns and salt. Pour in the vinegar, water and lemon juice, and bring to a boil over high heat. Then bake uncovered in the middle of the oven for 15 minutes, or until the fish are firm to the touch, basting them two or three times with the cooking liquid. Do not overcook. Let the fish cool to room temperature and cover tightly with foil or plastic wrap. Marinate in the refrigerator for at least 6 hours. Brush the onions and seasonings off the fish and, with a slotted spatula, carefully transfer the mackerel to a platter.

To debone the mackerel for easier serving, divide the top layer into individual portions with a fish server without cutting through the spine. Leave the tail intact. Lift up the portions with the fish server and a fork, and arrange them on a serving dish. Lift out the backbone in one piece and divide the bottom layer of fish into portions. Garnish each serving with a sprig of parsley.

Fish Pie

To serve 4 to 6

6 medium-sized baking potatoes (about 2 pounds), peeled and cut into quarters
7 tablespoons butter, softened, plus 2 tablespoons butter, cut into 1/4-inch bits
1 1/2 to 1 3/4 cups milk
1 teaspoon salt
Freshly ground black pepper
12 raw medium-sized shrimp
2 medium-sized onions, peeled and thinly sliced
3 tablespoons flour
1/4 cup heavy cream
3 tablespoons finely chopped parsley
2 teaspoons anchovy paste
1/4 teaspoon dried fennel seeds
Pinch of cayenne pepper
1/2 pound of fillets of any firm white fish such as sole, haddock or flounder, cut into 2-inch pieces
1/2 pound fresh or thoroughly defrosted frozen crab meat, or substitute one 7 1/2-ounce can crab meat, thoroughly drained

Drop the potatoes into enough lightly salted boiling water to cover them completely. Boil briskly, uncovered, until tender. Drain and return the potatoes to the pan. Shake over low heat until they are dry and mealy. Then mash them to a smooth purée with a fork, a potato ricer or an electric mixer. Beat in 4 tablespoons of the butter and 1/2 cup of the milk, 2 tablespoons at a time. Use up to 1/4 cup more milk if necessary to make a purée just thick enough to hold its shape in a spoon. Beat in the salt and a few grindings of black pepper, taste for seasoning, and set aside.

Shell the shrimp, and devein them by making a shallow incision down their backs with a small knife and lifting out their intestinal veins. Wash the shrimp under cold running water, and pat them dry with paper towels.

Preheat the oven to 400°. In a heavy 10- to 12-inch skillet, melt 3 tablespoons of the butter over moderate heat. When the foam has almost subsided, add the onions and cook, stirring frequently, for 5 minutes, or until they are soft and transparent but not brown. Thoroughly mix in the flour, pour in the remaining 1 cup of milk and the cream, and bring to a boil over high heat, stirring constantly with a whisk until the sauce is smooth and thick. Add the parsley, anchovy paste, fennel seeds and cayenne pepper, and stir until the anchovy paste dissolves. Then add the shrimp, fish and crab meat, and simmer slowly for about 5 minutes. Taste for seasoning, and pour the entire contents of the skillet into a 4- to 5-quart baking dish.

Spread the mashed potatoes evenly over the fish and smooth the top with a spatula. Make an attractive pattern on the potatoes with the tines of a fork, and dot with the remaining 2 tablespoons of butter cut into bits. Bake in the middle of the oven for about 20 minutes, or until the top of the pie is a light golden brown. Slide under the broiler for a few seconds to give the crust a deeper color, and serve at once directly from the baking dish.

Mackerel strewed with onion rings is ready for poaching and sousing (pickling) in vinegar, lemon juice, herbs and spices.

Scotch Woodcock

SCRAMBLED EGGS ON ANCHOVY TOAST

To serve 4

- 4 eggs
- 3 tablespoons heavy cream
- 1/8 teaspoon salt
- Freshly ground black pepper
- 3 tablespoons butter
- 4 slices hot buttered toast
- 2 tablespoons anchovy paste
- 8 flat anchovy fillets, thoroughly drained

In a small bowl, beat the eggs with a fork or whisk until they are well blended, then beat in the cream, salt and a few grindings of pepper. Place the skillet over low heat, and in it melt the 3 tablespoons of butter. Do not let the butter brown. Pour in the eggs and cook them over the lowest possible heat, stirring with the flat of a table fork or a rubber spatula, until they form soft, creamy curds. Do not overcook; the finished eggs should be moist. Quickly spread the toast with anchovy paste, arrange the slices on individual serving plates, and spread a layer of the scrambled eggs on top. Crisscross two anchovy fillets over each portion, and serve at once.

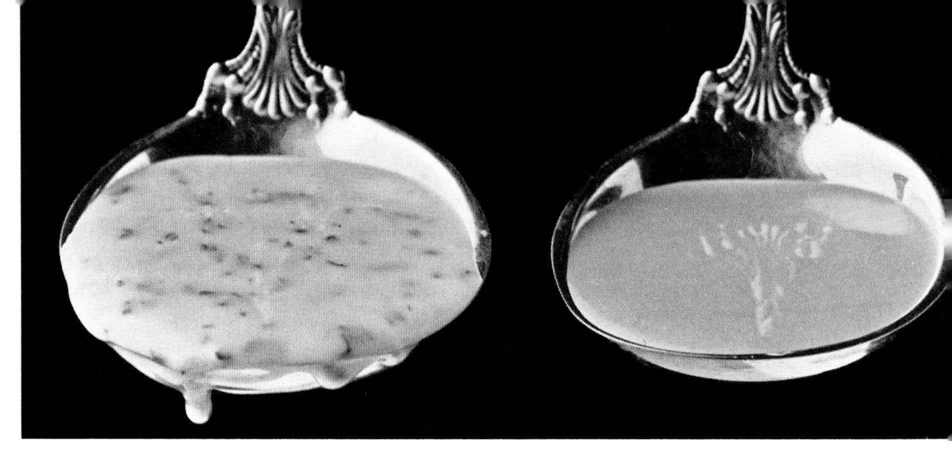

A FRAGRANT PARSLEY SAUCE (LEFT) OR A MUSTARD SAUCE IMPROVES MANY FISH DISHES.

Mustard Sauce

To make about 1½ cups

- 2 tablespoons butter
- 2 tablespoons flour
- 1 cup milk
- 4 tablespoons heavy cream
- 1 teaspoon distilled white vinegar
- 1 teaspoon Dijon-style prepared mustard
- 1 teaspoon dry hot English mustard
- ½ teaspoon salt
- Freshly ground black pepper

In a heavy 6- to 8-inch skillet, melt the butter over moderate heat. When the foam subsides, stir in the flour and mix together thoroughly. Pour in the milk and, stirring constantly with a whisk, cook over high heat until the sauce thickens heavily and comes to a boil. Reduce the heat to low and simmer for about 3 minutes, then beat in the cream, vinegar, prepared mustard, dry mustard, salt and a few grindings of pepper. Taste for seasoning and serve at once.

Mustard sauce may be served with a variety of fish dishes including Finnan haddie *(Recipe Index)*.

Baked Mullet

To serve 2

- 3 tablespoons butter, softened
- 3 cups peeled, chopped fresh tomatoes, or substitute 3 cups finely chopped, drained canned tomatoes
- 12 large peeled shallots (about ¼ pound)
- 2 tablespoons finely chopped parsley
- 1 teaspoon capers, drained and rinsed in cold water
- 1 teaspoon anchovy paste
- 1 teaspoon dry English mustard
- 2 whole 1-pound mullets, cleaned and scaled, but with heads and tails left on, or substitute any whole firm, white 1-pound fish
- ¼ teaspoon thyme
- ½ teaspoon salt
- Freshly ground black pepper
- 1 teaspoon fresh lemon juice

Preheat the oven to 350°. With a pastry brush and 2 tablespoons of the butter, coat the bottom and sides of an 8-by-12-by-2-inch casserole or a baking dish just large enough to hold the mullets comfortably.

In a heavy 2- to 3-quart saucepan, combine the chopped tomatoes, shallots, 1 tablespoon of the parsley, and the capers, anchovy paste and dry mustard. Bring to a boil over high heat, stirring constantly, then reduce the heat to low, and simmer uncovered, stirring occasionally, for 10 minutes, or until most of the liquid has evaporated and the sauce is thick. There should be about 2 cups.

Meanwhile, wash the mullets inside and out under cold running water and pat them thoroughly dry with paper towels. Lay the fish side by side in the casserole and score the top of each fish with three parallel diagonal cuts about an inch apart and ¼ inch deep. Sprinkle the fish evenly with the thyme, salt and a few grindings of pepper, and spread the sauce over them. Cover the dish and bake in the middle of the oven for 30 minutes, or until the fish is firm to the touch. (Lacking a cover, a sheet of buttered foil will do as well.)

With two wide metal spatulas, carefully transfer the fish to a heated serving platter. Remove the shallots from the sauce and strew them over the top.

With the aid of a rubber spatula, transfer the sauce remaining in the casserole to a small saucepan and briskly boil it over high heat, stirring constantly, until it is reduced to about ½ cup. Remove the pan from the heat, stir in the remaining 1 tablespoon of butter and 1 teaspoon of lemon juice, taste for seasoning, and pour over the fish. Sprinkle with the remaining tablespoon of parsley and serve at once.

Poached Haddock with Parsley Sauce

To serve 4 to 6

A 3- to 4-pound whole fresh haddock, cleaned and scaled, but with head and tail left on, or substitute any other 3- to 4-pound whole firm, white fish
2½ quarts water
1 cup malt vinegar
1 tablespoon salt
1 teaspoon black peppercorns
¼ cup finely chopped fresh fennel leaves or 1 tablespoon dried fennel seed

SAUCE
3 tablespoons butter
3 tablespoons flour
1½ cups milk
¼ cup finely chopped parsley
½ teaspoon salt
¼ teaspoon white pepper
1 tablespoon fresh lemon juice

Wash the fish inside and out under cold running water. Without drying it, wrap it in a long piece of damp cheesecloth of double thickness, leaving at least 6 inches of cloth at each end to serve as handles for lifting the fish. Twist the ends of the cloth and tie them with string. In a fish poacher or a deep covered roasting pan large enough to hold the fish comfortably, bring the water, vinegar, 1 tablespoon of salt, peppercorns and fennel to a boil over high heat.

Place the fish on the rack of the poacher or roasting pan, and lower it into the pan. The liquid should cover the fish by about 2 inches; add more boiling water if necessary. Cover, reduce the heat to its lowest point, and simmer slowly for 12 to 15 minutes, or until the fish feels firm when pressed lightly with a finger.

Meanwhile, prepare the sauce. In a heavy 8- to 10-inch skillet, melt the butter over moderate heat. When the foam begins to subside, stir in the flour and mix thoroughly. Pour in the milk and, stirring constantly with a whisk, cook over high heat until the sauce thickens and comes to a boil. Reduce the heat to low and simmer for about 3 minutes to remove any taste of raw flour. Then add the parsley, ½ teaspoon of salt and white pepper. Just before serving, stir in the lemon juice and taste for seasoning.

Using the ends of the cheesecloth as handles, lift the fish from the pan and lay it on a large board or platter. Open the cheesecloth and skin the fish with a small, sharp knife by making a cut in the skin at the base of the tail and gently pulling off the skin in strips from tail to gill. Holding both ends of the cheesecloth, carefully lift the fish and turn it over onto a heated serving platter. Peel off the skin on the upturned side.

Serve the fish from the platter, the sauce from a separate bowl. If you like, you may debone the fish for serving. Divide the top layer into individual portions with a fish server without cutting through the spine. Leave the head and tail intact. Lift out the portions with the fish server and a fork, and arrange them attractively on another plate or platter. Then gently remove the backbone in one piece, discard it, and divide the bottom layer of fish into individual portions as before.

Potted Shrimp

To serve 6

½ pound (2 sticks) plus 4 tablespoons butter, cut into ¼-inch bits
½ teaspoon mace
½ teaspoon ground nutmeg
⅛ teaspoon cayenne pepper
1 teaspoon salt
1 pound shelled, cooked tiny fresh shrimp (60 or more), or substitute 2 cups drained, canned tiny shrimp

In a 1½- to 2-quart saucepan, clarify ¼ pound of the butter by melting it slowly over low heat. Skim off the surface foam and let the butter rest off the heat for a minute or two. Then spoon the clear butter on top into a heavy 6- to 8-inch skillet and discard the milky solids at the bottom of the saucepan.

Melt the remaining ¼ pound plus 4 tablespoons of butter over moderate heat in a heavy 3- to 4-quart saucepan. When the foam begins to subside, stir in the mace, nutmeg, cayenne pepper and salt. Add the shrimp, turning them about with a spoon to coat them evenly.

Spoon the mixture into six 4-ounce individual baking dishes or custard cups, dividing the shrimp equally among them. Seal by pouring a thin layer of the clarified butter over each. Refrigerate the shrimp overnight or for at least 6 hours.

Potted shrimp are traditionally served with hot toast as a first course or at teatime.

Mussel Brose

MUSSEL SOUP

To serve 4 to 6

- 3 dozen mussels in their shells
- 1 cup finely chopped leeks, including 2 inches of the green
- 1/2 cup finely chopped celery
- 1/2 cup finely chopped onions
- 3 sprigs parsley
- 1 cup dry hard cider, preferably imported English cider
- 3 tablespoons butter
- 3 tablespoons flour
- 2 cups milk
- 2 tablespoons heavy cream
- Salt
- Freshly ground black pepper
- Ground nutmeg

Scrub the mussels thoroughly under cold running water with a stiff brush or soapless steel-mesh scouring pad. With a small, sharp knife scrape or pull the black ropelike tufts off the shells and discard them.

In a 6- to 8-quart enameled or stainless-steel pot, combine the leeks, celery, onions, parsley and cider. Drop in the mussels, cover, and bring to a boil over high heat. Reduce the heat to low and simmer for about 10 minutes, shaking the pot from time to time until the mussels open. Discard those that remain closed. With a slotted spoon transfer the mussels to a plate. Strain the stock through a fine sieve lined with a double thickness of cheesecloth, and return it to the pot.

Traditionally, the mussels are left in the half shell; to follow this method, remove and discard the upper half of each shell. Or you may remove the mussels from their shells entirely. In either case, cover the mussels with foil and set them aside. In a heavy 2- to 3-quart saucepan, melt the butter over moderate heat. Add the flour and mix together thoroughly. Pour in the milk and, stirring constantly with a whisk, bring to a boil over high heat. Reduce the heat to moderate and continue to cook, stirring, until the sauce is smooth and thick. Pour it into the strained stock, stir in the cream, and season lightly with salt and a few grindings of pepper and nutmeg.

Bring the soup to a simmer over low heat, stirring frequently. Then add the mussels and cook only long enough to heat them through. Taste for seasoning. Serve the soup from a heated tureen or individual soup plates.

Kipper Paste

To make 2 cups

- 1/4 pound butter plus 10 tablespoons butter cut into 1/2-inch bits and softened
- 2 pairs packaged smoked whole Scottish kippers (about 2 pounds)
- 4 teaspoons anchovy paste
- 1/4 teaspoon ground cloves
- 1/4 teaspoon ground mace
- 1/8 teaspoon cayenne pepper

In a 1 1/2- to 2-quart saucepan, clarify the 1/4 pound of butter by melting it slowly over low heat. Skim off the surface foam and let the butter rest off the heat for a minute or two. Then spoon the clear butter on top into a bowl or cup, and discard the milky solids at the bottom of the pan.

Bring 1 quart of water to a boil in a heavy 10- to 12-inch skillet. Add the kippers, reduce the heat to low, and simmer uncovered for 5 minutes, or until the fish flakes easily when prodded with a fork. Drain the kippers and remove the skin. With a fork, lift the meat away from the backbone and tail of each fish, but do not bother to remove the tiny bones. Discard the black roe.

Place the fish in the jar of an electric blender, and blend at high speed for 5 seconds. Add the anchovy paste, cloves, mace, cayenne pepper and 10 tablespoons of butter. Then continue to blend at high speed, stopping the motor occasionally to scrape down the sides of the jar with a rubber spatula, until the paste is smooth and creamy. (To make the paste by hand, mash the kippers as smoothly as possible with the back of a fork. Then beat in the bits of softened butter, a few pieces at a time, and finally the anchovy paste, cloves, mace and cayenne pepper.)

Spoon the kipper paste into a 2-cup serving dish at least 2 1/2 inches deep, filling the bowl to within 1/4 inch of the top. Seal by pouring the cooled clarified butter over the paste. Refrigerate for at least 6 hours, or until firm. Kipper paste may be served on thinly sliced toast, or it may be used as a filling for sandwiches. Refrigerated and tightly covered, the paste can be kept for a week to 10 days.

Mussels on the half shell swim in a soup based on hard cider and milk.

VIII

Noble Game and Succulent Birds

The man with the shotgun broke silently through the hedge that hemmed the meadow. The dog was so close to his master's heels that they made one shape, one movement, man and dog. The man's breath hung white on the freezing air and moved with them. The moon was up and the man could see for 500 yards. Snow covered the six-acre meadow like a lace tablecloth, and here and there clumps of grass broke through, diverse and irregular. He began to move up the field, across the iron ground, his boots crunching the thin veil of ice. The dog remained by the hole in the hedge. Suddenly the man began to run. There was a flurried movement as a pheasant broke cover and skimmed across the snow, honking like a klaxon. The gun was a light, single-barrel 12-bore, but the explosion split the dusk into a million fragments, and a huge echo rolled over the meadow, across country to the far hills and back again. The dog was streaking toward the bird even before it hit the ground, while the man ran back to the hole in the hedge. The dog, a black retriever, had cost the man five pounds and two years of careful training; they were a well-organized team, the poacher and his dog, and the bird would fetch a good price in town.

His eye out for a flash of gray in the underbrush, a hunter stalks rabbits in a Sussex woods on a Saturday in early spring. He is a member of a party engaged in a "rough shoot"—so called because it is an informal affair without paid beaters or strict rules.

The poacher was a friend of mine. I was 10, and he was about 40; quite recently someone told me that he was still alive and living in the same cottage, but he does not poach pheasant anymore. He was a real old-fashioned countryman—corduroy breeches, leather leggings and stout boots. He also wore a thick, tobacco-scented tweed coat and spoke with a soft Hertfordshire accent. He often carried with him, in the pocket of his coat, a sinuous yellow ferret with pink eyes, which he let down rabbit holes. The rabbits, ears back, eyes bulging with terror, would shoot out of their boltholes and into the nets that were pegged over the exits.

In those days the country people also set spring traps with steel teeth, carefully camouflaged in the grass, although these are now forbidden by law in England and Wales. But it was with the gun that he excelled. "My father," he used to say, "made me carry an empty shotgun for three years before I was allowed to shoot with it." He could hit a fast-moving rabbit at 60 yards in poor light almost before the butt of the gun had reached shoulder level. I've seen him do it. He would eviscerate the rabbit on the spot and put the carcass into the voluminous bag he carried on his shoulder. He knew many more wild birds and flowers than I did, knew in fact everything about the countryside that was worth knowing. He showed me how to set a snare and how to entice game birds with raisins soaked in rum. I'm glad to hear that he's still alive; he has plenty to remember.

A fair amount of poaching still goes on in the country. Sooner or later, by the law of averages, a poacher gets caught. Those after the big stuff—Scottish deer, for instance—are in for trouble in that event, and it usually means a fine. Repeated offenders are jailed. Unlike certain European countries, where the general rule for all wildlife sometimes seems to be "if it moves, eat it," England carefully protects birds and animals with closed seasons. It is unlawful in England, Wales and Scotland to kill grouse, partridge, pheasant and ptarmigan on a Sunday or Christmas Day. Wild duck, goose, snipe and woodcock are protected by game laws and closed seasons.

Wildfowl need no longer feed the yeomanry of England, for domestic poultry is plentiful and excellent. Inexpensive chickens and fine, fat geese (about which more later) are prepared in a number of distinctive ways, some recipes serving almost interchangeably for birds of either farm or forest. But game remains a delight of the British table, and hunting it one of the virile pleasures of English country life.

The first of September marks the opening of the partridge season, the first opportunity since the preceding winter for sportsmen to stumble through the turnip tops, blasting away at small birds (and sometimes each other). Many believe that one can see the real stuff of England then. In 1909, five years before the outbreak of World War I, a Cheshire farmer wrote: "Away from his ordinary business pursuits, the farmer is very largely given up to sport. It is bred in him, and is part of his very existence. And what a sportsman he is! No finer can be found in the three kingdoms [of England, Scotland and Wales]. The handling of the gun comes naturally to him. From boyhood his eye has been in, and to follow him through the turnips in the early days of September, when King Partridge is available, and watch the deadly effect of his shooting, is something not easily forgotten. Some of the deadliest game-shots are here found, whilst many of the young farmers are equally effective with the rifle. These young farmers are your men, Mr. Haldane [then Secretary for War]! They are, indeed, the Yeomen of England."

After a morning tiptoeing through the turnips, the farmers would take time out for lunch: cold roasts, meat pies, beer, wine, punch and port. Then: "A chat over a cigar, and we are back on the stubble, the birds getting up well, and everybody feeling that, after all, there is something to live for in this old country of ours."

At a break for lunch in the Blue Ship pub at Bucks Green, Sussex, men hunting informally, rough-shoot style, pool this morning's bag. These men hunt rabbits for sport and control of the rabbit population, which if unchecked would endanger crops. Properly prepared rabbit serves as the savory base for an excellent stew *(Recipe Index)*.

One of the great traditions was the dinner at the end of the day's shooting. These dinners displayed a great wealth of local produce. There were steaming goslings, ducklings, chickens, several roast pheasant *(Recipe Index)* and huge, juicy joints of beef, rare and tender, with the innumerable embellishments that the lady of the house took delight in preparing.

There were claret, ale and port, and the delicious, crumbling Cheshire cheeses from the farmers' own dairies. A rich and yeasty aroma of fresh, crusty bread mingled with that of hot apple pie and sugary damson pie, smothered in cream. "It has been a great day," our Cheshireman wrote, "and the night is much after our own heart . . . and we pass up the creaky old stairs and roll into bed, only turning occasionally in our sleep at the fancied cracking of the gun, and shouts of 'Mark,' 'A runner,' 'Good lass,' etc. Yes, the life of the farmer here is worth living!"

The folk in the villages had their own game to hunt. High above the villages in the swaying elm trees the black rooks flapped, squawked and quarreled among themselves as they built their nests in the fall. In spring the townsmen would come along with rook rifles to thin out the community, saving the young birds for the kitchen, where they were cleaned and placed in a pie dish with hard-boiled eggs, rashers of bacon, a piece of beefsteak and a few herbs. The pie was covered with a good puff pastry and cooked for two hours. Blackbirds were similarly treated, as the old nursery rhyme reminds us: "Sing a song of sixpence, a pocket full of rye; / Four and twenty blackbirds, baked in a pie." Rook pie is no longer so popular, but we still eat pigeons; they fall to the gun all year round and are baked in a pie or casserole, or made into pigeon pudding.

These days, pigeons, pheasant and partridge are so common that they are met with everywhere in the land, mainly because they are bred on a large scale. But we are talking about small fry. If you want the real game, then you must search in Scotland, where the weekend house parties of the nobility beat across the laird's shoot. There the red grouse feed on the wild cranberries, and the blackcock with his lyre-shaped tail bursts from cover as the line of guns advances. On the barren upper slopes of the mountains roam the big capercaillie and the white-winged ptarmigan, which takes some finding. Of all the game birds it is the red grouse, the Scots say, that has the best flavor. Before a Scottish cook roasts a young grouse, she often stuffs the bird with a handful of cranberries or adds a sprig of purple heather.

The mad blue mountain hare that leaps like a firecracker through the heather and juniper scrub also makes a splendid meal—if you can catch him. It is surprising how much meat there is on a hare. In England and Scotland the hare is eaten either roasted or jugged and is served with red currant jelly *(Recipe Index)* and forcemeat balls, a mixture of the hare's heart with suet, bread crumbs and herbs.

The general principle for all game is that it must be hung; it should be allowed to age for anything between three days and the time when you can stand it no longer, usually three weeks. In the days before refrigeration, game birds killed in warm weather had to be eaten almost immediately; in cool weather they were hung outdoors to age. Venison, like beef, was hung indoors where the flies could not get at it, either in the rafters high above the smoke of the fire or in the cool larders below ground level, until time had improved the flavor of the meat and made it tender.

The strong flavors of hare and venison demand a sweet adjunct—red currant jelly, for example, or the fruity Cumberland sauce made with oranges and port wine *(Recipe Index)*. Game birds, when roasted, are often served with crisp bacon, skirlie (oatmeal and chopped onion fried in fat), game chips (a form of potato chips, *Recipe Index)* and cranberry sauce.

Wild duck is always served with oranges. In fact I cannot recollect ever being served duck, either wild or domestic, without them. English restaurants seem to think that to omit the oranges would be to court disaster. It never occurs to them to cook a duck with prunes, with apples or with olives, ingredients that give fresh interest to the dish.

Game birds, with their strong flavor and dark meat, are a seasonal treat too rich and expensive for everyday eating—but worth waiting for. Poultry, on the other hand, is no longer the once-a-week treat of 20 years ago. Today most of our chickens are mass-produced in a strange (and cruel) world of even temperatures and artificial lights, a controlled environment where the true flavor of the meat is sacrificed to quantity and uniformity.

Those fat, dirt-scratching birds with their querulous voices and surprised expressions, the kind that my grandfather raised, have almost disappeared. There were 10,000 chickens on my grandfather's farm, and it took a whole morning to feed them. We boiled tons of potatoes in a huge copper boiler and added dry bran meal to make a thick, cereal mass. I can smell it to this day, along with the scent of autumn apples in the hayloft. We carried the chick feed in a hopper to the henhouse and poured it into the troughs. The hens were crazy about it.

When I got up really early I collected the newly sprung mushrooms from the fields, and we ate them for breakfast, fried with fresh eggs and bacon. On Sunday we had a chicken roasted with sage and onion stuffing, and served with roast potatoes. Not every Sunday though, for a chicken dinner was a luxury in those days. We rarely had duck, but one Christmas my grandfather killed the goose, a huge, bad-tempered bird that flew straight for anyone that came into the yard and stabbed at his ankles, making a formidable hissing noise. The goose was sacrificed to the ritual of the Christmas table, but once the proud, aggressive creature had been reduced to a plucked roast, we discovered that we had killed not merely a bird but a personality. My grandmother pushed away her plate. "I can't eat it," she said. The rest of us sat round the table, staring glumly at the fat, crisp goose surrounded by its attendant vegetables. It had had, as always, the last laugh.

Goose was the traditional Christmas dish long before the arrival of turkey. It was often served with applesauce and stuffed with a mixture of sage and onion. Unhappily, some English cooks stuff everything either with sausage meat or with sage and onion. Pork, chicken, duck and goose are similarly treated. It is too easy a way out, for in Britain the sage-and-onion mixture can be purchased in packets, requiring only hot water to reconstitute it. Bread sauce, a mixture of bread crumbs and milk simmered with cloves and a small onion, is another inevitable standby with most of our roasted poultry dishes. I am not myself overly fond of bread sauce, but many people are, and we have supplied a recipe for it *(Recipe Index).*

There's an apple stuffing worth trying, in which apples are cooked and mixed with butter, bread crumbs, spice and sugar. Then there's a veal-and-bacon stuffing, and a chestnut stuffing that includes puréed chestnuts blended with sausage meat, bread crumbs and butter—an excellent stuffing for large poultry, like goose or turkey.

A young chicken, though, needs a delicate stuffing and should be well buttered on the inside to prevent it from becoming too dry during roasting. I often place half a lemon and a sprig of thyme in a chicken before draping it with metal foil and placing it breast downward in the roasting pan. Gravity sees that the juices keep the breast meat moist, and the heat is better able to penetrate the legs and thighs of the bird, which always take longer to cook. Turn up the heat, baste the chicken with fat and allow 20 minutes for it to become nicely browned. One or two slices of streaky bacon packed against the breast before draping with foil give added flavor and juice for basting during cooking. This principle serves for all poultry and game, but remember that ducks and geese are well protected by a layer of fat; you should prick the skin with a sharp fork now and then during roasting to allow the fat to es-

Continued on page 140

With weapon poised and loader prepared to hand him another gun, a grouse hunter staunchly awaits the birds.

A Ritual Observance amid the Moorland Heather

Wherever heather grows on the moors, the natural habitat of grouse, Britons have for centuries hunted this bird for the pot. Since the late 19th Century, however, the grouse shoot has been an annual social affair for the affluent, on a par with the fashionable races at Ascot in June and the sailing at Cowes in early August, and is carried on with formalized rites. The hunter *(above)* at a Yorkshire shoot, where these pictures were taken, observes the rituals in every detail, wearing nondescript attire and exhibiting a proper reserve. Flanked by a brace of spaniels and backed by a loader, who has custody of the shell case *(left)* and is prepared to hand him another gun after he empties the first, the hunter maintains his position until beaters drive a covey of grouse in his direction. Before a break for lunch, the hunters at this shoot had managed a bag of nearly 40 birds *(right)*.

Using his shooting stick for a knee rest, the "gun," as a hunter is called during a shoot, takes a bead on a bird. Hitting a grouse requires a good eye as well as quick judgment and a steady hand; the birds are swift and erratic in flight.

In the middle of the grouse-shoot day, guns, beaters, dogs and distaff spectators take time out for a picnic lunch. The spread, packed by the ladies, includes fancy pâtés, cheeses and cakes, along with more solid fare. The lady at right, ignoring an imploring spaniel, is passing around her fruit cake. Plainer and less high-toned food is brought for the hired beaters, who eat separately after helping the dogs retrieve fallen birds *(left)*. The dinner in the manor house or lodge in the evening may include roast grouse from the previous week's bag; to ensure tenderness, grouse should always be hung for about a week before being cooked.

At the lunch break, the presence of the wives, who otherwise keep out of the action, is gratefully acknowledged. Opening the back doors and trunks of the Land Rovers and other cars, they break out elaborate dishes for the hungry guns.

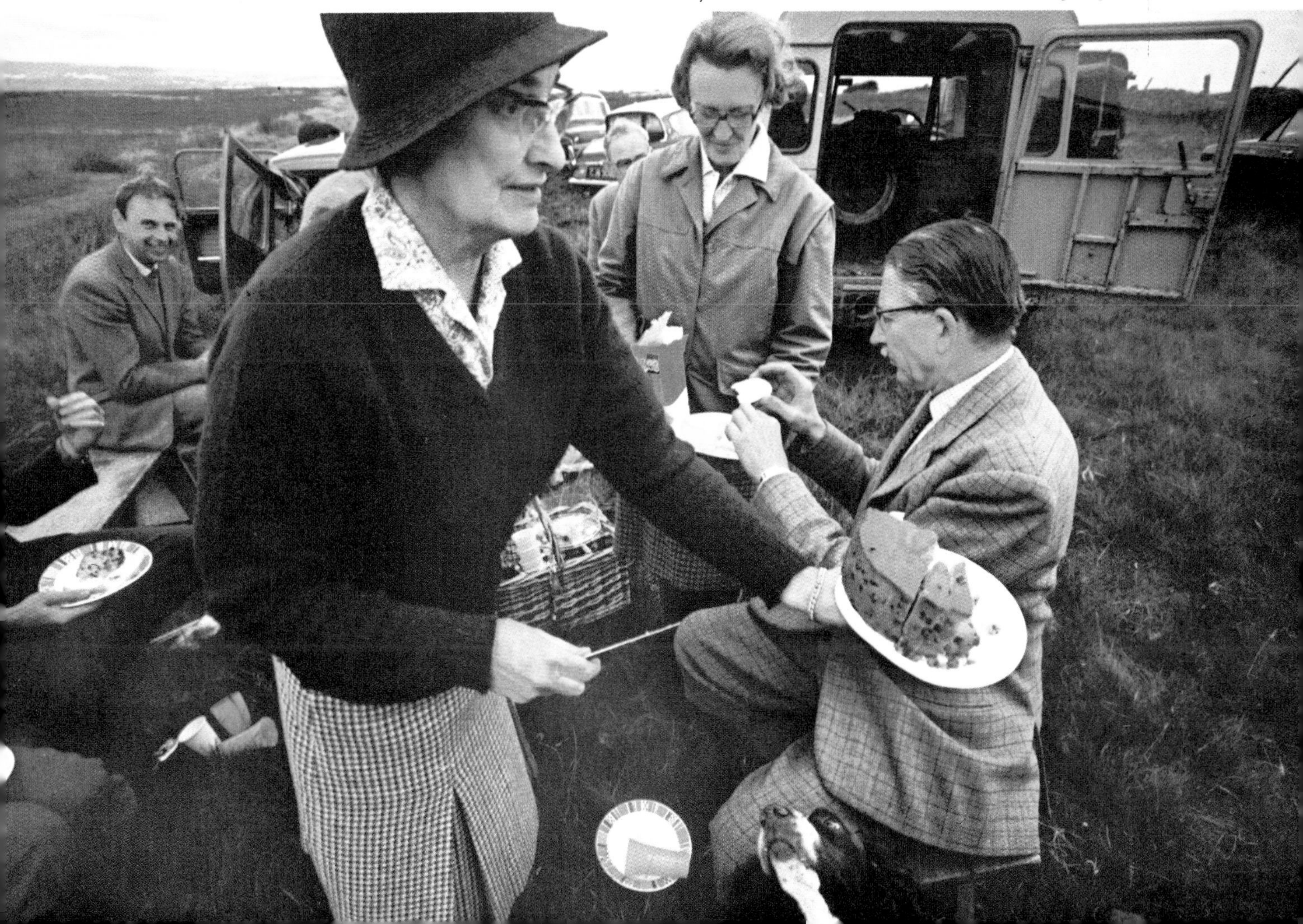

cape. Strongly flavored birds, such as the goose and certain wild fowl, do not require complete wrapping in foil.

Despite the fact that today's poultry may not have the flavor of the old hen that scratched among the nettles or the cockerel that strutted along the farmyard wall, there are many traditional recipes that will improve the taste. One not to be overlooked is cockaleekie, a warming Scottish soup containing leeks and sometimes prunes *(Recipe Index)*. Prunes also appear in a curious but delicious chicken dish called "hindle wakes" *(Recipe Index)*, from over the border down Lancashire way. The prunes are chopped and bits of the inner core of the pits are often added. A hen is stuffed with the fruit and is simmered until tender. It is usually served cold, coated with a lemon sauce, although one recipe suggests that the bird be given a final roasting wrapped in bacon and served hot. The origins of this dish are obscure, but the historian Dorothy Hartley thinks the recipe was brought to Lancashire by Flemish weavers who settled in the area in the 14th Century.

Since the leek is the national emblem of Wales, it is hardly surprising that the Welsh have several leek-and-chicken dishes. Leeks and chicken are made into a pie *(Recipe Index)*, and sometimes into a pudding. The famous Sussex steak-and-kidney pudding is simply a suet crust with a meat filling; chicken, goose, partridge or pheasant may be substituted for the beefsteak and kidneys that the recipe *(Recipe Index)* prescribes. Into such a pudding go mushrooms, onions, herbs and a good brown stock. If game is used, you might wish to add a little claret.

A fine game pie can last for several days. Game pies appear in picnic hampers at the Ascot races, and at the Glyndebourne Opera Festival in Sussex. Made with a hot-water crust in the manner of a veal-and-ham pie *(Recipe Index)* and filled with meat—hare or pheasant, grouse or deer—they are also part of the traditional hunt breakfast or shoot luncheon. When the pie is removed from the oven, an aspic jelly is poured through a hole in the top. The pie is eaten cold, with a glass or five of Burgundy and some salad (watercress and orange make an excellent accompaniment). A slice of game pie with its decorated, crisp and golden crust, rich meat and glistening aspic jelly is almost a meal in itself. Such dishes have medieval origins and stood on the Elizabethan table with roast peacock.

Many people seem to think that our Elizabethan ancestors dined exclusively on roast peacock and swan, though at that time the swan was protected as a royal bird; nobody was permitted to own one without the Queen's permission. Roast swan has nonetheless appeared from time to time on English tables through the centuries. The Victorians served it with a port-wine sauce, and if ever you are made a present of one I suggest you do the same. The sweet flavor of port-wine sauce and Cumberland sauce are fine complements to the strong, rich taste of game. The succulent dark meat (where often there lurks a tiny piece of lead shot) is the more enjoyable for its scarcity, like the transient fruits of summer.

That first grouse that falls to the gun on August 12, opening day of the season, heralds the approach of autumn, when the smell of wood smoke haunts the air, when copper-beech leaves are crisp underfoot, and flocks of geese call across the dark sky. It is, for many, a most nostalgic season. For the gun dog, whose wet coat steams before the fire, it is the best season of all.

Roast Pheasant

To serve 4 to 6

A 3½- to 4-pound oven-ready pheasant
½ teaspoon salt
Freshly ground black pepper
4 ounces ground beef
2 tablespoons butter, softened, plus ½ cup butter, melted
4 slices lean bacon

Preheat the oven to 350°. Wash the pheasant quickly under cold running water and pat it thoroughly dry inside and out with paper towels. Rub the inside of the bird with the salt and a few grindings of pepper and place the ground beef in the cavity. Close the opening by lacing it with skewers or sewing it with heavy white thread.

Fasten the neck skin to the back of the pheasant with a skewer, and, using a pastry brush, coat the skin of the bird evenly with the 2 tablespoons of softened butter. Drape the bacon slices side by side over the breast and wrap them around the bird, pressing the slices snugly against the body to keep them in place.

Place the pheasant, breast side up, on a rack in a shallow roasting pan just large enough to hold the bird comfortably. Roast undisturbed in the middle of the oven for 20 minutes, then increase the oven heat to 400°. Remove and discard the bacon slices. Using a pastry brush, baste the pheasant with 2 tablespoons of melted butter and roast it for about 20 minutes longer, basting generously every 5 minutes or so with a few tablespoons of the remaining melted butter.

To test whether the bird is done, pierce the thigh with the tip of a small, sharp knife. The juice should spurt out a clear yellow; if it is still pink, roast the pheasant for another 5 to 10 minutes.

Transfer the pheasant to a heated platter and let it rest for 10 minutes for easier carving. Discard the ground beef, which is used to keep the bird moist during the cooking and is not intended as a stuffing.

The roast pheasant is traditionally served with bread sauce *(Recipe Index)* and game chips *(below)*, and may be decorated with bunches of watercress and its own tail feathers before serving.

Game Chips

To serve 4 to 6

4 cups vegetable oil or shortening
6 medium-sized baking potatoes (about 2 pounds), peeled
2 teaspoons salt

Preheat the oven to 250°. Line a jelly-roll pan or large, shallow roasting pan with a double thickness of paper towels, and set it aside. In a deep-fat fryer or large, heavy saucepan, heat the oil to 360° on a deep-frying thermometer, or until a haze forms above it.

With a large knife or a vegetable slicer, cut the potatoes into slices 1/16 inch thick and drop them directly into cold water to remove the starch and prevent them from discoloring. When ready to use, drain them in a colander, spread them out in a single layer on paper towels, and pat them thoroughly dry with more towels.

Drop about ½ cup of the potatoes at a time into the hot fat and, turning the slices about with a slotted spoon, fry for 2 or 3 minutes, or until they are crisp and golden brown. Transfer the chips to the paper-lined pan and keep them warm in the oven while you proceed with the remaining batches.

To serve, heap the chips in a heated bowl and sprinkle them with the salt. Game chips are traditionally served with roasted birds, such as pheasant *(above)*, in which case they may be arranged in a circle around the bird and served on the same platter.

Overleaf: Soaring, black-marked brown plumes, added for decoration after the bird was cooked, identify this British dish as roast pheasant. Garnished with watercress and surrounded with crisp, homemade game chips—a variety of potato chips—the pheasant will be carved and served before the bread sauce *(at right of the platter)* is passed.

Game Pie

To serve 4 to 6

- 2 tablespoons butter, softened, plus 2 tablespoons butter
- 2 one-pound partridges, quartered, or substitute 2 one-pound grouse, pheasant, woodcock or other gamebirds
- 2 tablespoons vegetable oil
- 1 1/4 cups chicken stock, fresh or canned
- 3/4 pound veal scallops, cut 1/4 inch thick
- Salt
- Freshly ground black pepper
- 4 slices lean bacon
- 1/4 pound mushrooms, coarsely chopped
- 1 tablespoon coarsely chopped shallots, or substitute 1 tablespoon coarsely chopped scallions
- 1 tablespoon finely chopped parsley
- 2 teaspoons grated lemon peel
- 1/2 recipe rough puff pastry, made according to the directions below
- 1 egg lightly beaten with 1 tablespoon milk

Preheat the oven to 425°. Using a pastry brush, coat the bottom and sides of a 1 1/2-quart casserole or baking dish at least 2 inches deep with the 2 tablespoons of softened butter and set aside.

Wash the partridges under cold running water and pat the pieces completely dry with paper towels. In a heavy 10- to 12-inch skillet, melt the remaining 2 tablespoons of butter in the 2 tablespoons of oil over moderately high heat. When the foam begins to subside, brown the partridges a few pieces at a time, starting them skin side down and turning them with tongs. As the pieces become a deep golden brown, remove them to a plate.

Pour the stock into the skillet and bring it to a boil over high heat, meanwhile scraping in any brown particles clinging to the bottom and sides of the pan. Boil briskly for a minute or so; set the skillet aside off the heat.

Line the bottom of the baking dish with the veal scallops, sprinkle them with salt and a few grindings of pepper, and lay the bacon slices side by side over the veal. Arrange the partridge pieces skin side up on top. Mix the mushrooms, shallots, parsley, lemon peel, 1/4 teaspoon of salt and a few grindings of pepper together in a bowl and spread the mixture evenly over the partridge. Pour in the stock that you had set aside.

On a lightly floured surface roll the pastry out into a rough rectangle no more than 1/8 inch thick. Then cut two strips, each about 12 inches long and 1/2 inch wide, from the ends. Lay the strips end to end around the rim of the baking dish and press them firmly into place. Moisten them lightly with a pastry brush dipped in cold water.

Drape the remaining pastry over the rolling pin, lift it up, and unfold it over the baking dish. Trim off the excess with a small, sharp knife and, with the tines of a fork or your fingers, crimp the pastry to secure it to the rim of the dish.

Gather the scraps of pastry into a ball, reroll and cut them into simple leaf and flower shapes; moisten one side with the egg-and-milk mixture and arrange them decoratively on the pie. Then brush the entire pastry surface with the remaining egg-and-milk mixture, and cut a 1-inch round hole in the center of the pie.

Bake the pie in the middle of the oven for 20 minutes, reduce the heat to 375° and bake for 40 minutes longer, or until the crust is golden brown. Serve at once directly from the baking dish.

Rough Puff Pastry

- 2 cups sifted all-purpose flour
- 1/4 teaspoon salt
- 1/4 pound (1 stick) unsalted butter, thoroughly chilled and cut into 1/4-inch bits
- 1/4 cup lard, thoroughly chilled and cut into 1/4-inch bits
- 4 to 6 tablespoons ice water

Sift the flour and salt together into a large chilled mixing bowl. Drop in the butter and lard and, working quickly, use your fingertips to rub the flour and fat together until the mixture looks like flakes of coarse meal. Pour 4 tablespoons of ice water over the mixture all at once, and gather the dough into a ball.

If the dough crumbles, add up to 2 tablespoons more ice water, 1 teaspoon at a time, until the particles adhere. Dust lightly with flour, wrap the dough in wax paper and chill for 30 minutes.

Place the pastry on a lightly floured board or table, and press it into a rectangular shape about 1 inch thick. Dust a little flour over and under it, and roll it out into a strip about 21 inches long and 6 inches wide. Fold the strip into thirds to form a 3-layered rectangular packet, reducing its dimensions to about 7 by 6 inches.

Turn the pastry around so that an open end faces you and roll it out once more to a 21-by-6-inch strip. Fold it into thirds as before and roll it out again to a similar strip. Repeat this entire process twice more, ending with the pastry folded into a packet.

Wrap the pastry tightly in wax paper, foil or a plastic bag, and refrigerate it for at least 1 hour. The pastry may be kept in the refrigerator for 3 or 4 days before it is used.

Chicken-and-Leek Pie

To serve 4 to 6

- A 4- to 4½-pound roasting chicken or stewing fowl
- 1 large onion, peeled and quartered
- 1 small celery stalk including the leaves
- A bouquet of 8 parsley sprigs and 1 small bay leaf, tied together
- ¼ teaspoon thyme
- 1 tablespoon salt
- 10 medium-sized leeks, including 1 inch of the green stems, split in half and cut crosswise into 1-inch pieces
- ¼ pound cooked smoked beef tongue, cut into ⅛-inch slices
- 1 tablespoon finely chopped parsley
- Rough puff pastry *(above)*
- 1 egg yolk combined with 1 tablespoon heavy cream
- ¼ cup heavy cream

In a heavy 6- to 8-quart pot, combine the chicken or fowl, onion, celery stalk, bouquet of parsley and bay leaf, thyme and salt, and pour in enough cold water to cover the chicken by 1 inch. Bring to a boil over high heat, meanwhile skimming off all the foam and scum with a large spoon as they rise to the surface. Then reduce the heat to low and simmer partially covered until the bird is tender but not falling apart. (A roasting chicken should be done in about 1 hour; a stewing fowl may take as long as 2 hours or more, depending on its age and tenderness.)

Transfer the chicken to a plate and strain the stock through a fine sieve set over a bowl, pressing down hard on the vegetables and herbs with the back of a spoon before discarding them. Pour 2 cups of the stock into a heavy 2- to 3-quart saucepan and skim the surface of its fat. Add the leeks and bring to a boil over high heat. Then reduce the heat to low and simmer partially covered for 15 minutes, or until the leeks are tender.

With a small, sharp knife, remove the skin from the chicken and cut the meat away from the bones. Discard the skin and bones, cut the meat into 1-inch pieces, and arrange them evenly on the bottom of a 1½-quart casserole or baking dish at least 2 inches deep. Pour the leeks and their stock over the chicken and sprinkle lightly with salt. Arrange the slices of tongue side by side over the top, but leave a space about 1 inch square in the center. Sprinkle with the chopped parsley.

Preheat the oven to 400°. On a lightly floured surface roll out the puff pastry into a rough rectangle about ¼ inch thick. Then cut 2 strips, each about 12 inches long and ½ inch wide, from the ends. Lay the strips end to end around the rim of the baking dish and press them firmly into place. Moisten them lightly with a pastry brush dipped in cold water.

Drape the remaining pastry over the rolling pin, lift it up, and unfold it over the baking dish. Trim off the excess with a small, sharp knife and, with the tines of a fork or your fingers, crimp the pastry to secure it to the rim of the dish.

Gather the scraps of pastry into a ball, reroll and cut them into simple leaf and flower shapes; moisten one side with the egg-yolk-and-cream mixture and arrange them decoratively on the pie. Then brush the entire pastry surface with the remaining egg-yolk-and-cream mixture and cut a 1-inch round hole in the center of the pie.

Bake the pie in the middle of the oven for 1 hour, or until the crust is golden brown. Just before serving, heat the ¼ cup of cream to lukewarm and pour it through the hole in the crust.

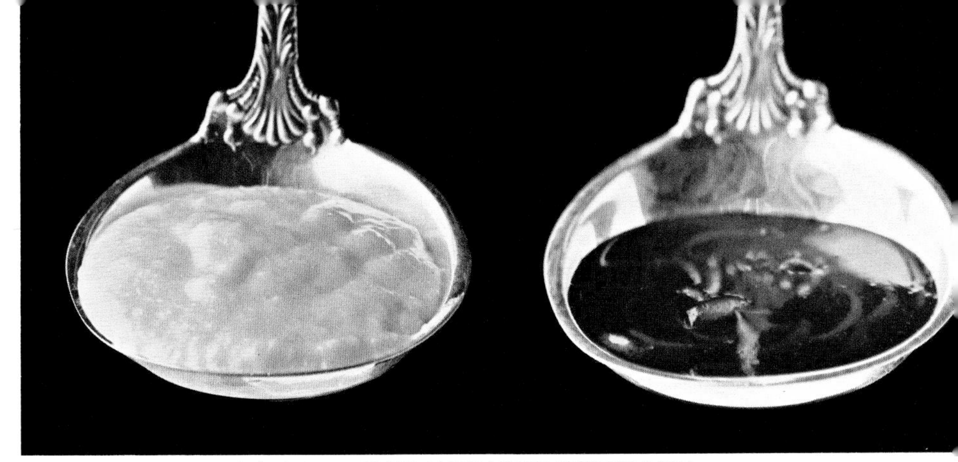

BOTH BREAD SAUCE (LEFT) AND CUMBERLAND SAUCE ARE GOOD WITH GAME.

Cumberland Sauce

To make about 1 cup sauce

- 1 medium-sized lemon
- 1 medium-sized orange
- 1 teaspoon sugar
- 1/3 cup port
- 2 tablespoons red currant jelly *(Recipe Booklet)*
- 2 teaspoons cornstarch
- 1 tablespoon cold water

Using a small, sharp knife or rotary peeler, remove the skin of the lemon and the orange, being careful not to cut so deep as to include the bitter white pith.

Cut the lemon and orange peels into strips about 1 inch long and 1/8 inch wide and drop them into enough boiling water to cover them completely. Boil briskly, uncovered, for 5 minutes. Drain in a colander and run cold water over them to set their color. Set aside.

Squeeze the juice from the fruit into a small, heavy saucepan. Add the sugar, port and currant jelly, and bring to a boil over high heat, stirring until the jelly dissolves completely. Reduce the heat to low and simmer uncovered for about 5 minutes.

Dissolve the cornstarch in the tablespoon of cold water, and stir it into the simmering sauce. Cook, still stirring, until the sauce comes to a boil, thickens and clears.

Strain the sauce through a fine sieve into a bowl. Stir in the lemon and orange peel and cool to room temperature. Then refrigerate for at least 1 hour, or until thoroughly chilled. Cumberland sauce is traditionally served with venison, ham and mutton.

Cockaleekie

CHICKEN-AND-LEEK SOUP

To make 4 to 5 quarts soup

- A 5½- to 6-pound stewing fowl
- 5 quarts cold water
- 10 large leeks, including 2 inches of the green stems, thoroughly washed to remove any hidden pockets of sand, and cut diagonally into ½-inch slices (about 8 cups)
- ½ cup barley
- 1 tablespoon salt
- 2 tablespoons finely chopped parsley

Wash the fowl thoroughly inside and out under cold running water. Remove and discard any chunks of fat from the cavity, and place the bird in a 10- to 12-quart soup pot. Pour in the 5 quarts of water and bring to a boil over high heat, meanwhile skimming off the foam and scum that will rise to the surface. Add the leeks, barley and salt, and reduce the heat to low.

Partially cover the pot and simmer for 3 to 3½ hours, or until the bird is almost falling apart. Then transfer it to a platter and, with a large spoon, skim almost all of the fat from the surface of the soup.

When the fowl is cool enough to handle, remove the skin and pull the meat from the bones with your fingers or a small knife. Discard the skin and bones and cut the meat into thin shreds about 2 inches long. Return the meat to the soup. Simmer for 2 or 3 minutes to heat the meat through and then taste the soup for seasoning.

To serve, pour the soup into a heated tureen or ladle it into individual soup plates, and sprinkle with chopped parsley.

Rabbit Stew

To serve 6 to 8

- 1/3 cup dry red wine
- 2 tablespoons olive oil
- 1 large onion, cut into 1/8-inch slices
- 3 whole juniper berries, wrapped in a kitchen towel and crushed with a rolling pin or crushed with a mortar and pestle
- 1 large bay leaf
- 1/2 teaspoon crumbled dried rosemary
- 1 1/2 teaspoons salt
- Freshly ground black pepper
- A 5- to 6-pound fresh rabbit or defrosted frozen rabbit, cut into 2-inch-square pieces, or substitute two 2 1/2- to 3-pound fresh or defrosted frozen rabbits
- 2 tablespoons flour
- 6 slices lean bacon, coarsely chopped
- 1/4 cup finely chopped shallots, or substitute 1/4 cup chopped onions
- 1/2 cup coarsely chopped celery
- 6 small carrots, scraped and coarsely chopped
- 1 1/2 cups chicken stock, fresh or canned
- 1 teaspoon dried thyme
- 2 teaspoons finely chopped parsley
- 2 small bay leaves
- 1/2 cup port
- 3 tablespoons red currant jelly *(Recipe Booklet)*

Combine the wine, olive oil, sliced onion, juniper berries, bay leaf, rosemary, 1/2 teaspoon of the salt and a few grindings of black pepper in a large bowl. Wash the rabbit under cold running water, pat it thoroughly dry with paper towels and place it in the bowl. Turn the pieces about with a spoon until they are thoroughly coated with the marinade, cover the bowl and marinate the rabbit for at least 6 hours at room temperature, or 12 hours in the refrigerator. In either case, turn the pieces about in the marinade occasionally to keep them well moistened.

Drain the rabbit in a colander set over a bowl. Reserve the liquid, but discard the onion and herbs. Pat the pieces of rabbit completely dry with paper towels, then coat them with the flour, shaking each piece vigorously to remove the excess.

In a heavy 4- to 5-quart flameproof casserole, cook the bacon over moderate heat, stirring occasionally, until crisp and brown. With a slotted spoon, transfer the bacon to paper towels to drain. Add the rabbit to the fat remaining in the casserole and brown it (in two batches, if necessary), turning the pieces with tongs and regulating the heat so that the rabbit colors quickly and evenly on all sides without burning. As the pieces brown, transfer them from the casserole to a plate.

Pour off all but 2 tablespoons of fat from the casserole, add the shallots, celery and carrots, and cook for 5 minutes, or until the vegetables are soft but not brown. Pour in the reserved marinade and the chicken stock and bring to a boil over high heat, meanwhile scraping in any brown particles clinging to the bottom and sides of the casserole. Add the thyme, parsley, bay leaves, teaspoon of salt and a few grindings of pepper, and return the rabbit and the bacon to the casserole.

Cover tightly and bake in the middle of the oven for 1 hour. Stir in the port and currant jelly, cover again, and bake for 30 minutes longer, or until the rabbit is tender but not falling apart. (If you are substituting small rabbits, they may cook much faster. Watch carefully that they do not overcook.) Taste for seasoning.

Serve the rabbit directly from the casserole. It may be accompanied by forcemeat balls *(below)*.

Forcemeat Balls

To make about 12 balls

- 1/8 pound fresh beef suet, finely chopped
- 1/4 cup finely chopped cooked smoked ham (about 1/8 pound)
- 2 cups fresh soft crumbs, made from homemade-type white bread, pulverized in a blender or shredded with a fork
- 2 teaspoons finely chopped parsley
- 1 teaspoon finely grated lemon peel
- 1/4 teaspoon ground thyme
- 1/4 teaspoon ground sage
- 1/2 teaspoon salt
- Freshly ground black pepper
- 1 egg, lightly beaten
- 2 tablespoons butter
- 2 tablespoons vegetable oil

In a large bowl, combine the suet, ham, bread crumbs, parsley, lemon peel, thyme, sage, salt and a few grindings of pepper. Stir thoroughly, then add the egg and mix together until the forcemeat can be gathered into a ball. Divide it into 12 equal pieces and, with lightly moistened hands, shape each piece into a ball about 1 1/2 inches in diameter.

In a heavy 10- to 12-inch skillet, melt the butter in the oil over moderate heat. When the foam has almost subsided, drop in the balls. Cook them for about 5 minutes, or until golden brown on all sides, turning them frequently with a spoon and regulating the heat so that they color slowly and evenly without burning. With a slotted spoon, transfer the balls to a double thickness of paper towels to drain briefly, and serve.

NOTE: Forcemeat balls traditionally accompany game dishes like rabbit stew *(above)*.

IX

"Blessed Be He That Invented Pudding"

Oh, puddings! Some day I will write a book just on puddings alone. Perhaps two books, for there are hundreds of English puddings. Each county has produced a wealth of puddings, large and small, hot and cold, all of them delicious. Rich golden ones topped with jam and cream; tender beef-and-kidney ones, steamed for hours and sometimes even containing a surprise of oysters. Puddings from country villages like those in Bedfordshire, where long ago the farmers' wives created a sausage-shaped object called a "clanger," containing meat and chopped vegetables at one end, and jam or fruit at the other; the men working in the fields could thus carry their entire lunch all in one piece. At Christmas we enjoy the flame-wreathed plum pudding, while the legendary Yorkshire pudding, a light cloud of hot, crisp batter, is the unsurpassed accompaniment to roast beef *(for both, see Recipe Index)*.

A pudding basin, a utensil indispensable to the English kitchen, is lifted from a steamed pudding, that ubiquitous English dessert. As the pudding is turned out, rivulets of raspberry jam stream down the sides. A steamed pudding may be varied by cooking it with currants or nuts and by adding any of a multitude of hot, sweet fruit sauces.

There is such a variety of puddings that there is even confusion about the term; to many of us in the British Isles "pudding" is a word applied to any sweet, filling and satisfying dish that follows a main course; thus even an apple pie might be considered a pudding. The confusion is compounded by the fact that different social classes in Britain use the word to mean different things. Moreover, while puddings are usually sweet, the word is also used for meat dishes—like steak-and-kidney pudding or rabbit pudding.

Meaty or sweet, each pudding has its individual flavor and every pudding eater has his favorite. Prized by many are the noble puddings that were no doubt cooked in the kitchens of Windsor Castle when Victoria was queen during the golden age of the English pudding: Windsor pudding, made of apples and rice and flavored with lemon; royal pudding, light as a soufflé; and empress pudding, a mixture of rice and fruit or jam, baked in a pastry shell. Bananas, suet, eggs and bread crumbs are mixed and steamed for an hour to create queen's pudding; duchess, on the other hand, is an airy, soufflélike creation with an unusual combination of marmalade, macaroons and pistachio nuts. Baroness pudding is rather heavy compared to the others: made of raisins and suet, it requires cooking for as long as five hours.

Some puddings are eaten plain, others are served with a sauce. These latter are light, spongy mixtures containing fruit or jam, or a simple flavoring such as chocolate, vanilla, orange or lemon, meant to be served with custard sauce. And when the weather turns really cold and damp we wheel on the armored brigade: puddings made of flour, shredded suet and dried fruit, boiled for several hours and served with custard or a jam sauce.

There is a pudding for everyone. Travelers can continue their journeys refreshed by omnibus pudding and railway pudding. There's a pudding for your favorite aunt—Aunt Martha, Aunt Nelly and Aunt Polly each has a pudding to her credit. A white suet pudding studded with raisins and currants was once likened to the Dalmatian dog and has been known ever since as spotted-dog pudding, or spotted Dick. There are also military and guard's puddings for soldiers, and admiral's pudding to be served on board.

Deprivation and invention joined to create queer-times pudding when times were hard and the cold, bony hand of poverty tightened belts yet another notch. If there was flour in the cupboard, and syrup, too, they were worked to a dense dough with water and baking soda, wrapped in a floured cloth, and boiled for hours. This was scarcely a taste treat, but as you see, even the poorest families insisted on their inalienable right to a pudding.

The names are frequently apposite; roly-poly pudding is so called because it is made from a sheet of rolled suet pastry, spread with fruit or jam, and rolled up before being placed in a cloth and boiled. Monday pudding utilized the remains of Sunday pudding, a preserved fruit pudding made several days beforehand and reheated on Sunday, thus observing the ethic of times past—"thou shalt not cook on the Lord's Day." And for the good country folk who followed that injunction and went to heaven there was sure to be brandy-and-spice-flavored paradise pudding when they arrived.

A pudding basin is shown filled with some of the ingredients out of which the countless puddings of Britain can be made: milk, sugar, dried fruit like raisins, eggs, a spice like freshly grated nutmeg, perhaps a lemon for added tang, and a dollop of butter.

In virtually every kitchen in every home in Britain you will find a deep bowl with a thick rim that we call a pudding basin. Into the basin goes the basic mixture of flour, butter and eggs, mixed to a batter and flavored in many different ways. For example, military pudding is made of bread, suet and lemon. So is a Shropshire pudding, except that a pinch of nutmeg is added. Both bachelor's and paradise puddings contain apples, lemon, spices and currants. But bachelor's lacks brandy; paradise has it. Albert and Alma puddings have flour, sugar, raisins and butter as their basic ingredients. Alma, however, contains currants.

Cabinet pudding *(Recipe Index)* is a little richer than most but still typically English. The basin is greased with butter and lined with a decorative pattern of *glacé* cherries, pieces of angelica and seedless raisins. The foundation of the pudding consists of pieces of bread or spongecake, macaroons or sweet biscuits, raisins and pieces of preserved fruits. To this dry base is added a rich egg custard, flavored with a little liqueur or wine. The top of the basin is then tightly covered with a cloth and the pudding steamed for about an hour. The cabinet pudding, with its colorful decoration of red cherries and green angelica, is then turned out onto a serving dish and sometimes served with a wine sauce.

Although most puddings are cooked by steaming or boiling, many others are baked. An apricot pudding is a combination pudding and pie. Apricots are puréed, mixed with a custard and poured into a pastry shell, then covered with meringue and baked in the manner of a lemon meringue pie. The renowned Yorkshire pudding is baked, too.

Quite recently a cook, writing about Yorkshire's pride in a magazine, had the audacity to suggest that the pudding originated in France. How ridiculous! Puddings have been around these islands for quite a while. It is likely that batter pudding was made by the early Saxons. Flour, eggs and milk were available to them, and it is known that simple batter puddings, perhaps sweetened with honey, were enjoyed long before the Normans arrived in 1066. By the 12th Century cooks for the drafty dining rooms of the castles of King Henry II were basting their roast mutton and fruits with batter, creating the prototype of Yorkshire pudding and the more complex puddings we know today. The pudding was on the threshold of history.

The monasteries of medieval times carried the dish a step further by making puddings of oatmeal combined with fruit from their orchards. Partly as a result of their endeavors, the pudding by the Elizabethan age had developed into a dish called plum porridge, made from a mixture of meat broth, fruit juice, wine, prunes, mace and bread crumbs, and when the Elizabethans tired of their plum porridge there were plenty of other sweet dishes to follow the main course, including apple pie (made from the big costard apples), fruit tarts, jam tarts, custards and creams. It has been suggested that such pastries and pies were invented to disguise meat, or other foods forbidden during Lent, from the prying eyes of the zealous, and that meat and fruit were frequently mixed together for this reason. By 1690 a French visitor, Misson de Valbourg, had this to say: "The pudding is a dish very difficult to be described, because of the several sorts there are of it; flour, with eggs, butter, sugar, suet, marrow, raisins, etc. are the most common ingredients of a pudding. They bake them in the oven, they boil them with the meat, they make them fifty several ways." Difficulties of definition aside, de Valbourg knew that he had found a supreme concoction: "Blessed be he that invented pudding! for it is a manna that hits the palates of all sorts of people; a manna better than that of the wilderness, because the people are never weary of it. Ah, what an excellent thing is an English pudding! *To come in pudding time,* is . . . to come in the most lucky moment in the world."

The puddings that de Valbourg so much enjoyed were, of course, not quite like those that we eat today, any more than England itself was. You must imagine rural England when much of the country was covered by thick forests, when a journey on horseback or by stagecoach was a hazardous adventure, when a villager might visit the local town once a year during fair time, or perhaps never. Every cottage was self-supporting and had its own cow, a few hens, a pig and a plot of land. The wife made her own cheese, her bread, her beer or fruit wine. From the simple ingredients available were launched the humble ancestors of a thousand puddings: frumenty, made from husked wheat and eaten with meat, with fruit, or with milk; or hasty pudding, made of milk, flour, eggs and butter, boiled until thick,

Two methods of pudding-making are shown in these illustrations. For a boiled pudding *(top),* the dough is wrapped in a floured cloth, tied with string, and gently boiled in a covered pot for several hours. (Tying the string to a handle of the pot makes the pudding easy to remove.) A steamed pudding is cooked, also for several hours, in a basin covered by a cloth within a covered pot. The water should come three quarters of the way up the sides of the basin, which sometimes rests on a stand.

Continued on page 154

Mrs. Richard Jones *(second from right)* carries on a family tradition in her Shropshire shop, where she and her staff sell meats,

savory meat puddings and pies. Displayed in the window, below hanging hams, is a selection of pork pies and black puddings.

poured onto a plate and eaten with a flavoring of cinnamon. Hasty pudding, which Daniel Defoe, author of *Robinson Crusoe,* reported he had been "regaled with" in the countryside 30 years after de Valbourg's visit, fed the hungry child and the plowman alike. This simple batter mixture was later improved when cooks baked or fired it, or put it into a basin and steamed it, just as we do today. The other basic ingredient was fruit. The wild blackberries whose woody brambles imprison the hedgerows in prickly profusion, as well as strawberries, damsons and gooseberries, added another dimension.

Remember, most of these were winter puddings. Nevertheless, we did manage to invent a summer pudding, just to fill in between seasons, as it were. Although most cooks call it summer pudding, some refer to it as hydropathic pudding because it was served to patients in nursing homes and at spas where, it seems, pastry was not permitted. I prefer to believe that it was the simple invention of the British cook who just happened to have a garden full of fresh summer fruit, a loaf of bread and a pudding basin. The bread, cut into slices, lined the sides of the bowl. Raspberries, red currants or blackberries, gently combined with fine sugar, filled the bowl to the brim. More slices of bread covered the top, and the whole pudding was pressed down with a weight and left to get cold. Later the pudding was turned out onto a dish. By this time, the bread had soaked up the fruit juice and the pudding had set into a homogeneous mass of rich sweet fruit, over which the cook poured thick cream. This too is a true English pudding *(Recipe Index),* and to echo Misson de Valbourg, blessed be he that invented it.

The age of the stagecoach helped to widen the variety of the English pudding, and some stage inns created their own special dishes. If you stopped at Chester you would probably look forward to Chester pudding, followed by Cheshire cheese. At Exeter you would be transfixed by the sticky richness of Exeter pudding. Those en route to the east coast from London might stop off at Ipswich, where, in the kitchens of the White Horse Inn, Ipswich puddings were baking in the ovens. A traveler to Ireland by way of Holyhead would demand a large portion of the rich Wrexham pudding to sustain him in his journey across wild north Wales, where several towns offered Snowdon pudding. To the south, in the oak forest of Dean, stood the Speech House Inn where Speech House pudding was the specialty.

The Speech House Inn is still there, boasting enormous four-poster beds in its rooms, but the pudding is a part of the past. Nevertheless, we include a recipe for it *(Recipe Index)* because Speech House pudding has the classic qualities and ingredients demanded of an English winter pudding, created to reward an appetite provoked by a day's tramping in winter fields. In the 18th Century Speech House served, as it still does, to house a court of law that assembles from time to time to settle disputes among the foresters, and in the Verderer's Court Room there is a large fireplace where roasts once turned on the spit. Into the room the coach travelers crowded to sit near the fire, knocking the snow off their boots, huddling deep in their coats. They needed the roast meat and the gravy, mulled ale or rum punch, toasted cheeses and, finally, the specialty: Speech House pudding, made of eggs, butter and white flour, steamed for a couple of hours and served with a hot jam sauce. That was a delight appreciated by a traveler in a cold 18th Century winter.

The Englishman's love of puddings, particularly the very sweet ones, is a heritage not only of history but of upbringing. His taste is formed today, as it has been for centuries, in the nursery and the school dining room. The childish habits remain with us and the now middle-aged schoolboy enjoys his habitual meals in the club dining room or the factory canteen. He makes no effort to conceal his fondness for the sticky, baked marmalade roll, or the boiled suet pudding, down whose sides runs Tate & Lyle's golden syrup in rivulets of warm delight. Certainly the finest of sweet dishes is the pudding called "burnt cream," a rich baked custard cream, strewed with sugar, and caramelized under the broiler. The origin of the dish has often been disputed. Since it can rank among the world's great desserts, the French lay claim to its creation and call it *crème brulée;* others maintain that it is a New Orleans specialty, and some writers say that it came from Aberdeenshire in the 1860s.

Our taste for such food is ingrained. The dishes our mothers cooked for us we in turn cook for our children, a practice that ensures the survival of a national cuisine. Strange, is it not, how so many of us yearn for the foods on which we were nurtured? An Englishman spends half his life in the jungles of Africa, and dreams of steak-and-kidney pudding, followed by jam sponge and custard. I know a New Yorker who has lived for 15 years in Paris and whose eyes swim moistly at the mere mention of cheesecake.

Pudding is more than a beloved dish in Britain. The word also describes a course in a meal. When a British child asks, "What's for pudding?" he is expressing his interest in the sweet dish that follows the main course. Another child might ask about the "sweet" or the "dessert." All three terms refer to sweet dishes like American desserts, but that may be served during the meal, sometimes followed by a "savoury" course—any one of various nonsweet dishes ranging from anchovies to Welsh rabbit. The three terms—pudding, sweet, and dessert—do not always include the same dishes, however. "Dessert" means strictly fruit, candy or ices.

The use of these words can also reveal distinctions of class. What we eat and how we eat are still dictated by that many-headed hydra, the English class system. In Evelyn Waugh's novel *Brideshead Revisited* a character remarks: "It is purely out of respect for your Aunt Philippa that I dine at this length. She laid it down that a three-course dinner was middle-class . . . your Aunt ordained that at home I must have soup and three courses; some nights it is fish, meat and savoury, on others it is meat, sweet and savoury—there are a number of possible permutations."

The middle- and upper-class Victorian—verbose, pompous and acutely class-conscious—would have had something sweet for his "dessert" or "sweet." The factory worker or the agricultural laborer came home to a meal that might consist of meat and potatoes or fish and potatoes, followed by a sweet dish he would have called "pudding."

The upper classes now use the word "pudding" instead of "sweet." To compound the confusion, "sweet" now is commonly used by the middle classes, and the working class makes use of all three words—pudding, sweet and dessert—to describe what Americans call the dessert course.

Among the many things that Americans would not consider puddings, but the British do, are pies. That inventive American Thomas Alva Edison, who was inordinately fond of apple pie, once charged that the "English are not an inventive people; they don't eat enough pie." It was an unreasonable complaint, for English pies are many and varied, and the English actually in-

Luncheon at Christ's Hospital, which is not a hospital but a school for boys in Horsham, Sussex, is a major daily event. Every noon a band *(above)* escorts the more than 800 pupils from the quadrangle of classroom buildings to the main dining hall. There they are served a solid meal prepared under the supervision of chef Charles Bold *(opposite)*, who displays a few of the scores of steak-and-kidney pies he prepares for one day's lunch. At the dining tables the decorum of the bluecoats, as the boys are called because of their ankle-length uniforms, is reinforced by the paintings of former masters and historic British figures who look down from the walls—and by the presence of the faculty, who eat at the table in the background.

vented pie more than 600 years ago. If they had never invented anything since, they would have earned a place in history.

A pie is usually made in a deep dish lined with pastry, then filled with either meat or fruit and covered with additional pastry. A fruit pie—one made with damsons, for instance—would probably have a little sugar added to the pastry. Tradition demands that meat pies be decorated with pastry leaves or other ornaments. Fruit pies must be left plain, or simply dusted with sugar; in this way one can tell whether a pie contains fruit or meat.

A tart may look like a pie, but it is always a sweet dish made with fruit or jam. Tarts range from small, jam-filled hollows of pastry to large plate-sized pastry shells containing perhaps a layer of apples, apricots or plums, or a solid layer of raspberry jam. Tarts are usually left open-faced—that is, uncovered by pastry. But hard-and-fast rules cannot be applied. Some tarts are covered, some pies are open-faced. Often a jam tart is decorated with strips of pastry in a variety of designs: lattices, stars or whorls *(see Chapter 11)*. As a general guide, though, if the dish is shallow, call it a tart, if it is deep, call it a pie.

"Hand-raised pies," such as game pie, pork pie and mutton pie, are made with durable hot-water pastry that can be worked like potter's clay and shaped by hand into the boxlike casing that encloses the meat filling. These raised pies, called "coffyns" in the Middle Ages, are cooked for hours in a slow oven, and topped with a rich aspic jelly after being taken from the oven. There is also a good old rural dish, frequently seen on pub counters at lunchtime and known as cottage pie or shepherd's pie. This is made of minced beef and onion, cooked in a deep pie dish, and covered not with pastry, but with fluffy mashed potato.

Meat pies like this one arise out of a long tradition. Piers Plowman de-

scribed the eating of "hote pies" in the 14th Century. The Elizabethans cooked hand-raised pork and mutton pies of this type, often adding sugar and apples. They made the pastry with butter, and filled the pies with clarified butter. Thyme, sage and marjoram were used for flavoring, and so were spices, but not too many, for "a man all virtue, like a pie all spice will not please," as the saying went when George III was king in the late 18th Century.

Until quite recent times, meat pies were vended all over England by traveling piemen. Simple Simon met one during the mid-18th Century and Victorian housewives were warned to beware of them. This was because such pies were meant to be topped off, after baking, with aspic or butter forced through a vent in the crust; this seal blocked air from reaching the contents, thus preventing the pie from spoiling before sale. Piemen who failed to top off their pies, and some did, occasionally poisoned their customers.

Most pies are now mass-produced and eaten by the thousand every day. There is a pork-pie belt right across the Midlands, extending from Nottingham to the Welsh border. In Nottingham, Pork Farms Ltd. makes what are reputed to be the best pork pies in England from a family recipe handed down for generations. The company refuses to reveal the secret of its recipe, but those wishing to taste its ware can find them all over the country. It is easy to buy a factory-produced pork pie, and many of them are excellent. Yet a freshly made, hand-raised pie with a real pork jelly and a crisp crust, egg golden and light, is unbeatable, and I urge you to try making your own *(Recipe Index)*, for if we lose the English tradition of handmade puddings and pies, we are all one step nearer to the day when we reach for the deep freeze and the can opener because we have forgotten what the rolling pin is for, and the cake tins will gather rust at the bottom of the cupboard.

Burnt Cream

CARAMEL CREAM DESSERT

To serve 6 to 8

6 egg yolks
6 tablespoons sugar
3 cups heavy cream
1 tablespoon vanilla extract

Preheat the oven to 350°. With a whisk or a rotary or electric beater, beat the egg yolks and 2 tablespoons of the sugar together in a mixing bowl for 3 or 4 minutes, or until the yolks are thick and pale yellow.

Heat the cream in a heavy 1½- to 2-quart saucepan until small bubbles begin to form around the edges of the pan. Then, beating constantly, pour the cream in a slow stream into the beaten egg yolks. Add the vanilla extract and strain the mixture through a fine sieve into a 1-quart soufflé dish or other baking dish 6 to 7 inches in diameter and at least 2 inches deep.

Place the dish in a large shallow pan on the middle shelf of the oven and pour enough boiling water into the pan to come halfway up the sides of the dish. Bake for about 45 minutes, or until a knife inserted in the center of the cream comes out clean. Remove the dish from the water and cool to room temperature. Then refrigerate for at least 4 hours, or until the cream is thoroughly chilled.

About 2 hours before serving, preheat the broiler to its highest point. Sprinkle the top of the cream with the remaining 4 tablespoons of sugar, coating the surface as evenly as possible. Slide the dish under the broiler about 3 inches from the heat, and cook for 4 or 5 minutes, or until the sugar forms a crust over the cream. Watch carefully for any signs of burning and regulate the heat accordingly. Cool the cream to room temperature, then refrigerate it again until ready to serve.

A crunchy topping of partially caramelized sugar adds flavor and texture to the rich custard dessert known as burnt cream.

Cornish Pasty

To make 16 six-inch pasties

1 tablespoon butter, softened

PASTRY

4 cups all-purpose flour

1/8 teaspoon salt

1 1/2 cups lard (3/4 pound), chilled and cut into 1/4-inch bits

8 to 10 tablespoons ice water

FILLING

1 cup coarsely chopped white or yellow turnips

2 cups finely diced lean boneless beef, preferably top round

1 cup coarsely chopped onions

2 cups finely diced potatoes

1 1/2 teaspoons salt

1 teaspoon freshly ground black pepper

1 egg, lightly beaten

Preheat the oven to 400°. Using a pastry brush, coat a large baking sheet with the 1 tablespoon of softened butter. Set aside.

In a large chilled bowl, combine the flour, salt and lard. Working quickly, rub the flour and fat together with your fingertips until they look like coarse meal. Pour in 8 tablespoons of ice water all at once, toss together, and gather the dough into a ball. If the dough crumbles, add up to 2 tablespoons of water, 1 teaspoonful at a time, until the particles adhere. Dust the pastry with a little flour and wrap it in wax paper. Refrigerate for at least 1 hour.

On a lightly floured surface, roll out the dough into a circle about 1/4 inch thick. With a pastry wheel or sharp knife, cut the dough into 6-inch rounds using a small plate or pot lid as a guide. Gather the scraps together into a ball, roll it out again, and cut it into 6-inch rounds as before.

With a large spoon, toss the turnips, beef, onions, potatoes, salt and pepper together. Place about 1/4 cup of the mixture in the center of each pastry round. Moisten the edges of the rounds with a pastry brush dipped in cold water, then fold the rounds in half to enclose the filling completely. Press the seams together firmly and crimp them with your fingers or the tines of a fork. Place the pasties on the baking sheet, and cut two slits about 1 inch long in the top of each. Brush lightly with the beaten egg and bake in the middle of the oven for 15 minutes. Reduce the heat to 350° and bake for 30 minutes, or until the pasties are golden brown. Serve hot or at room temperature.

Fresh Fruit Fool

PURÉED FRUIT DESSERT

To serve 6 to 8

1 quart fresh ripe gooseberries, raspberries or blackberries (about 1 1/2 pounds)

1 cup sugar

3 cups heavy cream

Pick over the berries carefully, removing any stems and discarding berries that are badly bruised or show signs of mold. Place the fruit in a heavy 3- to 4-quart saucepan and cook over low heat for 30 minutes, stirring and mashing the fruit against the bottom and sides of the pan to extract its juices. Stir in the sugar and simmer until dissolved. Taste and add more sugar if desired. Then purée the fruit, a cup or so at a time, in a blender, or force it through a fine sieve or food mill set over a bowl. Cover and refrigerate.

Just before serving, beat the cream with a whisk or a rotary or electric beater until it forms stiff peaks on the beater when it is lifted from the bowl. With a rubber spatula gently fold the puréed fruit into the cream but do not overmix; the intermingled streaks of purée and cream should create a marbled effect. Serve at once in parfait glasses or individual dessert bowls.

Custard Sauce

To make about 1 1/2 cups sauce

1 1/2 cups milk

2 teaspoons cornstarch

1 tablespoon sugar

1 egg yolk

1/2 teaspoon vanilla extract

In a heavy 1- to 1 1/2-quart saucepan, combine 1/4 cup of the milk and the cornstarch, and stir with a whisk until the cornstarch is dissolved. Add the remaining 1 1/4 cups of milk and the sugar, and cook over moderate heat, stirring, until the sauce thickens and comes to a boil. In a small bowl break up the egg yolk with a fork and stir in 2 or 3 tablespoons of the sauce. Then whisk the mixture back into the remaining sauce. Bring to a boil again and boil for 1 minute, stirring constantly. Remove the pan from the heat and add the vanilla. Custard sauce is served hot with such desserts as blackberry-and-apple pie, apple dumplings or jam sponge *(for all, see Recipe Index)*.

For summer pudding, line a mold with bread slices cut to fit. Place the fruit in a bowl.

Sugar the fruit and stir until the grains dissolve.

Summer Pudding

FRUIT-FILLED BREAD PUDDING

To serve 6 to 8

2 quarts (about 3 pounds) fresh ripe raspberries, blackberries, blueberries or red currants
1¼ cups superfine sugar
10 to 12 slices homemade-type white bread
1 cup heavy cream

Pick over the fruit carefully, removing any stems or caps and discarding any berries that are badly bruised or show signs of mold. Wash in a colander under cold running water, then shake the berries dry and spread them out on paper towels to drain. Place the berries in a large mixing bowl, sprinkle with the 1¼ cups of sugar, and toss them about gently with a large spoon until the sugar dissolves completely. Taste, and add more sugar if necessary. Cover tightly and set the berries aside.

With a small, sharp knife, cut 1 slice of bread into a circle or octagon so that it will exactly fit the bottom of a 2-quart English pudding basin, a 2-quart deep bowl, or a charlotte mold, and set it in place. Trim 6 or 7 slices of the bread into truncated wedge shapes 3½ to 4 inches wide across the top and about 3 inches wide across the bottom. Stand the wedges of bread, narrow end down, around the inner surface of the mold, overlapping them by about ¼ inch. Ladle the fruit mixture into the mold, and cover the top completely with the remaining bread. Cover the top of the mold with a flat plate, and on it set a 3- to 4-pound kitchen weight, or a heavy pan or casserole. Refrigerate the pudding for at least 12 hours, until the bread is completely saturated with the fruit syrup.

To remove the pudding from the mold, place a chilled serving plate upside down over it and, grasping the plate and mold firmly together, quickly invert them. The pudding should slide out easily. In a large chilled bowl, beat the cream with a whisk or a rotary or electric beater until it holds its shape softly. Serve the whipped cream separately with the pudding.

NOTE: If the berries are not fully ripened and soft, combine the fruit and sugar in a heavy 3- to 4-quart saucepan, and cook over low heat for about 5 minutes, shaking the pan frequently.

Trifle

CAKE, FRUIT AND CUSTARD DESSERT WITH WHIPPED CREAM

To serve 6 to 8

A piece of homemade poundcake about 5 inches long, 4 inches wide and 3 inches high, or substitute a 12-ounce packaged poundcake
4 tablespoons raspberry jam
1 cup blanched almonds, separated into halves
1 cup medium-dry sherry
¼ cup brandy
2 cups heavy cream
2 tablespoons superfine sugar
A double recipe of custard sauce *(page 159)*, chilled until firm
2 cups fresh raspberries, or 2 ten-ounce packages frozen raspberries, defrosted and thoroughly drained

Cut the poundcake into 1-inch-thick slices and spread them with the raspberry jam. Place 2 or 3 of the slices, jam side up, in the bottom of a glass serving bowl 8 or 9 inches across and 3 inches deep. Cut the remaining slices

Place the fruit in the mold and top with bread slices, a plate and a weight.

Refrigerate overnight; then slide the pudding from the mold.

of cake into 1-inch cubes, scatter them over the slices, and sprinkle ½ cup of the almonds on top. Then pour in the sherry and brandy and let the mixture steep at room temperature for at least 30 minutes.

In a large chilled bowl, whip the cream with a whisk or a rotary or electric beater until it thickens slightly. Add the sugar and continue to beat until the cream is stiff enough to form unwavering peaks on the beater when it is lifted out of the bowl.

To assemble the trifle, set 10 of the best berries aside and scatter the rest over the cake. With a spatula spread the custard across the top. Then gently smooth half of the whipped cream over the surface of the custard. Using a pastry bag fitted with a large rose tip, pipe the remaining whipped cream decoratively around the edge. Garnish the cream with the 10 reserved berries and the remaining ½ cup of almonds.

The trifle will be at its best served at once, but it may be refrigerated for an hour or two.

Bread-and-Butter Pudding

To serve 6 to 8

8 tablespoons butter, softened
12 thin slices homemade-type white bread
½ cup dried currants
½ cup white raisins
⅛ teaspoon ground cinnamon
5 eggs
3 cups milk
1 cup heavy cream
¼ cup sugar
A pinch of nutmeg

With a pastry brush, coat the bottom and sides of a 7-by-10-by-2½-inch baking dish with 2 tablespoons of the butter.

Trim and discard the crusts from the bread, and butter it liberally on both sides. Place 4 slices of the bread side by side on the bottom of the dish, and trim them to fit snugly. Toss the currants, raisins and cinnamon together in a small bowl, and strew half of the mixture over the bread. Add a second layer of bread, strew the remainder of the fruit over it, and top with a final layer of bread.

With a whisk or a rotary or electric beater, beat the eggs to a froth in a large mixing bowl. Beat in the milk, cream, sugar and nutmeg, and then pour the mixture evenly over the bread. Let the pudding rest at room temperature for at least 30 minutes, or until the bread has absorbed almost all of the liquid.

Preheat the oven to 350°. Cover the pudding with a lightly buttered sheet of foil and bake in the middle of the oven for 30 minutes. Then remove the foil and bake for 30 minutes longer, or until the top is crisp and golden brown. Serve hot, directly from the baking dish.

To serve 4 to 6

2 pounds lean boneless beef chuck or top round, cut into 1-inch cubes
1 pound veal or lamb kidneys, peeled and trimmed of fat, and cut into 1-inch cubes
2/3 cup flour
1/4 teaspoon ground nutmeg
1 1/2 teaspoons salt
1/4 teaspoon freshly ground black pepper
1/4 pound large fresh mushrooms, trimmed and cut into quarters, including the stems
1/2 cup coarsely chopped onions
1/4 cup finely chopped parsley
Suet pastry *(below)*
1 1/2 cups boiling water

Steak-and-Kidney Pudding

Place the cubes of beef and kidney in a large mixing bowl. Combine 1/3 cup of the flour with the nutmeg, salt and pepper, and sift it over the meat. Then toss together with a large spoon to coat the pieces evenly. Stir in the mushrooms, onions and parsley. Set aside.

On a lightly floured surface, roll out about two thirds of the suet pastry into a rough circle 14 inches in diameter and 1/4 inch thick. Drape the pastry over the rolling pin and unfold it slackly over a 6-cup English pudding basin or a plain 6-cup mold about 7 inches in diameter and 4 inches deep. Gently press the pastry into the bowl, being careful not to stretch it. Roll out the remaining pastry into an 8-inch circle, and set it aside.

Ladle the beef-and-kidney mixture into the mold, filling it to within 1/2 inch of the top. Mound the meat in the center, and pour in the water.

With a sharp knife, trim the excess pastry from the rim of the mold and lightly moisten the rim with a pastry brush dipped in cold water. Carefully place the 8-inch circle of pastry over the mold and trim the edges again. Then crimp the pastry all around the rim with your fingers or the tines of a fork to seal it tightly. Lay a lightly buttered 10-inch circle of parchment paper or foil over the top of the pudding, turning the edges down all around its circumference to hold it in place.

Now dampen a cloth kitchen towel with cold water and wring it dry. Spread the towel flat, sprinkle it evenly with the remaining 1/3 cup of flour, and shake it vigorously to dislodge the excess flour. Spread the towel, floured side down, over the top of the pudding. Bring the ends of the towel down around the sides of the basin or mold and tie them in place about 1 1/2 to 2 inches down the side (just below the rim if you are using a pudding basin) with a long length of kitchen cord. Bring up two diagonally opposite corners of the towel and tie them together on top of the pudding. Then bring the remaining corners together and tie them similarly.

Place the pudding in a large pot and pour in enough boiling water to come three fourths of the way up the side of the mold. Bring to a boil, cover the pot tightly, reduce the heat to its lowest point, and steam for 5 hours. From time to time replenish the water in the pot with additional boiling water.

To serve, lift the pudding out of the water (holding it by the looped cloth if you are using a basin with a rim) and remove the towel and paper or foil. Wipe the mold completely dry and wrap it in a clean linen napkin. Serve at the table directly from the basin or mold.

1/2 pound finely chopped beef suet, thoroughly chilled
4 cups all-purpose flour
1 teaspoon salt
Freshly ground black pepper
6 to 8 tablespoons ice water

Suet Pastry

In a large chilled mixing bowl, combine the suet, flour, salt and a few grindings of pepper. With your fingertips rub the flour and fat together until they look like flakes of coarse meal. Pour 6 tablespoons of ice water over the mixture all at once, knead together vigorously and gather the dough into a ball. If the dough crumbles, add up to 2 more tablespoons of ice water, 1 teaspoon at a time, until the particles adhere.

Gather the dough into a ball and place it on a lightly floured surface. Knead, pressing the dough flat, pushing it forward and folding it back on itself for 6 to 8 minutes, or until it is smooth and satiny. Dust the suet pastry with a little flour and wrap it in wax paper. Refrigerate at least 1 hour before using.

Steak-and-kidney pudding *(recipe, opposite)* is made much as it was in Dickens' day—though it is no longer likely to contain oysters, much less larks. The English steam it in a pudding basin *(above)*, but you can use any plain mold. First press the pastry lining into the mold *(1)*. Fill with beefsteak and kidney and trim the rim *(2)*. Top the pudding with a circle of pastry *(3)*, and cover that with buttered paper. To ensure a tight seal, spread a kitchen towel across the mold *(4)*, bring it down around the sides, and tie it in place with string. Lift two diagonally opposite corners of the towel and tie them over the mold *(5)*. Then tie the two other corners above the first knot *(6)*. The finished pudding shown at right has been turned out and the crust cut away to display its contents.

To serve 6 to 8

2 tablespoons butter, softened
2 pounds lean boneless veal, cut into 1/4-inch cubes
1 pound lean smoked ham, cut into 1/4-inch cubes
1/4 cup finely chopped parsley
6 tablespoons brandy
6 tablespoons fresh or canned chicken or beef stock
2 tablespoons fresh lemon juice
1 teaspoon finely grated lemon peel
1 teaspoon crumbled dried sage leaves
2 teaspoons salt
1/4 teaspoon freshly ground black pepper
Hot-water pastry *(opposite)*
4 hard-cooked eggs
8 to 10 pickled walnuts (optional)
1 egg yolk combined with 1 tablespoon heavy cream
1 envelope unflavored gelatin
2 cups chicken stock, fresh or canned

Veal-and-Ham Pie

Preheat the oven to 350°. Using a pastry brush, coat the bottom and sides of a 10-by-5-by-4-inch loaf mold with the butter. Set aside. In a large bowl, combine the veal, ham, parsley, brandy, stock, lemon juice, peel, sage, salt and pepper. Toss the ingredients about with a spoon until thoroughly mixed.

Break off about one third of the hot-water pastry and set it aside. On a lightly floured surface, roll out the remaining pastry into a rectangle about 20 inches long, 10 inches wide and 1/4 inch thick. Drape the pastry over the rolling pin, lift it up, and unroll it slackly over the mold. Gently press the pastry into the mold. Roll the pin over the rim to trim off the excess pastry.

Spoon enough of the veal and ham mixture into the pastry shell to fill it a little less than half full. Arrange the hard-cooked eggs in a single row down the center of the mold, and line up the pickled walnuts, if you are using them, on both sides of the eggs. Cover the eggs with the remaining meat mixture, filling the shell to within 1 inch of the top.

Roll the reserved pastry into a 4-by-13-inch rectangle 1/4 inch thick. Lift it up on the pin and drape it over the top of the mold. Trim off the excess with a small knife and, with the tines of a fork or your fingers, crimp the pastry to secure it to the rim of the mold. Then cut a 1-inch round hole in the center of the pie. Roll out the scraps of pastry and cut them into leaf and flower shapes. Moisten their bottom sides with the egg-and-cream mixture and arrange on the pie. Brush the entire surface with the egg-and-cream mixture.

Bake the pie in the middle of the oven for 2 hours, or until the top is a deep golden brown. Remove from the oven and cool for 15 minutes.

Meanwhile, in a 1- to 1 1/2-quart saucepan, sprinkle the gelatin over 2 cups of cold chicken stock and let it soften for 2 or 3 minutes. Then set the pan

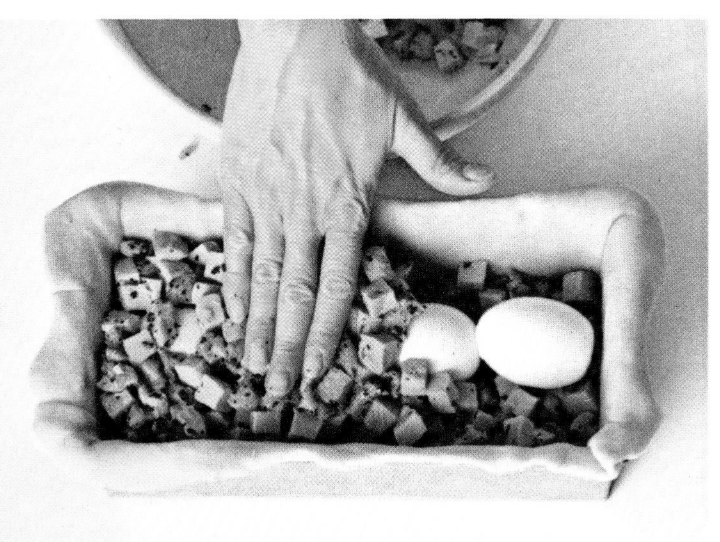

1 To assemble a veal-and-ham pie, line a large loaf mold with hot-water pastry, then fill it half full of the meat mixture. Arrange hard-cooked eggs in a row down the center and add the rest of the meat, patting the filling gently to spread it and smooth the top.

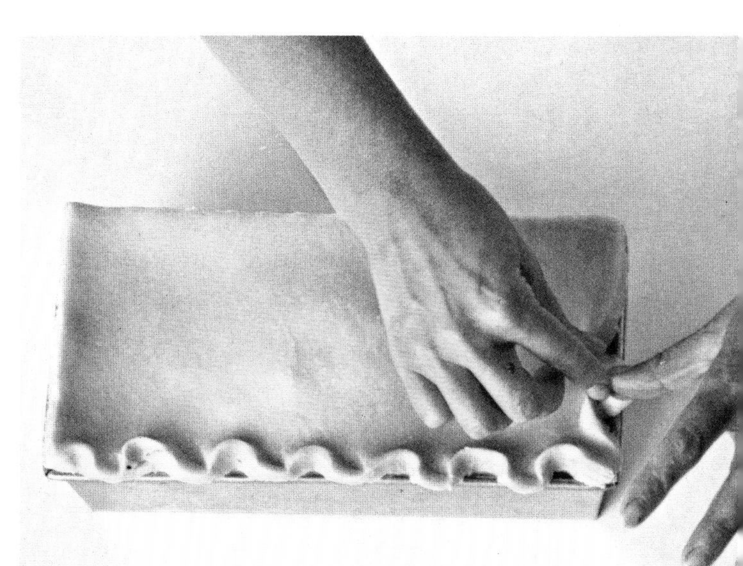

2 Cover the pie with pastry and trim the excess from the rim of the mold with a small knife. Crimp the edge of the pastry by pinching it between your thumb and forefinger to make a rope-like scallop all around the pie. This also seals the pastry shell securely.

over low heat and cook, stirring constantly, until the gelatin dissolves completely. Pour the gelatin through a funnel into the opening of the pie. Cool the pie to room temperature, then refrigerate it for at least 6 hours, or until the aspic is set. Ideally the pie should be removed from the refrigerator about 30 minutes before being served.

To unmold and serve the pie, run the blade of a sharp knife around the inside edges of the mold and dip the bottom of the mold in hot water. Wipe the mold dry, place an inverted serving plate over it and, grasping mold and plate together firmly, quickly turn them over. Rap the plate on a table and the pie should slide out easily. Turn the pie over and serve, cut into ½-inch-thick slices.

NOTE: Traditionally, veal-and-ham pies are "raised pies." That is, the pastry casing for the pie is "raised," or shaped, around a wooden mold.

Hot-Water Pastry

5 cups all-purpose flour
½ teaspoon salt
10 tablespoons lard
6 tablespoons milk
2 tablespoons water

In a deep bowl, combine the flour and salt. Warm the lard, milk and water in a saucepan over moderate heat, and stir until the lard melts. Beat the mixture, a few tablespoons at a time, into the flour, and continue to beat until the dough can be gathered into a compact ball. On a lightly floured surface, knead the dough for 2 or 3 minutes by pressing it down, pushing it forward, and folding it back on itself until it is smooth and elastic. Again gather it into a ball. Place it in a bowl and drape a dampened kitchen towel over it. Let the dough rest for 30 minutes before using.

NOTE: This pastry is traditionally used for veal-and-ham pie *(above)* and pork pie.

3 Cut a hole in the top and trim it with flower petals cut from scraps of pastry. Then brush the pie with the egg-and-milk mixture and bake it. After aspic is poured in the hole and the pie chilled, serve it in thick slices; they will look like the cross section at right.

X

Your Pleasure, Gentlemen?

The Scots farmer held his glass up to the light and closed one eye, while the other appraised the pale, almost colorless liquid, with its faint tint of amber. "Cheers," I said. "Oh, aye," he responded. "Down the hatch." He drained his glass at one gulp. I did the same. The spirit penetrated every corner of my soul, instantly and forever. Fire spread from the soles of my feet to the roots of my hair. My scalp crinkled.

The Scotsman smiled. He appeared totally unaffected. "That's a fine whisky," I managed to say. "What is it?" The farmer avoided my gaze with a shifty glance out the window. "Och," he said, "it has nae a name."

For the first time it occurred to me that the Scots still make their own brew, as do the Irish, in illicit stills hidden in the mountains. Or maybe the farmer had run a secret pipe from a distillery vat to a tap over the sink. It wouldn't be the first time it had been done; I could see the roofs of one distillery from where I was standing in the farm kitchen.

Order a "ploughman's lunch" in any village inn or pub in the British Isles and you can expect freshly baked bread, a foaming pint of bitter ale, a generous portion of Cheddar cheese and a couple of pickled onions. Plowing into it will give you plenty of energy to last until teatime.

"It has nae a name." Well, if he made his own whisky it wouldn't have a name. But this was Scotch whisky, not the murderous liquor called poteen that the Irish brew from grain or potatoes, but the real McCoy, so to speak.

Nobody in Scotland or in Ireland will admit to knowing anything about illicit stills hidden in the mountains, but poteen was being made a few years ago, when I last visited Ireland. I traveled from the village of Glenbeigh, on the Ring of Kerry, as the hills that surround the blue Lakes of Killarney, the diamonds in the ring, are known, and sat next to the driver in a big truck, bumping down the mountain road. Rain, driven by the wind from the west, smashed against the windscreen so we could barely see where we were going. It was like driving under the sea. After a while it cleared slightly and we could see the town of Killarney and the lakes below us, gray that day like pools of cold lead. The driver had not said a word for hours, but now he spoke, pointing to a tree. "See that tree?"

I nodded. The driver said, "We was driving along this road won day, me and my mayt, when I saw this pig high up in that tree. I didn't say anything to my mayt, thinking—'Ah, 'tis the poteen has a hold of me.' Some months later it turned out that he'd seen the pig, too, but didn't say so, for he thought it was the drink in him."

"Can ye believe that?" he asked. "How could a pig climb a tree?" "Maybe it was a flying pig," I suggested. The driver looked at me suspiciously. "Ar, now, there's no such thing as a flying pig." We drove on in total silence until we eventually reached Killarney. The driver said, "This is Killarney; tell me, is there a flying pig?"

"No," I said.

"Yes," said the driver, "I knew all along 'twas the drink."

Concoctions even more hallucinogenic have been made to do in a pinch. When some of the Irish emigrated to England and settled in Liverpool 50 years ago they were cut off from their natural supply of poteen and whiskey, and introduced a quaint brew that I would not recommend to Caligula. Called "red biddy," it was a cocktail comprised of one part of methylated spirit and one part chlorodyne, the latter being a patent anesthetic obtainable in pharmacies, but I don't suggest that you try it, not even for kicks. Its inclusion in this chapter is simply to illustrate the extent of these isles' invention where drink is concerned.

Perhaps no other people on earth enjoy such a variety of alcoholic beverages. When a barmaid in a British pub asks, "Your pleasure, gentlemen?" she is in a position to serve a great variety of pleasant potables. England is the spiritual home if not the actual birthplace of gin, which still carries a trace of the wickedness it connoted in 18th Century London. There also are beers in several forms—stout, porter, bitter, mild—and hard cider as well. In country homes you may be offered wine made of turnips or plums, or perhaps even a sip of the old medieval honey wine called mead. Everywhere, besides the fine wines of the Continent, is the peculiarly British port, made in Portugal but mostly by English-dominated firms to suit English tastes. But the most famous of all the drinks of the British Isles, and deservedly so, are the whiskeys. Irish—not poteen but the real Irish whiskey, always spelled with an "e"—has a roguish charm of its own. Good as it is, its fame is eclipsed by that of the mellow golden Scotch whisky, always spelled without the "e." In many parts of the world when you ask for whiskey you get Scotch; no other kind is known.

To this day the rivalry between Scottish and Irish distillers is deeply rooted. The Irish are often credited with the invention of whiskey, and they gave it its generic name. In the 16th Century, Irish settlers established distilleries on the coasts of Wales and Scotland, and so Irish whiskey can be said to have been made in Wales, and even in Scotland. But today everyone, even the Irish, acknowledges the world supremacy of Scotch whisky.

The real stuff can be made only in Scotland; it is impossible to imitate, although many have tried. I have had "Scotch whisky" that was made in

Japan, and the bottle bore more than just a faint resemblance to Johnny Walker. There is a story that one such bottle, purchased in Tokyo, bore a label asserting that "this Scottish Whisky was made in Buckingham Palace by their Majesties the King and Queen of England."

Unlike Irish whiskey, which is rarely blended, the Scotch whiskies that most of us know are blends of two types, malt whisky—so called because the barley from which it is made is "malted," or germinated, before fermentation—and whiskies made from other, unmalted grains.

The blends made Scotch a popular drink during the 1870s and 1880s when brandy, then the tipple of the upper-class Englishman, became unavailable because the vineyards of France were threatened with extinction by a parasite called *Phylloxera* that preyed upon the vines. Some years earlier a few distillers, seeking wider markets, had begun to blend grain whiskies produced in the Lowlands of Scotland with the unblended malt brewed in the Highlands to create what we today call Scotch, which took the place of brandy. For this, I suppose we must thank America, since the species of *Phylloxera* that attacked the French vines was a native of the United States.

Unblended malt whisky is still the drink of the Highland Scots, and one that most Scots take very seriously indeed, knocking it back undiluted, without ice, in single determined gulps. It has a distinctive, smoky flavor, derived (it is frequently contended) from ingredients that can be found only in Scotland—the barley of the counties of Aberdeen and Angus, the clear mountain water of the Highlands, and the peat fire over which the barley is dried after malting. It is said that even the shape of the copper pot stills in which the stuff is brewed has an effect on its flavor, and a still that has been accidentally dented will produce a whisky of greatly altered taste. Mind you, there's much more to the making of Scotch than all this; if there weren't, you and I would be making it in the kitchen and, believe me, I've tried.

As a result each brand of malt, more than the somewhat standardized blended Scotches, has very individualistic characteristics. Laphroaig, for example, comes from the tiny island of Islay off the west coast of Scotland and possesses so distinctive a flavor that it can never be mistaken for any other brand. Every Scotsman is sure of his own choice. I remember being in the bar of a tiny hotel by Loch Awe in Argyll when a huge Scots engineer came in. He looked at the glass in my hand.

"What's that ye are drinking?"

"It's whisky," I said, my English accent coming over loud and clear.

"Aw, I know that, but what *kind* of whisky?"

I mentioned a well-known brand.

The engineer said, "That's no bloody whisky, that's the muck they drink doon in Glasgow."

He yelled at the barman, and pointed, "Gie us that bottle." The bottle turned out to be a different, but equally well-known brand.

"That's the stuff to drink," he said. "Never ask for any other, it's the best in Scotland." But whatever a man's preference, all Scots would agree that Scotch in general is a concoction beyond compare. Perhaps the last word on that subject should be left to Robert Burns, who was an officer of the Customs and Excise, a gauger of barrels and detector of smugglers, a drinker of some renown, and one of the greatest poets in the world: "O thou, my

Muse! guid auld Scotch drink; / Whether thro' wimplin' worms thou jink, / Or, richly brown, ream owre the brink, / In glorious faem, / Inspire me, till I lisp an' wink, / To sing thy name!"

Day after day, the big whisky trucks lumber over the border into England to refill empty glasses, and inspire the world as they did Robbie Burns. Even the taciturn English are inspired; and Englishmen primed with a few glasses of "whusky" will talk your arm off, a phenomenon usually achieved only after several pints of beer. But in England beer wins in popularity; it, rather than whisky, is the national drink.

One of the most famous English beer-making centers lies in the Midlands. There the River Trent rises among the little black houses high on Biddulph Moor and swings down from the "five towns" of Stoke, bordering the Black Country's mill towns to reach for the mouth of the Humber. Like many rivers, the Trent undergoes a change of character according to the area; it is by turns an industrial river, a navigable canal, a rural waterway. Seated firmly on its upper reaches is the great brewery town of Burton-on-Trent, which owes its renown to water, and not the water of the River Trent but the hard, gypsum-impregnated water that springs from the hills around the town and first gave Burton beer its character.

To brew a good pale ale like the Burton bitter you need gypsum-rich water; the Benedictine monks who built Burton Abbey more than 950 years ago somehow realized this, and perhaps that's why they built the abbey here, for they made a lot of beer and prospered from their Saxon customers. Today the monks are gone, but there are eight huge beer-makers that produce millions of barrels each year for the home market, and this is only a fraction of the national consumption.

The beer made there—Ind Coope's Double Diamond for instance—is sent to all parts of England, either bottled or in kegs as draft beer, and it is a standard product, well-liked in most of the country. Yet tastes vary from district to district, even within a few miles of one another. The farther north you go, the stronger the brewers generally make the beer. Porter, popular in London, is somewhat sweet and has about 4 per cent alcohol. The beer called "mild" is what its name implies. Yorkshire Stingo is a strong beer similar to a type known as barley wine. Imperial Russian stout, as brewed by Courage Barclay & Simonds in London, is one of the strongest beers we have in England; it is heavy, black, sweet and very potent—so potent, in fact, that some pubs won't allow you more than a few. This is probably similar to a type of beer drunk by the Elizabethans, who brewed various strengths: there were "single" beer, "double" beer, and "double-double" beer.

The most popular and widely drunk beer today is that called "bitter," a draft beer served in pubs all over England. In appearance it is a clear, honey-colored beer, but usually darker than American beer. It has richness, body, quite a strong and distinctive flavor, a stronger alcoholic content than American beer, and much less carbon-dioxide gas. It is never meant to be served chilled (much to the alarm of American visitors), but at cellar temperature. Chilled, the beer would lose much of its special slightly bitter flavor of malted barley, hops and yeast, a flavor entirely English, and a taste well worth the trouble of acquiring.

There are a great many brands of bitter, each slightly different in flavor, and if you go into an English pub, for which there is no substitute in all the world, you will see a row of tall, slender handles along the serving side of the bar. Some are made of colored and decorated ceramics while others may be of black ebony with a silver band in the middle. These are the identifying handles of the pumps that draw the beer from the selection of barrels in the cellar up to the bar, and into your glass. If you are a regular customer you might have your beer presented in your personal pewter mug, but most of us today drink our beer from a glass.

In mug or glass, Englishmen drink a lot of beer. The pottery workers in Staffordshire, who fire the great kilns and work in high temperatures, are said to be able to drink around 14 pints of beer in an evening, provided that the beer is not too strong, and not over-hopped. They prefer their beer light in color, while the Tyneside shipbuilders like a strong, dark beer that they, too, consume by the gallon.

Mulled ale is a drink for wintry weather, made by thrusting a red-hot poker into an earthenware pitcher of spiced ale. It is traditionally downed from a silver or pewter tankard.

This staggering capacity is nothing new. During the 18th Century a Frenchman in England wrote, "Would you believe it, though water is to be had in abundance in London, and of fairly good quality, absolutely none is drunk? The lower classes, even the paupers, do not know what it is to quench their thirst with water. In this country nothing but beer is drunk, and it is made in several qualities." Another commentator remarked: "Very frequently, after having drunk to the health of their friends, they drink to the ruin and damnation of their enemies. There is then no sort of mad pranks they do not think of, to excite one another to drink."

This was strong beer that was being consumed, even the "small beer" served to children, which is stronger than modern lager. It was especially good on the farms, which malted their own barley and made beer for the men who brought in the harvest. The Reverend James Woodforde, that indefatigable chronicler of 18th Century rural life, gives an idea of the quantities the country folk brewed for their own use in those days: "Busy this morning and day in brewing some Ale being the first time of brewing since I came to Weston. I had my Malt and Hopps of Mr. Palmer of Norton. I brewed only one vessel of 36 gallons and I allowed one coomb [approximately four bushels] of Malt and one Pound and a half of Hops, which I think will make a tolerable good Ale. . . ."

A country family in this period all drank beer, the men, women and children alike, at breakfast, at noon and in the evening. In winter the beer might be served mulled—that is, heated with a red-hot poker thrust into the jug, which caused the cloudy, thick brew to hiss and foam. Spices and a little sugar were added, and on especially important occasions like Christmas, a dram or two of brandy.

By Parson Woodforde's day, "beer" and "ale" had come to mean the same thing in Britain, as they still do there today, but long ago "beer" referred solely to a brew containing hops, ale being without hops. In the 15th Century, some experimenters began adding hops to ale, but for nearly 100 years drinkers opposed this newfangled notion of adding a strange, aromatic flower to their brew. In the end hops won; they added an extra flavor to the ale, and they were discovered to have preservative qualities, so the brew could be kept for longer periods.

By this time hundreds of commercial houses were supplementing the production of the home brewers, and successive monarchs attempted to enforce

Continued on page 176

This thatch-roofed cottage serves as both pub and grocery store in the village of Castlebar, in County Mayo, Ireland. Mrs. John T. Clarke, wife of the publican, chats at the door with two villagers.

Pubs and Stout: A Part of the Islands' Landscape

Dotted across the rural and urban landscape of the British Isles are two institutions without which the islands would not be recognizable: the pub and the billboard proclaiming "Guinness is good for you." In the pubs, the talk flows as freely as the stout (a malt liquor) offered by Guinness and other breweries. Here, in John T. Clarke's County Mayo pub, a philosophic patron pauses between quaffs to weigh the words being exchanged by Mrs. Clarke, the pub's acting barmaid, with an unseen customer. At the right, an equally philosophic gentleman is inadvertently blocking the good out of Guinness.

Overleaf:

An air of formality lends serenity to Henekey's Bar, a pub on the edge of the City, London's financial district. Famous as the "long bar," Henekey's has allotted some of its space to booths for ladies and privacy-seekers. But most of the businessmen who frequent the place do their quiet drinking while standing up.

standards. Local authorities kept an eye on prices, while aleconners—testers—are said to have judged the quality by pouring some of the beer onto a bench and sitting in the puddle in their leather breeches. If they stuck to the chair the beer was considered to have been adulterated by the addition of sugar. Why these aleconners did not rely on taste alone has never been explained to my satisfaction.

The need for governmental control was plain, however, for many murderous liquors were sold. On the grounds of Winchester Cathedral, there is a tomb erected in memory of a soldier who died of inferior beer, and inscribed on the tomb are these words, "An honest soldier never is forgot, whether he die by musket or by pot." Some ales acquired meaningless nicknames like "huff-cap" or "nippitatum". Such brews provoked statements like this one: "To quench the scorching heat of our parched throtes, with the best nippitatum in this toun, which is commonly called huff-cap, it will make a man look as though he had seen the devil and quickly move him to call his own father. . . ." Today, of course, you can drink with confidence whatever the barmaid draws for you. It's not the quality of the beer that need be of concern, only your own capacity.

In an English pub you get matter-of-fact service on an order that, in an American bar, would break up the house with laughter. Try asking for a pint of cider, for instance. In England this is hard cider, and some of it is quite powerful, containing as much as 8 per cent alcohol. It too is scarcely a new beverage. Down in the West Country the people tell the following legend: Joseph of Arimathea came to Britain and founded a center of Christianity in Somerset at Glastonbury, a place that Arthurian legends called Avalon. Avalon means "isle of apples," and the legend says that Joseph stood on Glastonbury Tor eating an apple, the pips of which he spat into Somerset. Where the pips fell cider-apple trees sprang out of the ground, and from these few trees eventually sprang the vast cider-apple orchards today found in Hereford, Somerset and Devon.

There can be little doubt that this Christian legend was forged to explain an old pagan worship of the apple as a fruit of fertility, and the ritual still survives in the form of "apple wassailing" on Twelfth Night. This rite is supposed to promote the apple crop and maybe it does. Who am I to scorn the success of centuries of British paganism? I regret that I have never attended an apple wassailing, for it sounds like quite an event; the villagers gather round the largest tree in the orchard, which is hung with pieces of toast soaked in cider. These are offerings to the robins, the good spirits of the tree, who have probably learned by now to be as far away from an apple orchard during Twelfth Night as they can get. Next, cider is poured on the roots of the tree, and down the throats of the villagers, who link hands and dance around, chanting an ancient toast that they probably don't understand, while men in various parts of the orchard blast away with shotguns to frighten away the evil spirits of the tree—there's a lot more to making cider than the crushing of apples.

Rituals and legends are only one indication of the antiquity of the cider apple in Britain. The Romans, when they came to the island, planted many varieties of apple trees, of which some of today's 300 cider types are descendants. Cider apples have beautiful names: Redstreak (which Isaac Newton tried

to introduce into Cambridgeshire), Redstreak-Blackstreak, Kingston Black (in Devon called "Sheep's Nose"), Yarlington Mill, Dabinett, Stoke Red, Sweet Coppin and Sweet Alford; and much older varieties like the pearmain, the Moile, the White Swan, the Slack-My-Girdle, the codling and the French Longtail. Cider apples differ from dessert and cooking apples in that they have a sweet juice and an acid pulp. The acid is malic acid—very important in cider making, for a good cider, like a good cheese, must have the right proportion of acid to correct and improve the flavor. A cider apple should not be too sweet.

Many years ago hundreds of farms made their own cider, just as farms made their own cheese, and perhaps there were as many different ciders in England then as there now are cheeses in France. Cider, like local cheese, must have varied considerably in flavor from district to district. Many farmers still make cider for their own use, but most of the cider that we drink in England now comes from the cider factories, which use six or seven varieties of apple to blend a more or less standard type of cider.

Cider-making time is the "black end" of the year—September to Christmas. In the Quantock Hills, along the Vale of Taunton and around Norton Fitzwarren the orchards annually bear a heavy crop. Taunton cider makers crush 100 tons of apples a day during harvest time, squeezing out 16,000 gallons of juice, and the perfume of crushed apples in the farms and factories around the town is heavy and intoxicating.

After the initial crushing the pulp is spread on straw or on wooden racks and cloths, piled layer upon layer like a sandwich: this is traditionally called a "cheese." The cheese is put into a cider press and afterward the juice, extracted under pressure, is allowed to ferment. The working cider hums and bubbles in the vats—"singing low and sweetly," the country people used to say—until the fermentation ceases.

"Cider is really a wine," a Somerset cider maker told me, "and most peo-

The drinks that contribute to the mellow friendliness of a British pub are less often whiskey or gin than milder potations: hard cider and a wide variety of beers like lager, ale, stout and porter. These popular pub beverages usually are sold by the pint, often in mugs or tankards. The 10 examples lined up in the window of The Carpenters Arms, a London pub, are *(from left):* draft Guinness (a stout), another brand of stout, mild (a kind of ale), barley wine (not a wine, in fact, but a strong, dark ale with the barley-malt base common to all beers), brown ale, bitter (a strong ale), light ale, bottled lager, cider and draft lager.

Continued on page 180

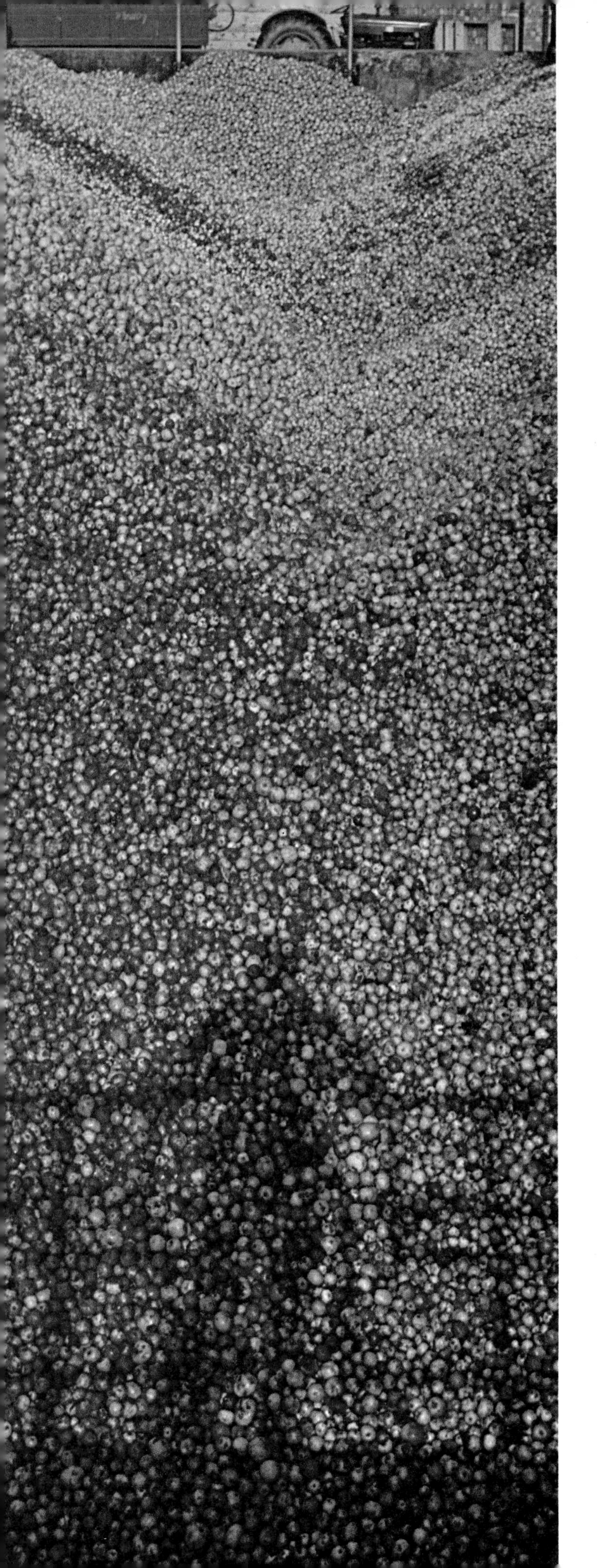

Cider: Innocent Drink to Surprise the Unwary

British bottled cider, gold in color with a fizzy tang, combines an innocent look with a mild kick that sometimes overtakes the unwary. Unlike the sweet, cloudy, nonalcoholic variety familiar to Americans, English cider is usually clear and hard, with an alcohol content as high as 8 per cent. Most of it comes from the acres of orchards that roll across England's West Country, which each autumn yield great quantities of bittersweet apples. As shown in these pictures, taken in the Bulmer works in Hereford, the largest cider producer in the world, the harvested apples are first collected in gigantic concrete bins *(left)*, each holding 1,500 tons of the fruit (their capacity can be gauged by the size of the man's shadow in the foreground). The apples are conveyed to chopping machines and hydraulic presses from which the freshly squeezed juice and pulp flow into receiving tanks *(below)*. The mixture is then piped into huge vats *(opposite, top)* where the pulp and other sediments settle to the bottom. Next the juice is allowed to ferment for three weeks in smaller casks. The resulting cider, actually an apple wine, is blended to ensure uniform quality and then bottled for sale. Bulmer, like other cider manufacturers, also produces a draft that is shipped in barrels for consumption in West Country pubs.

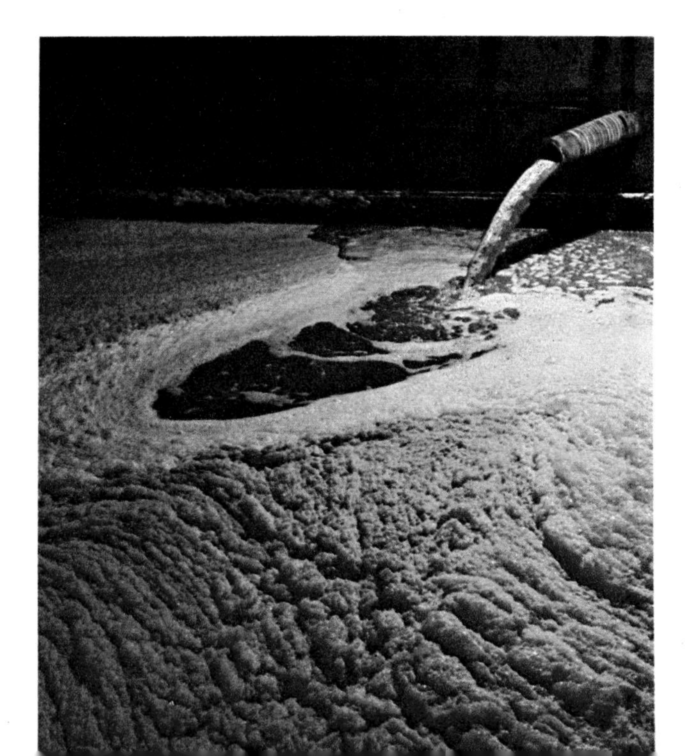

Unfermented apple juice is stored in the Bulmer factory's 121 enormous settling vats of seasoned oak. So intricately arranged and decorated that they resemble a pop-art maze *(above)*, the 22-foot-high tanks are named after honored employees, apples, birds and even countries. Arrows indicate exits from the maze. Unblended cider from fine apples is bottled much like champagne and labeled Pomagne *(right)*.

ple forget this fact. It is the fermented juice of the apple, just as French wines are the fermented juice of the grape." Most ciders are weaker than wine, but one company has been making a stronger variety that was in the past known all over England as "Merrydown vintage" cider. The Merrydown Company sold the product in secondhand champagne bottles and wooden casks, at the same time warning customers and pub owners that it was more potent than average cider, and should be sold as a wine.

Despite the warning most pubs offered Merrydown by the pint and half pint, just as they would an ordinary cider or a beer, with the result that many a customer became paralytic before the evening was half gone. I have seen hardened drinkers felled like trees after a few pints of Merrydown. Then in 1956 the tax laws changed in such a way that it became more profitable for the company to increase the alcohol content by four percentage points, and call Merrydown, not cider, but what it really was all along: apple wine. Customers still buy and drink it in quantity and are still felled like trees, but at least they know what to expect.

Even ordinary cider can be insidious, as I learned when I was 10 years old on a drive with my father somewhere in Somerset, or perhaps it was Devon. I remember that it was a summer day, one of those country days in the 1930s when the interior of a motorcar smelled of hot leather, petrol and oil, and when the slow, sputtering airplanes took a long time to cross the blue sky. When my father stopped for cider I asked for some, too, and so he went into the bar and ordered a pint for me. Out he came into the street, carrying in his hand a large flagon. "Scrumpy," the locals called it, rough, cloudy and strong. I managed half quite easily but had to leave the rest, for scrumpy is a bit too strong for a 10-year-old, a fact that became obvious when I tried to walk back to the car.

I am not surprised that the French distill their Normandy cider, and that most of their cider produce goes to make the powerful spirit that is called Calvados. Why, I once asked a Taunton cider maker, don't the English do the same? Do we not make a mistake neglecting to distill our excellent cider to make a type of Calvados? He smiled. "Maybe we do, and then maybe we don't," he said. "I am not in the position to say. But I will tell you this: Down here in the West Country we make the best cider in the world. It would be a shame to turn it into something else."

My recollection of a youthful introduction to cider prompts a similar memory of my first drink of wine. It was at a small farm in Hertfordshire owned by two sisters, the Misses Edmonds they were called, and they made the most delicious wine. It was their custom to offer a glass of homemade wine to a visitor, and children were no exception, and so I sat on the ladderback chair in the farm kitchen, my feet barely touching the floor, and sipped the heady wine from a red glass. (Curious how memory stores details like the color of a glass, or the design of a chair.) The wine—I believe that it was cherry—was strong and sweet. It was perhaps 10 years until my next introduction to English country wine, and that's a long time between drinks. On this occasion it was made from potatoes—yes, potatoes—and had lain brooding and grumbling in a cellar, biding its time, before being served to guests at a party on a houseboat in Oxford. The boat was leaking rapidly and going down by the stern, but nobody aboard seemed to mind in the least; it wasn't noticed until the river began lapping around our ankles. We drank potato wine by the bucketful; people fell into the water both inside and outside the boat; eventually the wine had shown no mercy, but gathered its strength and struck. The guests recovered, although the houseboat and the recipe—perhaps fortunately—are lost forever.

In spite of this cautionary tale, most English wine is kind and gentle. We make it from practically anything you care to name—carrots, oranges, tea leaves. There are elderberry wine and currant wine. We make cherry and sloe and oak-leaf wine. Turnips, plums, raspberries, apples, red currants and damsons all go to make individual and excellent wines. French and Italian visitors to Britain consider our wine a curiosity, refusing to concede that wine can be made of anything but the grape, but they would be hard put to tell the difference between a good Rhine wine and an English dandelion wine. We also make grape wine, though not as much as we did centuries ago. Around the time of the Norman Conquest grapes grew readily over large areas of Britain, and they were put to good use. Fruit wines were made then, too, and esteemed for their medicinal properties. Wine made from elderberries was administered as a palliator for colds and coughs; the wine from cowslip seeds was supposed to promote sleep. Parsnip wine was a laxative, while a large glass of parsley wine was drunk by the country bride and groom as a sure-fire aphrodisiac and promoter of fertility.

In those days a common wine was mead, made by fermenting honey (and often scraps from the hive that help the fermentation process) in hot water. Herbs and spices like cinnamon, ginger and coriander were then added. The result was a light, clear drink with a fine white head that did much to keep Robin Hood and his merry men merry. A book published as late as 1669 listed more than 100 recipes for mead and related drinks, but today this fine old wine is a rarity.

Port also ought to be counted as a British wine, even though it is not made in the British Isles. Its story begins, oddly enough, with a dispute between England and France in the late 17th Century. King William of Orange, a Dutchman who assumed the throne of England with his wife Mary in 1689, was a Francophobe who heavily taxed imports of French wines, forcing thirsty Englishmen to turn to Portugal for their drink. The Portuguese product proved unpalatable, however, until someone hit upon the idea of "fortifying" the wine with brandy and then aging it in a stoppered bottle. The result was port, a rich mellow drink that is just right for the damp cold of a British winter.

The prohibitive taxes on French liquors that inspired the invention of port introduced another drink to Britain. This was gin. Originally prepared in Holland as a medicine, its potent effects and simplicity of manufacture quickly made it the solace of London's lower classes. Shops selling gin spread like a malignant rash across London. By the year 1735 gin was being distilled at the rate of 5.4 million gallons per annum—or nearly a gallon per head of the population, including children.

Such quantities, it appears, were insufficient. Gin shops began to make gin substitutes to satisfy the huge demand and to counter the taxation later imposed by the government. Thousands died from the effects of such lethal concoctions as a mixture of sulfuric acid, oil of turpentine, oil of almonds, brandy, lump sugar, lime water, rose water, alum and salt of tartar. Gin shops openly advertised the price of oblivion. "Drunk for a penny, dead drunk for twopence, clean straw for nothing." It is hardly surprising that true gin took a long time to shake off its evil reputation.

Today gin, like vodka, which it resembles, is a pure, clean spirit, but with flavoring added by "botanicals"—such ingredients as juniper berries from Italy, coriander seed, orange peel, cassia bark, angelica, licorice and orris root. The proportions are the jealously guarded secret of every distiller, the secrets upon which the success of a particular brand is based. For my taste the most individual gin in Britain is the medium-dry type made in Plymouth by Coates, which prepares its gin from English grain, malted and distilled in Scotland, and finally mixed in Plymouth with a unique herbal flavoring described as "Plymouth's best-kept secret." It was in the Coates distillery that the Pilgrim Fathers gathered before their journey in the *Mayflower* to the New World, only in those days the building was a monastery. Where devout monks prayed, copper pot stills now bubble, carrying off the pure, clean spirit to be bottled for the delight of us all.

Gin is a popular tipple of the English middle class—Army and Navy officers, colonial civil servants and business executives. If you ever spot a ship of the Royal Navy displaying a green and white pennant, lose no time in getting on board, for the flag's message really means "welcome aboard for a gin." Don't ask for a whiskey, or even a rum, for gin is what you will get—iced, colored pink, and bitter from Angostura bitters. It is a drink known throughout the fleet as pink gin, an invention of the Navy.

Ashore gin and tonic is a favorite of businessmen and London advertising executives during the lunch hour. Considered to be an effective hangover remedy, it owes its origin to Britain's imperial adventures in the tropics.

The tonic part of gin and tonic came about because of Jacob Schweppe, a Swiss-born chemist who, in 18th Century Bristol, started a brisk trade selling soda water in bottles. The soda water was a great success and, in the 1860s, a small quantity of quinine, the antimalaria drug, was added by his successors. This experimental product was first marketed in the British colonies in Africa and India, where malaria was a constant hazard. To make the taking of one's medicine a pleasure rather than a chore, the quinine tonic water was inevitably combined with gin. Gin was also one of the most popular foundations of the "chota-peg" (literally, "little drink") sipped on the veranda during the Indian summer of the British raj, while watching the sun sink behind the banyan groves.

Gin is a very definite kind of drink, with its own distinctive flavor; either you like it, or you don't. I had a great-aunt who liked it, and who always kept a drop in a stone hot-water bottle under her bed, in case she got thirsty in the night. Auntie was a Victorian skeleton in the family cupboard, for gin had a long way to go toward respectability, and she was, it was whispered, a Secret Drinker! The poor old thing was ahead of her time, for today it is most respectable to drink gin, though not in considerable quantities—and never out of a stone hot-water bottle.

Auntie's drinking habits might not have been talked about so had she limited herself to Grant's cherry brandy, England's liqueur. It was so well thought of that Queen Victoria permitted her likeness to appear on the label. The creator of this genteel drink, Thomas Grant, was an austere Victorian businessman, but a very inventive one. I prefer to think of him as one of mankind's happy barmen, mixing drinks for us all. He owned a distillery and a bonded warehouse in Dover, and until one of the famous white cliffs fell on it in 1853, burying the distillery under 90,000 tons of chalk, his talents were undeveloped and unremarked. He moved to Maidstone, in the heart of the county of Kent, called the "garden of England," where apples, hops and fat cherries flourish in season. While at Dover he had been thinking that advantage might be taken of the fine Kentish Morella cherries, using them to make liqueur spiked with brandy, and from this idea was eventually born Grant's Morella cherry brandy. During the years that followed, Grant mixed, stirred, blended and tasted. He made cherry whiskey, sloe gin, ginger brandy, ginger cognac, orange gin and cognac, Hollands gin, cherry jam and cherry marmalade—and finally Grant's cherry brandy itself. In August, the ripe and delicate cherries were delivered to the Maidstone distillery for pressing. The stones were cracked and added to the cherry pulp, for these impart a distinctive almond flavor, and the whole fruity mass was left to macerate in French brandy for two months. Sugar syrup was added and the liqueur was left to mature in oak vats, which sweat and dribble slightly during the heat of summer.

Delighted customers wrote to the firm, praising the drink, and extolling its virtues. "Were its good qualities known in America," wrote one, "where so many remedies are employed to counteract the ill effects of the climate, I have no doubt whatever that it would eventually be found in every home in the land." For some inexplicable reason, it has not been taken to heart by Americans. This is the New World's everlasting loss, for few drinks go down as well as Grant's, which clings to the side of the glass, warm, sweet and glowing like a ruby, to cosset, comfort and console you during the chill months of winter, and what more can you ask?

XI

Foods of Feast and Festival

The winter sun, a disk of pale fire, climbs but a short way up the cold marble arch of our British sky. At sunset the horizon is inflamed, the color tinting the snow that lies on the frozen fields, and the entire landscape is washed in a frigid pink. Only the evergreen shrubs and trees, the holly and the ivy, and those sacred birds of winter, the robin and the wren, show that life still exists. The earth lies dormant, and sleeps.

It is all very terrifying; who among us is daring enough to prophesy with certainty that the earth will reawaken in spring? To our ancestors the ancient Britons, the onset of winter meant death, and they tried to hold back the darkness by lighting fires on the hills and offering sacrifices, real or symbolic; when months later the light and life of spring returned, they welcomed the bright new season with dancing and feasting. From harvest time to Christmas and from the beginning of Lent to Easter, the observances and festivals of the British year lie in the shadow of long-forgotten rites of the Celts, Germans, Romans and even older peoples. Bound inextricably to these customs is what we eat at such times: ritual foods, in a sense, many of which are satisfying, comforting, stomach-quelling foods.

Early in November, the Celtic Druids used to celebrate the start of their year with great symbolic fires, built to give power to the declining sun. Today in England on each November 5 we commemorate an effort by Guy Fawkes to blow up the Houses of Parliament in 1605 by burning him in effigy on big bonfires, to the accompaniment of blazing fireworks and the children's shrieks of delight. The real Fawkes was executed by hanging, not by burning, but it is the ancient fire rite that prevails. The Celts called their au-

The festive midday meal over, Dr. and Mrs. Barry Child and their daughters wait in their Sussex home for tea to steep on a Christmas afternoon. Mrs. Child baked an elaborate Christmas cake like the one pictured on page 191 besides the small mince pies and spongecake on the table in the foreground.

Continued on page 188

A Skirling Salute to a National Dish

A steaming haggis, the dish that Scotland claims as its own, is skirled to dinner by members of the Pride of Murray Pipe Band, a group of London Scotsmen. Haggis, a sheep's stomach stuffed with a pudding made of sheep's innards and oatmeal, is traditionally served at Hogmanay (New Year's Eve) celebrations held by Scottish regiments and on national occasions like Burns Night, which commemorates the birthday of the great Scots poet Robbie Burns. Behind the bearer of the haggis marches the bearer of the Scotch whisky. When the ceremonious entry is completed, the host slits the haggis open with his *skean d'hu (above)* while repeating a salutation to haggis written by Burns. After the haggis is served, the diners drench their individual portions with the Scotch, giving an additional lilt to the skirl of the pipes and the flavor of the haggis.

tumnal feast Samhain, and its proximity to Guy Fawkes Day and other modern autumn holidays—Allhallows Eve and the feasts of All Saints and All Souls, when witches fly across the sky—is all too close for comfort, betraying our subliminal instinct for ancestral modes of worship.

On those Celtic autumnal fires in prehistory, sacrifices—both human and animal—were made to some pastoral deity. Now the sacrifice consumed on Guy Fawkes Day is spicy gingerbread baked in the shape of a man. Ancient sacrificial customs are also recalled by relics of the old, world-wide business of setting out provisions for the dead; as late as the 19th Century, on the eve of the feast of All Souls, households set out "soul cakes" and glasses of wine for the spirits of the departed, who were believed to return to their earthly homes that one night of the year. In some villages children went "souling" through the streets crying: "soul, soul, for a soul cake; pray you, good mistress, a soul cake." Only a few country cooks still bake soul cakes, a pity, for these rich round buns, made with eggs, milk and spices, were a good treat.

The power of superstition is such that it diverts reason, and forges habit. Today, when an English housewife prepares her mixture for the Christmas pudding, the family all take turns in the stirring—and each makes a secret wish. But we must stir clockwise, the direction in which the sun was assumed to proceed around an earth at the center of the universe, for to stir in the opposite direction—"widdershins" as one local dialect has it—is to ask for trouble. In the same way, in certain districts of Britain, a countrywoman making jam would never dream of stirring the hot mixture counterclockwise, for such an error would ensure the failure of the jam.

Perhaps the most fascinating evidence of all of our culinary ties to the pagan past lies in the decorations on our many festive cakes, all of which have religious or mythological origins. The most obvious is, of course, the Eastertime hot cross bun *(Recipe Index)*. Its cross-shaped topping has ties extending far back into pre-Christian times. The cross has long been thought to have represented both sun and fire, the sun symbol being a circle that was bisected by two right-angled lines into four quarters, which represented the four seasons. Both the Greeks and the Romans had festive cakes that bore such a symbol. Other cakes were marked with yet another powerful fire-sun symbol that was later Christianized, a central disk like a wheel. Roman bread so marked has been found buried under the preservative volcanic ash in the ruins of Herculaneum.

One of the world's oldest festival cakes, a Shrewsbury simnel, is decorated with 12 balls of marzipan. It is traditionally baked in Britain on Mothering Sunday, a holiday antedating Mother's Day, but the cake's origins can be traced to the customs of Classical Greece.

Venerable not only in design but even in recipe is the rich, spicy cake known as Shrewsbury simnel. Baked of a very fine white flour and topped with 12 decorative balls of marzipan, it has preserved its identity through the many variations on one particular kind of holiday for thousands of years. In Britain today it is often served on Mother's Day and Easter as well. Not long ago it marked Mothering Sunday, the fourth Sunday in Lent, a day when homage was paid to the patron saint of the local church, and when children paid respects to their parents with gifts of flowers and simnel cakes. Long before that the Romans were using a fine white flour that they called *simila* to bake special ball-topped cakes for the Matronalia; on this festival, dedicated to Juno, protectress of the home, Roman wives entertained their slaves and received presents from their husbands. The significance of the 12 balls on their cakes could have been lost on the Romans, for this decoration may be a part of a still older tradition. The Athenians are said to have had a cake bearing 12 balls, perhaps in honor of the original gods of the Greek pantheon—the Titans, from whom sprang Zeus and all the rest.

Only a few festivals have foods like simnel cake with traditions so easy to trace back from culture to culture. But there is one holiday with more than its share of varied and cherished customs—a complex mixture of both ancient and fairly modern customs and symbols, many of them obscure and taken for granted—and that is Christmas. The robin appears on our Christmas cards because it and the wren were symbols of life; the robin was a sacred bird whose breast was reddened by contact with Christ's blood on the Cross. The evergreen is also a symbol of life, and when we bring evergreen and mistletoe into our houses we are performing, whether we know it or not, a very old rite. When we take a sprig of holly and stick it on top of the flaming Christmas pudding, we are said to be reminding ourselves of Christ's crown of thorns. The red holly berries are His blood.

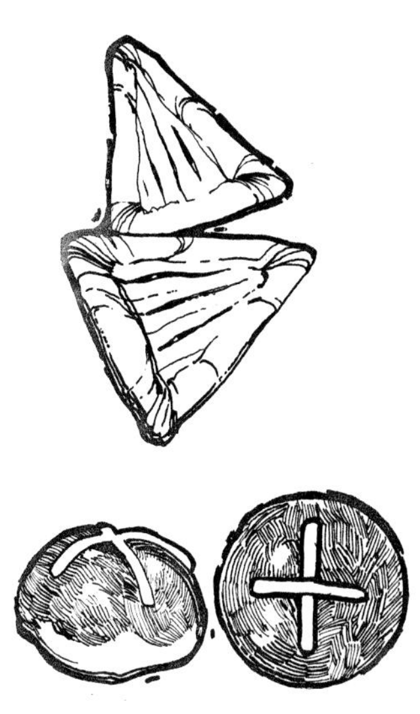

A gift to godchildren from godparents on New Year's Day, Coventry godcakes are depicted here above the hot cross buns prepared and served during Lent.

The tenacity of these traditions was brought home to me not long ago in a Christmas card I received from Australia, where Christmas is celebrated in the heat of summer. The card bore a picture of a Regency stagecoach rattling through an English village at night during a heavy fall of snow. Candles illuminated the windows of the timbered cottages and Christmas trees stood around, hung with lights. Although the picture depicted the middle of the night, a robin sat singing cheerfully on the gatepost! This is the scene that the word Christmas evokes in the minds of all Englishmen, whether they live in Borneo or in Bedfordshire.

The old-fashioned traditional Christmas does live on, most noticeably in the country. Here is the Christmas of log fires, of snow piling up outside the door; here we do indeed find the traditional bowls of hot punch, roast goose, plum pudding, port wine and nuts, and the once-a-year treat of muscat raisins, dried figs and dates, Carlsbad plums and mince pies. The faithful, blowing on numbed fingers, stamp their way to church on the bright, crisp Christmas morning. The vicar intones his message of Christmas cheer, and the hearts of the congregation are warmed by the playing of the merry organ, the sweet singing in the choir. They are also thinking of the roast turkeys and hams, the spicy puddings and rich cakes of Christmas dinner, preceded by a warming glass at the village pub.

There's very little room at the inn, for the bar is packed to capacity. It is also full of friendly talk. Colored paper decorations hang from the oak-beamed ceiling. A farmer buys his plowman a drink.

"What'll you have, Fred?"

"Thank 'ee Mr. Rose, since you're paying, oil 'ave a pint of the usual." Those standing around chuckle. "Go on, Fred, have a whisky." But Fred, the old countryman, won't change the habits of a lifetime, not even at Christmas; he's drunk beer all his life—whisky's for the gentry. Old Fred will have Christmas dinner with his daughter, who married a young farmer over Chipping Campden way. Christmas is family, you see, and his son-in-law will drive over and fetch the old man from the pub, for nobody should be alone at Christmas, and Fred's wife died these five years back. "Anyway," thinks the old man, "there will be the children, a good log fire and a glass of mulled ale," or maybe he'll have ginger wine, for the cold fair nips at you when you are nearing 70.

Continued on page 193

An Elegant English Christmas Cake

To an Englishman, Christmas cake always means a large, rich dark fruitcake—and it is as much a part of the holiday tradition as a yule log. In the northern shires, the cake is simply decorated with toasted almonds or marzipan and perhaps a sprig of holly. But in the south the adornment is elaborate, as these pictures show, though the cake underneath is much the same. The recipe is on page 198. At left, the basic cake rests on a pedestal surrounded by such ingredients as candied fruit, raisins, eggs, nuts and spirits. To add the decoration, the first step is to paint the top and sides with a glaze of jam. Carefully fit a

1

2

rolled-out round of the almond-based marzipan over the top *(1)*. Next, gently turn down the edges of the marzipan lid and wrap the sides of the cake in a strip of marzipan *(2)*. The cake is now ready for the frosting. Spread it lavishly on the cake, roughing it up around the sides *(3 and 4)* to resemble drifting snow. The frosting will harden into a crisp coating over the soft marzipan underneath. Before bringing the cake to the table, decorate the top with small Christmas ornaments such as the tiny trees shown at right. For a finishing touch, pipe a holiday greeting onto the cake with red-tinted frosting.

3

4

Later, while sitting in the back of the car, a rug over his knees, he thinks of the past, and little of the future. His daughter never made a Christmas spread as good as his old lady did, but then times are changing, even in the country. Today they'll have a big, fat turkey, but he would rather have a roast goose, its crisp skin and rich dark meat fragrant with that sweet applesauce-and-sage stuffing.

The jolly, rollicking feasts of Christmases past that old Fred remembers so fondly were those of the sort that Charles Dickens immortalized in *A Christmas Carol*. In the gaiety and good eating that went on at Bob Cratchit's humble household can be seen the pleasure that made the old-fashioned English Christmas a true tradition:

> Mrs. Cratchit made the gravy (ready beforehand in a little saucepan) hissing hot; Master Peter mashed the potatoes with incredible vigor; Miss Belinda sweetened up the apple-sauce; Martha dusted the hot plates. . . . At last the dishes were set on, and grace was said. It was succeeded by a breathless pause, as Mrs. Cratchit, looking slowly all along the carving-knife, prepared to plunge it in the breast; but when she did, and when the long-expected gush of stuffing issued forth, one murmur of delight arose all round the board, and even Tiny Tim, excited by the two young Cratchits, beat on the table with the handle of his knife and feebly cried, Hurrah!
>
> There never was such a goose. Bob said he didn't believe there ever was such a goose cooked. Its tenderness and flavor, size and cheapness, were the themes of universal admiration. Eked out by apple-sauce and mashed potatoes, it was a sufficient dinner for the whole family; indeed, as Mrs. Cratchit said with great delight (surveying one small atom of a bone upon the dish), they hadn't ate it all at last! Yet every one had had enough, and the youngest Cratchits, in particular, were steeped in sage and onion to the eyebrows! But now, the plates being changed by Miss Belinda, Mrs. Cratchit left the room alone—too nervous to bear witnesses—to take the pudding up, and bring it in.
>
> Suppose it should not be done enough! Suppose it should break in turning out! Suppose somebody should have got over the wall of the back yard, and stolen it, while they were merry with the goose—a supposition at which the two young Cratchits became livid! All sorts of horrors were supposed.
>
> Hallo! A great deal of steam! The pudding was out of the copper. A smell like a washing-day! That was the cloth. A smell like an eating-house and a pastry-cook's next door to each other, with a laundress's next door to that! That was the pudding! In half a minute Mrs. Cratchit entered—flushed but smiling proudly—with the pudding, like a speckled cannon-ball, so hard and firm, blazing in half of half-a-quarter of ignited brandy, and bedight with Christmas holly stuck into the top.
>
> Oh, a wonderful pudding! Bob Cratchit said, and calmly too, that he regarded it as the greatest success achieved by Mrs. Cratchit since their marriage . . . they were happy, grateful, pleased with one another, and contented with the time. . . .

Opposite:
Flaming cognac forms a soft halo on a solid Yuletide dessert, a plum pudding based on suet and dried and candied fruits *(Recipe Index)*. Many British families identify this dish so firmly with the holiday season that they call it Christmas pudding, and make their own versions according to personal, handed-down recipes.

Even today in the farms around Fred's village you may be offered a dinner like that, and the drinks to go with it. You might find fruit wines that have been maturing through the year in casks and bottles, for visitors will be offered winter potations designed to keep the frost out, to warm the blood and redden the nose, the most warming and nose-reddening of which is Scotch and ginger wine, known as "whisky Mac." At this holiday season, also, mulled ale and the dark, strong ales come into their own: Stingo, Russian stout and barley wine. There's cherry brandy, and there's gin flavored with the tart, dark-purple sloes of the hedgerows—sloe gin. And, of course, there is punch, perhaps a "bishop" punch, for which an orange, studded with cloves, is steeped in hot port wine.

It was the country gentlemen of the late 17th Century who discovered the pleasures of the holiday punch bowl, soon after rum was first brought to England from Jamaica. The huge silver bowl of hot punch containing rum and brandy, ale, oranges and lemons, and mixed spices was the feature of every squire's Christmas hospitality, of every fox-hunting household and gentlemen's club. Songs were composed to the glory of the flowing bowl, urging drinkers to: "Heap on more coal there/And keep the glass moving/The frost nips my nose,/Though my heart glows with loving/Here's the dear creature,/No skylights—a bumper;/He who leaves the heeltaps/I vote him a mumper./With hey cow rumble O,/Whack! populorum,/Merrily, merrily, men,/Push round the jorum."

"No skylights—a bumper" meant a brimful glass. "Heeltaps" referred to a glass not drained to the last drop. A "mumper" was a beggar, and "jorum" referred to a punch bowl.

Christmas in the country is the time and the place to feast on local specialties. The country shires all have their own contributions to Christmas eating. In Yorkshire they eat Yule bread, a sweet dough filled with currants and candied peel. With it is served cheese, orange jelly with cream, gingerbread with ginger wine, and the cake called parkin. This dark-brown, sweet biscuitlike cake of oatmeal and flour, flavored with ginger, dark syrup and cinnamon will keep for weeks—even months—and improves with keeping. Yorkshire people will tell you that their recipe is the only "true" one, but the parkin made over the border in Lancashire tastes just as good to me. But how would I know? I'm only a southerner. Similarly, Cumberland gave us rum butter to have with our Christmas pudding, and also from Cumberland came "standing pie," or "sweet pie," filled with chopped mutton, apples and raisins, the grandfather of the mince pie. The Scots follow Christmas with a New Year celebration at which everyone eats haggis with his whisky; the Scots also relish "black bun," a rich fruit cake in a coat of pastry.

If some of these foods are eaten mainly in their native shires, to every table in the land comes one holiday dish: the Christmas pudding, mystic, dark, and wreathed in flames. Today the Christmas pudding is a fruity, brandy-soused offering. But it was a plum porridge when Shakespeare was a lad, made of meat broth, fruit juice, wine, prunes, mace and bread crumbs, and served in a semiliquid state. Charles II saw plum porridge solidify into the true Christmas pudding in the late 1600s. The fruity alcoholic aroma of the royal Christmas pudding delighted George I when it was served to him at 6 o'clock in the evening of December 25, 1714, his first Christmas in England after his arrival from Hanover to take the throne. In those days the pudding was shaped into a ball, simply wrapped in a cloth, and boiled. One hundred and fifty years were to pass before the Victorians put it in a basin to boil it, as we still do today *(Recipe Index)*.

Another traditional Christmas treat eaten the length and breadth of the land is mince pie *(Recipe Index)*. It, like the Christmas pudding, has changed in shape and content over the years. Three centuries ago mince pie was a huge dish called "Christmas pye," and described as "a most learned mixture of Neats-tongues [ox tongues], chicken, eggs, sugar, raisins, lemon and orange peel, various kinds of Spicery, etc." Over the years the pies grew smaller, and the meat content was gradually reduced until the pies were simply filled with a mixture of suet, spices and dried fruit, previously marinated in brandy. This filling was then put into little pastry cases that were covered with lids of additional pastry and the pies were then baked in an oven. Essentially, this is today's mince pie.

Mince pies are nowadays rarely eaten except at Christmas time, but a much larger version made on a plate and containing the same mixture is frequently met at all times of the year, particularly in pubs, where it is usually served with custard. Custard, that sweet, yellow sauce, often made today from a packaged mix, is ubiquitous in Britain; it was probably this sauce that prompted Count Carrocioli, the 18th Century Neapolitan ambassador to London, to remark: "There are in England sixty different religions, and only one sauce."

The modern festal board contains many reminders of tradition. The rich Elizabethans prized the Saturnalian boar's head, garlanded with branches of laurel in the Roman fashion, as their Christmas centerpiece, just as today we have a turkey, now garlanded with sausages. They drank from the wassail bowl, full of spiced ale with roasted apples floating in it, a custom borrowed from the Saxons who drank from it to the toast of "Waes Hael!"—"Good Health!" The Elizabethans also enjoyed stuffed pike and oysters, game, beef, sweet syllabub and mead, milk and fruit puddings, cheesecakes and currant cakes, dried figs and dates.

But half a century after Elizabeth there came a bleak time when we enjoyed no boar's head, no wassail—and in fact no Christmas at all. The Puritans under Oliver Cromwell abolished the whole thing. The streets of London echoed not to caroling but to town criers' braying, "No Christmas! No Christmas!" And when Londoners still decked their houses and streets with evergreen boughs, the Lord Mayor had all the greenery gathered up and burned. Fortunately, Cromwell and such nonsense didn't last.

The turkey had been introduced to us from the New World via Spain around a century before that, but it took the bird a long time to replace the boar's head, of which Queen Anne's physician, Dr. William King, still sang praises in 1709: "At Christmas time be careful of your Fame,/See the old Tenant's Table be the same:/Then if you would send up the Brawnwer's Head,/ Sweet Rosemary and Bays around it spread:/His foaming tusks let some large Pippin grace,/Or 'midst these turnd'ring spears an Orange place,/ Sauce like himself, offensive to its Foes,/The Roguish Mustard, dang'rous to the Nose,/Sack and well-spic'd Hippocras the Wine,/Wassail the Bowl with antient Ribbands fine,/Poridge with Plumbs, and Turkeys with the Chine [backbone]."

Personally, I am on the side of the Queen's physician; turkey, to my mind, is one of the least interesting exports from the New World to the Old, and should come last in any listing of Christmas favorites. Like old Fred the plowman and many other Britons I prefer to see the more traditional goose upon my Christmas table. For my taste the turkey is too tough a bird for roasting, but you might try another method suggested by this Old English saying: "Turkey boiled is turkey spoiled./And turkey roast is turkey lost,!/But for turkey braised!/The Lord be praised." Braising is one of the best ways of cooking a meat that is inclined toward dryness during roasting, for braising helps to retain the natural flavor and keep the juices within the meat.

The stuffed turkey, browned in butter, is placed on a bed of chopped, sautéed vegetables—tomato, celery, onion, carrot and leek—in a casserole large enough to receive it. Strips of bacon should be laid over the bird, and a bouquet of herbs (thyme, marjoram, bay leaf) added to the pot, as well as a cupful of water or stock. Then the casserole is covered and cooked in a slow oven until the turkey is tender and moist as it should be for a proper Christmas dish.

A characteristic of the Christmas meal is not so much variety of choice as the quantity of food consumed. Rarely is there a soup, an hors d'oeuvre, a piece of fish, or any other overture. In most British homes we get down right away to the basics, to the turkey or the goose with its accompaniment of sausages; stuffing; roast, mashed or boiled potatoes; brussels sprouts and green peas; lashings of gravy. Many cooks—my mother included—frequently serve a large boiled ham in addition. A second helping of everything for everyone is the rule, perhaps a third helping for big appetites.

The Christmas drinks that precede or accompany the meal have given us courage to face whatever follows the mighty meat course. And what comes next? Christmas pudding, of course! How can we possibly meet such a challenge? Yet here is the pudding, heavy with fruit, drenched in brandy, wreathed in a smile of pale-blue flames and wearing its sprig of red-berried holly. The spoon scoops a moist, generous portion of flaming pudding on to the proffered plate. There is little doubt that plates will be scraped clean, just in time for that second helping. In our family the pudding is served with either a cream or a hard sauce. A hard sauce is made of creamed butter and sugar with rum or brandy. One of the most famous hard sauces is Cumberland rum butter *(Recipe Index)*. The rum butter has been chilling for a while in the refrigerator; the combination of the cold hard sauce and the hot, soft pudding is too enticing to resist.

Christmas puddings are often made months in advance, and the fruit frequently ferments, increasing the proof of the pudding. I have a pudding made some years ago that for some reason we never got around to eating; it has been gathering strength for so long that I am almost afraid of it.

Following the pudding on most Christmas tables, comes a plate piled with hot little mince pies, dusted with sugar. Also on the table you might find boxes of sticky dates, Turkish delight, Chinese figs, muscat raisins and Carlsbad plums. Bowls of assorted nuts are offered with the port or with the coffee and brandy. Everyone is given a Christmas snapper to pull, and he who pulls hardest generally gets a paper hat and a slip of paper bearing a joke or motto. The jokes are uniformly bad, but on Christmas Day no one, especially the children who haven't heard them before, seems to mind: "An elephant saw a mouse for the first time. 'My,' said the elephant, 'aren't you small?' 'Oh, well,' replied the mouse, 'I've been ill.' "

After such a meal most of us grope for an armchair and sit transfixed, bemused and stunned, watching television and wearing foolish grins. The elderly stagger up to bed while the children, as only children can, their reserves of energy unaffected by food, play with their new toys. Some of us, hardy, go out and walk it off.

Then, late in the afternoon at teatime, there is rich Christmas cake *(Recipe Index)*. There are some people who can manage a slice or two at tea, but I never can, and anyway, I don't really like it. No one in our family likes it, yet in spite of this my mother bakes a huge Christmas cake every year, mainly because she always has. Tradition is another way of saying habit. A Christmas cake is always a large, dark fruitcake. In the North of England it is generally decorated with toasted almonds or marzipan and a sprig of holly, but no white icing, for only wedding cakes are iced in the north. In the south, however, you'll usually see a Christmas cake that is heavily iced with a white, hard icing, roughed up to resemble an expanse of snow, and decorated with little figures: evergreen trees, Santa Claus, reindeer, a robin; a big frilly ribbon may go around the cake.

The day after Christmas is Boxing Day, when some of us go out to visit relatives and friends, and unless our timing is good we may be offered another Christmas dinner, but usually it's cold goose or turkey, ham and sausages. Slices of yesterday's Christmas pudding, now just like cake, are served with what remains of the brandy butter, and more mince pies are popped in the oven for a few minutes. A great combination is the cold goose, chutney and hot bubble and squeak *(Chapter 5)*.

This, then, is Christmas. It has meant weeks of preparation and cooking, the results to be devoured in two short days. A man lies asleep in an armchair. On his head a yellow paper hat from a Christmas snapper slips down over one eye. He snores. A cigar from a gift box is wedged, unlit, between two fingers. Logs crackle and hiss in the fire. For the man and the children, Christmas comes but once a year; and the women washing the dishes in the kitchen are glad; but for those of us who revel in the glories of British food, it is still the best of all possible days.

CHAPTER XI RECIPES

To make one 12-inch round fruitcake

CAKE

- ½ pound (2 sticks) plus 4 tablespoons butter, softened
- 2 cups finely chopped mixed candied fruit peel (about 10 ounces)
- 2 cups white raisins (about 10 ounces)
- 1½ cups dried currants (about 8 ounces)
- 1 cup seedless raisins (about 5 ounces)
- ½ cup candied cherries, cut in half (about 4 ounces)
- ½ cup finely chopped candied angelica (about 4 ounces)
- 2 cups all-purpose flour
- ½ teaspoon double-acting baking powder
- ½ teaspoon salt
- 1 cup dark-brown sugar
- 1 cup shelled almonds (about 6 ounces), pulverized in a blender or with a nut grinder or mortar and pestle
- 4 eggs
- ¼ cup pale dry sherry, rum or brandy

GLAZE

- ¼ cup red currant jelly *(Recipe Booklet)*

MARZIPAN

- 2 cups almond paste
- 1 teaspoon almond extract
- ½ teaspoon salt
- 1 cup light corn syrup
- 7 cups confectioners' sugar (2 pounds), sifted

ICING

- 6 cups confectioners' sugar, sifted
- 4 egg whites
- 1 tablespoon strained fresh lemon juice
- ⅛ teaspoon salt

English Christmas Cake

Preheat the oven to 325°. Using a pastry brush, coat the bottom and sides of a 12-by-3-inch springform cake pan with 2 tablespoons of the softened butter. Coat one side of a 20-inch strip of wax paper with 2 tablespoons of butter, and fit the paper, greased side up, inside the pan.

In a large bowl, combine the fruit peel, white raisins, currants, seedless raisins, cherries and angelica. Sprinkle the fruit with ½ cup of the flour, tossing it about with a spoon to coat the pieces evenly. Set aside. Then sift the remaining 1½ cups of flour with the baking powder and salt. Set aside.

In another large bowl, cream the remaining ½ pound of butter with the brown sugar by mashing and beating them against the sides of the bowl until they are light and fluffy. Add the pulverized almonds, then beat in the eggs one at a time. Add the flour-and-baking-powder mixture, a half cup or so at a time, then beat the fruit mixture into the batter. Finally, add the sherry and pour the batter into the springform pan. It should come to no more than an inch from the top. If necessary, remove and discard any excess.

Bake in the middle of the oven for 1 hour and 45 minutes, or until a cake tester inserted in the center of the cake comes out clean. Let the cake cool for 30 minutes before removing the sides of the springform, then slip it off the bottom of the pan onto a cake rack to cool completely. Then carefully peel off the paper.

Heat the currant jelly in a small saucepan over moderate heat until it reaches a temperature of 225° on a candy thermometer or is thick enough to coat a wooden spoon lightly. With a small metal spatula, spread the hot glaze evenly over the top and sides of the cake.

To make the marzipan, use an electric mixer, preferably one equipped with a paddle. Crumble the almond paste in small pieces into the bowl, add the almond extract and ½ teaspoon of salt, and beat at medium speed until well blended. Gradually add the corn syrup in a thin stream, beating constantly until the mixture is smooth. Then beat in the 7 cups of confectioners' sugar, ½ cup at a time. As soon as the mixture becomes so stiff that it clogs the beater, knead in the remaining sugar with your hands. From time to time it will be necessary to soften the marzipan as you add the sugar by placing it on a surface and kneading it for a few minutes. Press the ball down, push it forward, and fold it back on itself, repeating the process as long as necessary to make it pliable.

On a clean surface, roll out half the marzipan into a circle about ½ inch thick. Using a 12-inch pan or plate as a pattern, cut a 12-inch disc out of the circle with a pastry wheel or small, sharp knife. Roll and cut the remaining marzipan into a 36-by-3-inch strip. Gently set the disc of marzipan on top of the cake and press it lightly into place. Wrap the strip of marzipan around the cake, pressing it gently to secure it. If the strip overlaps the top, fold the rim down lightly *(pictures, pages 190-191)*.

Wrap the cake in foil or plastic, and let it stand at room temperature for at least 48 hours before icing. The cake may be stored for longer periods; it improves with age, and can be kept for several months.

Just before serving, ice the cake. Combine the 6 cups of confectioners' sugar, egg whites, lemon juice and 1/8 teaspoon salt in a large mixing bowl. With a whisk or a rotary or electric beater, beat until the mixture is fluffy but firm enough to stand in soft peaks on the beater when it is lifted out of the bowl. With a small metal spatula, spread the icing evenly over the sides and top of the cake. Then decorate the cake to your taste with swirls of icing, fresh or artificial holly and mistletoe, candied fruits, or even small china reindeer, people and houses.

Plum Pudding

To make 4 puddings

- 1 1/2 cups dried currants
- 2 cups seedless raisins
- 2 cups white raisins
- 3/4 cup finely chopped candied mixed fruit peel
- 3/4 cup finely chopped candied cherries
- 1 cup blanched slivered almonds
- 1 medium-sized tart cooking apple, peeled, quartered, cored and coarsely chopped
- 1 small carrot, scraped and coarsely chopped
- 2 tablespoons finely grated orange peel
- 2 teaspoons finely grated lemon peel
- 1/2 pound finely chopped beef suet
- 2 cups all-purpose flour
- 4 cups fresh soft crumbs, made from homemade-type white bread, pulverized in a blender or shredded with a fork
- 1 cup dark-brown sugar
- 1 teaspoon ground allspice
- 1 teaspoon salt
- 6 eggs
- 1 cup brandy
- 1/3 cup fresh orange juice
- 1/4 cup fresh lemon juice
- 1/2 cup brandy, for flaming (optional)

In a large, deep bowl, combine the currants, seedless raisins, white raisins, candied fruit peel, cherries, almonds, apple, carrot, orange and lemon peel, and beef suet, tossing them about with a spoon or your hands until well mixed. Stir in the flour, bread crumbs, brown sugar, allspice and salt.

In a separate bowl, beat the eggs until frothy. Stir in the 1 cup of brandy, the orange and lemon juice, and pour this mixture over the fruit mixture. Knead vigorously with both hands, then beat with a wooden spoon until all the ingredients are blended. Drape a dampened kitchen towel over the bowl and refrigerate for at least 12 hours.

Spoon the mixture into four 1-quart English pudding basins or plain molds, filling them to within 2 inches of their tops. Cover each mold with a strip of buttered foil, turning the edges down and pressing the foil tightly around the sides to secure it. Drape a dampened kitchen towel over each mold and tie it in place around the sides with a long piece of kitchen cord. Bring two opposite corners of the towel up to the top and knot them in the center of the mold; then bring up the remaining two corners and knot them similarly.

Place the molds in a large pot and pour in enough boiling water to come about three fourths of the way up their sides. Bring the water to a boil over high heat, cover the pot tightly, reduce the heat to its lowest point and steam the puddings for 8 hours. As the water in the steamer boils away, replenish it with additional boiling water.

When the puddings are done, remove them from the water and let them cool to room temperature. Then remove the towels and foil and re-cover the molds tightly with fresh foil. Refrigerate the puddings for at least 3 weeks before serving. Plum puddings may be kept up to a year in the refrigerator or other cool place; traditionally, they were often made a year in advance.

To serve, place the mold in a pot and pour in enough boiling water to come about three fourths of the way up the sides of the mold. Bring to a boil over high heat, cover the pot, reduce the heat to low and steam for 2 hours. Run a knife around the inside edges of the mold and place an inverted serving plate over it. Grasping the mold and plate firmly together, turn them over. The pudding should slide out easily.

Christmas pudding is traditionally accompanied by Cumberland rum butter or brandy butter *(next page)*. Small paper-wrapped coins (such as sixpences and threepenny bits) are sometimes pressed into the pudding as good-luck pieces just before it is served.

If you would like to set the pudding aflame before you serve it, warm the 1/2 cup of brandy in a small saucepan over low heat, ignite it with a match and pour it flaming over the pudding.

Cumberland Rum Butter

To make about 3/4 cup

- 4 tablespoons unsalted butter, softened
- 1/2 cup light-brown sugar, rubbed through a sieve
- 1/4 cup light rum
- 1/8 teaspoon ground nutmeg

Combine the butter, sugar, rum and nutmeg in a bowl, and beat with an electric beater until smooth and well blended. (By hand, cream the butter by beating and mashing it against the sides of a mixing bowl with a spoon until it is light and fluffy. Beat in the sugar, a few tablespoons at a time, and then the rum and nutmeg.) Refrigerate for at least 4 hours, or until firm. Cumberland rum butter is traditionally served with plum pudding *(preceding page)*.

Brandy Butter

To make about 3/4 cup

- 4 tablespoons unsalted butter, softened
- 1/2 cup superfine sugar
- 3 tablespoons brandy
- 1/2 teaspoon vanilla extract

Combine the butter, sugar, brandy and vanilla in a bowl, and beat with an electric beater until the mixture is smooth and well blended. (By hand, cream the butter by beating and mashing it against the sides of a mixing bowl with a spoon until it is light and fluffy. Beat in the sugar, a few tablespoons at a time, and continue beating until the mixture is very white and frothy. Beat in the brandy and vanilla.) Refrigerate at least 4 hours, or until firm. Brandy butter is traditionally served with plum pudding *(preceding page)*, and may be sprinkled with ground nutmeg before serving.

Spiced Beef

To serve 8 to 12

- 1/4 cup dark-brown sugar
- A 3- to 4-pound lean fresh brisket of beef
- 1/4 cup whole juniper berries
- 1 tablespoon whole allspice
- 1 tablespoon whole black peppercorns
- 1/4 cup coarse (kosher) salt
- 3/4 cup cold water

NOTE: This old traditional recipe is a comparatively simple one, but the beef does require almost 2 weeks of marination.

With your fingertips, firmly press the brown sugar into the brisket. When the meat is well coated on all sides, place it in a 5- to 6-quart casserole or baking dish. Cover and refrigerate undisturbed for 2 days.

With a mortar and pestle, crush the juniper berries, allspice, peppercorns and salt together, or wrap them in a towel and crush with a rolling pin. Once a day for 9 days, press about 1 tablespoon of the spice mixture into the surface of the meat, cover and return it to the refrigerator.

On the 12th day, preheat the oven to 275°. Rinse the beef under cold running water to remove any spices adhering to it, and pour off all the accumulated liquid in the casserole. Return the beef to the casserole and add the 3/4 cup of water. Cover and bake undisturbed in the middle of the oven for 3 1/2 hours, or until the meat is tender and shows no resistance when pierced with a fork. Then cool the meat to room temperature and wrap it in foil. Place a flat plate or board on top of it, and weight it with a heavy pan or casserole weighing at least 3 or 4 pounds. Refrigerate the weighted meat overnight or for at least 12 hours. To serve, carve the beef into the thinnest possible slices and accompany it with freshly baked bread and butter.

Tightly wrapped in foil and refrigerated, spiced beef will keep for as long as 4 weeks. When the beef is fully chilled, the weight may be removed.

Mince Pies

To make eight 2 1/2-inch pies

- 8 teaspoons butter, softened
- Short-crust pastry *(page 107)*
- 1 1/2 cups mincemeat *(opposite)*

Preheat the oven to 375°. With a pastry brush, coat the bottom and sides of eight 2 1/2-inch tart tins with the softened butter, allowing 1 teaspoon of butter for each tin. (These mince pies are most successful baked in specialized tart tins, available in well-stocked housewares stores; check the size by measuring the diameter of the bottom, not the top.)

On a lightly floured surface, roll out the pastry into a circle about 1/8 inch thick. With a cookie cutter or the rim of a glass, cut sixteen 3 1/2-inch rounds of pastry. Gently press 8 of the rounds, 1 at a time, into the tart tins. Then spoon about 3 tablespoons of mincemeat into each pastry shell. With a pastry brush dipped in cold water, lightly moisten the outside edges of the pastry shells and carefully fit the remaining 8 rounds over them. Crimp the edges of the pastry together with your fingers or press them with the tines of a fork. Trim the excess pastry from around the rims with a sharp knife, and cut two 1/2-inch long parallel slits about 1/4 inch apart in the top of each of the pies.

Arrange the pies on a large baking sheet, and bake them in the middle of the oven for 10 minutes. Reduce the heat to 350° and bake for 20 minutes longer, or until the crust is golden brown. Run the blade of a knife around the inside edges of the pies to loosen them slightly, and set them aside to cool in the pans. Then turn out the pies with a narrow spatula and serve.

NOTE: Mince pies are traditional Christmas fare, often served with whipped cream, Cumberland rum butter or brandy butter *(both opposite)*.

Mincemeat

To make about 3 quarts

- 1/2 pound fresh beef suet, chopped fine
- 4 cups seedless raisins
- 2 cups dried currants
- 1 cup coarsely chopped almonds
- 1/2 cup coarsely chopped candied citron
- 1/2 cup coarsely chopped dried figs
- 1/2 cup coarsely chopped candied orange peel
- 1/4 cup coarsely chopped candied lemon peel
- 4 cups coarsely chopped, peeled and cored cooking apples
- 1 1/4 cups sugar
- 1 teaspoon ground nutmeg
- 1 teaspoon ground allspice
- 1 teaspoon ground cinnamon
- 1/2 teaspoon ground cloves
- 2 1/2 cups brandy
- 1 cup pale dry sherry

Combine the suet, raisins, currants, almonds, citron, dried figs, candied orange peel, candied lemon peel, apples, sugar, nutmeg, allspice, cinnamon and cloves in a large mixing bowl and stir them together thoroughly. Pour in the brandy and sherry, and mix with a large wooden spoon until all the ingredients are well moistened. Cover the bowl and set the mincemeat aside in a cool place (not the refrigerator) for at least 3 weeks. Check the mincemeat once a week. As the liquid is absorbed by the fruit, replenish it with sherry and brandy, using about 1/4 cup at a time. Mincemeat can be kept indefinitely in a covered container in a cool place, without refrigeration, but after a month or so you may refrigerate it if you like.

Irish Christmas Cake

To make one 9-inch round white fruitcake

- 3/4 pound (3 sticks) plus 2 tablespoons butter, softened
- 1 1/4 cups plus 2 tablespoons all-purpose flour
- 2/3 cup coarsely chopped candied cherries
- 1 1/4 cups seedless raisins
- 1 1/4 cups white raisins
- 1 1/4 cups dried currants
- 1/4 cup finely chopped mixed candied fruit peel
- 2 tablespoons finely chopped candied angelica
- 1 1/4 cups sugar
- 7 eggs
- 1 teaspoon ground allspice
- 1 tablespoon salt
- 1 cup finely chopped walnuts

Preheat the oven to 300°. Using a pastry brush, coat the bottom and sides of a 9-by-3-inch springform cake pan with 2 tablespoons of the softened butter. Sprinkle 2 tablespoons of the flour into the pan, tip it from side to side to spread the flour evenly, then invert the pan and rap it sharply on the bottom to remove excess flour. Combine the cherries, seedless and white raisins, currants, candied peel and angelica in a bowl, add 1/4 cup of the flour, and toss the fruit about with a spoon to coat the pieces evenly. Set aside.

In a large bowl, cream 3/4 pound of softened butter and the sugar and 2 more tablespoons of the flour together by mashing and beating them against the sides of the bowl until they are light and fluffy. Beat in the eggs, one at a time, then slowly beat in the remaining flour, the allspice and the salt. Combine the nuts with the fruit mixture and add the mixture to the batter, about 1/2 cup at a time, beating well after each addition. Pour the batter into the prepared pan, spreading it out with a spatula. Bake in the middle of the oven for 1 1/2 hours, or until the top of the cake is light golden in color or a cake tester inserted in the center comes out clean. Cool the cake completely before removing it from the pan.

ALE: Originally applied to a variety of malt drinks brewed without hops but now used by most Englishmen interchangeably with "beer."

ANGELS ON HORSEBACK: A "savory" (see entry, below) consisting of oysters rolled in bacon and grilled.

BANBURY CAKE: A flat, round pastry with a filling of spiced and sugared dried fruits.

BANNOCKS: Flat, round Scottish cakes of oat, rye or barley meal, baked on a hearth or griddle or in the oven.

BATH OLIVER: A thin wheat cracker eaten with cheese, first made at Bath by, legend says, one Dr. Oliver.

BEEF TEA: A nutritious beef broth made from beef extract and often given to invalids and convalescents.

BISCUIT: A hard, flat cracker or cookie.

BITTER: A rich amber-colored beer, strongly flavored with hops, and Britain's most popular.

BLACK BUN: A rich Scottish fruitcake baked in a case of short-crust pastry (see entry, below).

BLACK PUDDING: A sausage made of pig's blood, suet and oatmeal.

BOXTY: Irish potato pancakes.

BRAWN: A cold aspic made with fleshy bits of meat clinging to the knuckles, feet and other bones of an animal, cooked with onions and spices. Frequently made with a pig's head and feet. Similar to American head cheese.

BUBBLE AND SQUEAK: A dish of leftover cabbage and potatoes, chopped and fried together.

BUNS: Small, light, sweet cakes made from a yeast dough and often with dried fruits.

CHIPS: French-fried potatoes, as in fish and chips.

CIDER: Fermented apple juice, often sparkling, with an alcohol content as high as 15 per cent.

CLARET: Commonly used term covering all the red wines of Bordeaux.

COCKALEEKIE: A Scottish soup made from a stewing hen and leeks.

COLCANNON: An Irish dish made of potatoes, cabbage and scallions.

COTTAGE LOAF: A traditional crusty loaf of white bread, made by placing a small ball of dough on top of a large one, producing a loaf with a topknot.

COTTAGE PIE: A meat pie, also known as shepherd's pie, made of ground leftover meat and onions and topped with mashed potatoes.

CRISPS: Potato chips.

CRUMPETS: A small, flat breadlike cake, somewhat similar to what Americans call an English muffin. The British variety is thinner and spongier than the American.

DAMSON CHEESE: A paste made from the fruit of the damson tree.

DEVILED: Used to describe dishes prepared with spicy sauce or seasoning, as in deviled kidneys. British spelling: *devilled*.

DESSERT: Originally a sweet course —usually consisting of fruit, candies or ices—that concluded a meal, and still used by some in this sense. Or, any sweet course in a meal.

FLAN: A shallow shell of pastry filled with any of a variety of jellied fruits or custards.

FOOL: A thick purée made from soft fresh fruit and sugar and mixed with cream or custard. Served chilled.

GAME CHIPS: Potato chips served with game.

GOLDEN SYRUP: A lightly caramelized syrup of cane sugar.

HAGGIS: A rich meat pudding made of sheep's innards, oatmeal, suet, herbs and spices cooked in a sheep's stomach.

HOT POT: A traditional oven-baked casserole made of cheap cuts of meat, onions and potatoes.

JOINT: A roast of meat and the main dish of a meal.

JUGGED: Traditional method of cooking game, poultry or meat in a covered jug, jar or other earthenware vessel.

KEDGEREE: A dish made of fish (often smoked), rice, eggs and seasonings.

KIPPERS: Herring that have been split, salted, dried and smoked. A Scottish specialty.

MAIDS OF HONOR: Small, round pastry tarts with a rich almond filling. British spelling: *honour*.

MASH: Colloquialism for mashed potatoes.

MILD: The cheapest of British beers; it is low in alcohol and is mildly flavored with hops.

MINCE: Colloquialism for ground, or "minced," meat; not to be confused with mincemeat, the term for pie filling that may or may not contain meat.

MULLED: Characterizes wine or ale heated (originally with a red-hot poker) with sugar and spices and served as a hot punch.

MULLIGATAWNY: A rich soup made from chicken or lamb stock highly seasoned with curry powder; the name comes from the days of British India and derives from two colloquial Indian words meaning "pepper" and "water."

PARKIN: A flat biscuitlike cake made of oatmeal and spices. A specialty of the North of England.

PASTY: A small pillow-shaped pastry pie filled with meat, onions and potatoes, as in Cornish pasty.

PIE: A baked pastry consisting of a mixture of meats or game or fish or vegetables or fruit covered with or enclosed in a crust. One version, meat or game in aspic in a shell of hard "hot-water" pastry, was originally raised around a mold by hand and hence was known as a raised or hand-raised pie.

PIPPIN: A well-known variety of English eating apple, as in Cox's Orange Pippin.

POTTED: Used to describe fish, meat, poultry or game pounded with lard or butter into a coarse or smooth paté and preserved in jars or pots.

PUB: Colloquialism for "public house," i.e., a place in which the public is served drinks and sometimes food, as distinct from a private establishment like a club.

PUDDING: A term often used to describe the sweet course following the main course in a meal, also sometimes called the sweet or dessert course. Also, a very broad term encompassing a number of steamed, boiled or baked dishes (as distinct from courses in a meal) that may be based on anything from custards and fruits to meats and vegetables.

RAISED PIE: See *Pie*.

RISSOLES: Patties of ground meat or fish rolled in eggs and bread crumbs and fried. The equivalent of croquettes.

ROUGH PUFF PASTRY: A flaky, puffy crust made from a rich, buttery dough that has been rolled out a number of times.

SAVORY: A nonsweet course, served in a meal after a sweet course, perhaps a small canapé-like dish such as angels on horseback or Welsh rabbit. British spelling: *savoury*.

SCONE: A teacake made with baking powder.

SCOTCH WOODCOCK: A savory (see entry, above) of toast spread with anchovy paste and scrambled eggs.

SHEPHERD'S PIE: See *Cottage pie*.

SHORTBREAD: A sweet, buttery Scottish biscuit.

SHORT-CRUST PASTRY: Standard British pastry crust made from butter, lard, flour and water.

SILVERSIDE: A cut of beef from the round, traditionally pickled in brine. Used as the basic ingredient in boiled beef and carrots.

SIMNEL: A rich fruitcake baked with almond paste and traditionally served on Mothering Sunday, the fourth Sunday in Lent. Now more frequently served at Easter.

SKIRLIE: A mash of oatmeal and chopped onion fried in fat.

SLOE: The fruit of the blackthorn, a small, dark-purple plum with a yellow, very tart flesh. Used in the making of sloe gin.

SODA BREAD: An Irish bread that uses baking soda instead of yeast as the raising agent.

SOUSE: To pickle.

STINGO: A strong, almost black beer from Yorkshire.

STOUT: The richest, heaviest and darkest of British beers, and one of the most potent.

SUGAR: The British employ the following terms to describe different types of sugar: castor (superfine white), icing (confectioners'), loaf (white lump), Demerara (crystals of unrefined brown), Barbados (also unrefined brown, but with a finer, softer, moister texture than Demerara).

SWEET: The sweet course, also called by some the "pudding" or "dessert" course, following the main course of a meal. Also a hard candy.

SYLLABUB: A light, frothy dessert made of whipped cream, wine, spice, lemon and sugar.

TART: A baked shallow round pastry shell containing any of a variety of sweet fillings of fruit, custard and preserves.

TOAD-IN-THE-HOLE: A dish of sausages or pieces of meat, cooked in batter.

TREACLE: Thick molasses.

TROTTERS: Pigs' feet.

WASSAIL BOWL: Hot, strong punch of ale, sherry, spices and roasted apples. Traditionally served on Christmas Eve.

WATER BISCUIT: See *Biscuit*. "Water" is believed to be a corruption of "wafer."

WHITEBAIT: Silvery fish about an inch long, usually eaten whole after deep-frying.

WHORTLEBERRY: A dark blue-black berry, also called a bilberry or blaeberry.

Recipe Index

NOTE: An R preceding a page refers to the Recipe Booklet. Size, weight and material are specified for pans in the recipes because they affect cooking results. A pan should be just large enough to hold its contents comfortably. Heavy pans heat slowly and cook food at a constant rate. Aluminum and cast iron conduct heat well but may discolor foods containing egg yolks, vinegar or lemon. Enamelware is a fairly poor conductor of heat. Many recipes therefore recommend stainless steel or enameled cast iron, which do not have these faults.

Preserves

Vegetables and Pickles

Cheese

Breads, Buns and Cakes

Fish

Meat, Poultry and Game

Savory Puddings and Pies

Sweet Puddings and Pies

Sauces

General Index

Numerals in italics indicate a photograph or drawing of the subject mentioned.

Credits and Acknowledgments

The sources for the illustrations in this book are shown below. Credits for the pictures from left to right are separated by commas, from top to bottom by dashes.

All photographs in this book are by Anthony Blake except: 4—Frank Apthorp—Charles Phillips, Kurt Miehlmann. 13—Map by Gloria du Bouchet. 98,99—Anthony Blake, courtesy The National Trust. All drawings in this book are by Adrian Bailey.

For their help in the production of this book the editors wish to thank the following: *in Great Britain,* Aberdeen Angus Cattle Society; Mrs. Anne Angus; F. R. Smith of Leadenhall Market; H. P. Bulmer, Ltd.; Coates & Company (Plymouth) Ltd., Devon; Elizabeth David; Mrs. Trudy Day; Len Deighton; the English Country Cheese Council; Fatstock Marketing Corporation (Meat) Ltd.; Mrs. Paddy Folkard; Glyndebourne Festival Opera; Robin Grant; Thomas Grant & Sons of Maidstone, Kent; G. Hutchinson of Whitchurch, Shropshire; Ind Coope, Ltd., of Burton-on-Trent, Staffordshire; The Irish Fisheries Board; T. Cotton, Harbourmaster of Newlyn, Cornwall; Mrs. Georgette Matthews; The Merrydown Wine Company of Horam, Sussex; The National Federation of Women's Institutes, Mrs. M. Millard; The National Trust; The National Farmers' Union; Martin Orskey; The Royal Horticultural Society; The Taunton Cider Company Ltd.; J. L. Ward of the English Vineyards Association; *in New York City,* B. Altman & Company; Richard Camp; Jean Silversmiths, Inc.; R. H. Macy & Company; Plummer McCutcheon; Mrs. Elisabeth Lambert Ortiz.

Sources consulted in the production of this book include: *Talking about Cakes* by Margaret Bates; *Mrs. Beeton's Household Management* by Isabella Beeton; *British Bouquet* by Samuel Chamberlain; *Cooking the British Way* by Joan Clibbon; *The Englishman's Food* by J. C. Drummond and Anne Wilbraham; *The Art of British Cooking* by Theodora FitzGibbon; *Food in England* by Dorothy Hartley; *Soups* by Robin Howe; *Cookery for Every Household* by Florence Jack; *Recipes from Scotland* and *The Scots Kitchen* by F. Marian McNeill; *Movable Feasts* by Arnold Palmer; *Farmhouse Fare,* recipes from *The Farmer's Weekly: Sunday Telegraph Cookery Book* by Jean Robertson; *Drink* and *Food* by André Simon; *The Romance of Tea* by William Ukers; *Good English Food* and *Good Things in England* by Florence White.

XX
Printed in U.S.A.